Selected
Short Stories

D. H. Lawrence

Edited by Michael Lockwood

Series Editor: Judith Baxter

CAMBRIDGE
UNIVERSITY PRESS

The publishers would like to thank Nicholas McGuinn and
Jane Ogborn for their help as consulting editors for the series.

PUBLISHED BY THE PRESS SYNDICATE OF THE UNIVERSITY OF CAMBRIDGE
The Pitt Building, Trumpington Street, Cambridge CB2 1RP, United Kingdom

CAMBRIDGE UNIVERSITY PRESS
The Edinburgh Building, Cambridge CB2 2RU, United Kingdom
40 West 20th Street, New York, NY 10011-4211, USA
10 Stamford Road, Oakleigh, Melbourne 3166, Australia

This edition first published 1997

Printed in the United Kingdom by Scotprint, Musselburgh, Scotland

Typeset in Sabon 10/13 pt and Meta

Prepared for publication by Stenton Associates

A catalogue record for this book is available from the British Library

ISBN 0 521 57505 2   paperback

CONTENTS

━━━━━━━━━━━━━━━━ ◆ ━━━━━━━━━━━━━━━━

CAMBRIDGE LITERATURE

This edition of D. H. Lawrence's short stories is part of the Cambridge Literature series, and has been specially prepared for students in schools and colleges who are studying the book as part of their English course.

This study edition invites you to think about what happens when you read the short stories, and it suggests that you are not passively responding to words on the page which have only one agreed interpretation, but that you are actively exploring and making new sense of what you read. Your 'reading' will partly stem from you as an individual, from your own experiences and point of view, and to this extent your interpretation will be distinctively your own. But your reading will also stem from the fact that you belong to a culture and a community, rooted in a particular time and place. So, your understanding may have much in common with that of others in your class or study group.

There is a parallel between the way you read these stories and the way they were written. The Resource Notes at the back are devised to help you to investigate the complex nature of the writing process. This begins with the author's first, tentative ideas and sources of inspiration, moves through to the stages of writing, production and publication, and ends with the text's reception by the reading public, reviewers, critics and students. So the general approach to study focuses on five key questions:

Who has written the short stories and why?

What type of texts are they?

How were they produced?

How do the short stories present their subjects?

Who reads them and how do they interpret them?

D. H. Lawrence's short stories are presented complete and uninterrupted. You will find some words in the text asterisked: these are words which may be unfamiliar because they have a particular cultural or linguistic significance. They are explained in the Glossary section at the back.

The Resource Notes encourage you to take an active and imaginative approach to studying these short stories both in and out of the classroom. As well as providing you with information about many aspects of them, they offer a wide choice of activities to work on individually, or in groups. Above all, they give you the chance to explore these compelling stories in a variety of ways: as a reader, an actor, a researcher, a critic, and a writer.

Judith Baxter

INTRODUCTION

These short stories are a small selection from more than 70 which David Herbert Richards Lawrence wrote. Lawrence is best known as a novelist, the author of books such as *Sons and Lovers* (1913), *The Rainbow* (1915) and *Lady Chatterley's Lover* (1928), which broke new ground in their portrayal of emotional and sexual relationships. But in addition to his twelve novels, Lawrence also wrote more than a thousand poems, ten plays, four travel books, and many other works of non-fiction. So what is the value of studying Lawrence's short stories, in particular?

The stories offer you the opportunity to enjoy and study Lawrence's craft as a writer of fiction on a small canvas. In his tales, as Lawrence called them, he had to shape his narratives in a different way from his long novels, with more economy and restraint. The stories are *not* unfinished or miniature novels. They represent a different art form, with its own techniques and disciplines, which Lawrence worked at and developed throughout his career. He started off writing about the people and places he knew from his childhood, but towards the end of his life he wrote stories set in exotic locations, which have the structure and language of myths. He also accepted commissions from editors to write ghost and murder stories.

These stories offer variety. They deal with characters of different ages (from a little boy to an old lady) in very different situations who behave in different ways at different times. However, running through these diverse fictions you will soon begin to notice Lawrence's own unique preoccupations and concerns. Lawrence is interested in the underlying emotional logic which makes people behave as they do, sometimes in ways which go against their better judgement. He is also interested in how these emotions link us to our environment, both natural and industrial. So, in all of these short stories, you will find Lawrence trying to get under the surface of characters

7

to reveal their unconscious motivation. Readers can usually identify with the feelings which are revealed, and this gives the stories a universality within the variety of fictional situations.

The ten short stories in this collection come from different periods of Lawrence's life, and are arranged in chronological order according to when they were first begun. While the collection is designed to show Lawrence's overall development as a writer of stories, it also seeks to present some of the best stories from one of this century's most individual and influential storytellers. For the first time in a one-volume selection, the stories are printed in the authoritative texts established by the Cambridge Edition of Lawrence's works.

The White Stocking

I

"I'm getting up, Teddilinks," said Mrs. Whiston, and she sprang out of bed briskly.

"What the Hanover's° got you?" asked Whiston.

"Nothing. Can't I get up?" she replied animatedly.

It was about seven o'clock, scarcely light yet in the cold bedroom. Whiston lay still and looked at his wife. She was a pretty little thing, with her fleecy, short black hair all tousled. He watched her as she dressed quickly, flicking her small, delightful limbs, throwing her clothes about her. Her slovenliness and untidiness did not trouble him. When she picked up the edge of her petticoat, ripped off a torn string of white lace, and flung it on the dressing-table, her careless abandon made his spirit glow. She stood before the mirror and roughly scrambled together her profuse little mane of hair. He watched the quickness and softness of her young shoulders, calmly, like a husband, and appreciatively.

"Rise up," she cried, turning to him with a quick wave of her arm – "and shine forth."

They had been married two years. But still, when she had gone out of the room, he felt as if all his light and warmth were taken away, he became aware of the raw, cold morning. So he rose himself, wondering casually what had roused her so early. Usually she lay in bed as late as she could.

Whiston fastened a belt round his loins and went downstairs in shirt and trousers. He heard her singing in her snatchy fashion. The stairs creaked under his weight. He passed down the narrow little passage, which she called a hall, of the seven and sixpenny house which was his first home.

He was a shapely young fellow of about twenty-eight, sleepy now and easy with well-being. He heard the water drumming into the kettle, and she began to whistle. He loved the quick way she dodged the supper cups under the tap to wash them for breakfast. She looked an untidy minx, but she was quick and handy enough.

"Teddilinks," she cried.

"What?"

"Light a fire, quick."

She wore an old, sack-like dressing-jacket of black silk pinned across her breast. But one of the sleeves, coming unfastened, showed some delightful pink upper-arm.

"Why don't you sew your sleeve up?" he said, suffering from the sight of the exposed soft flesh.

"Where?" she cried, peering round. "Nuisance," she said, seeing the gap, then with light fingers went on drying the cups.

The kitchen was of fair size, but gloomy. Whiston poked out the dead ashes.

Suddenly a thud was heard at the door down the passage.

"I'll go," cried Mrs. Whiston, and she was gone down the hall.

The postman was a ruddy-faced man who had been a soldier. He smiled broadly, handing her some packages.

"They've not forgot you," he said impudently.

"No – lucky for them," she said, with a toss of the head. But she was interested only in her envelopes this morning. The postman waited inquisitively, smiling in an ingratiating fashion. She slowly, abstractedly, as if she did not know anyone was there, closed the door in his face, continuing to look at the addresses on her letters.

She tore open the thin envelope. There was a long, hideous, cartoon valentine. She smiled briefly and dropped it on the floor. Struggling with the string of a packet, she opened a white cardboard box, and there lay a white silk handkerchief packed neatly under the paper lace of the box, and her initial, worked in heliotrope, fully displayed. She smiled pleasantly, and gently put the box aside. The third envelope contained another white packet – apparently a cotton handkerchief neatly folded. She shook it out. It was a long white stocking, but there was a little weight in the toe. Quickly, she thrust down her arm, wriggling her fingers into the toe of the stocking, and brought out a small box. She peeped inside the box, then hastily opened a door on her left hand, and went into the little, cold sitting-room. She had her lower lip caught earnestly between her teeth.

With a little flash of triumph, she lifted a pair of pearl ear-rings from the small box, and she went to the mirror. There, earnestly, she began to hook them through her ears, looking at herself sideways in the glass. Curiously concentrated and intent she seemed as she fingered the lobes of her ears, her head bent on one side.

Then the pearl ear-rings dangled under her rosy, small ears. She shook her head sharply, to see the swing of the drops. They went chill against her neck, in little, sharp touches. Then she stood still to look at herself, bridling her head in the dignified fashion. Then she simpered at herself. Catching her own eye, she could not help winking at herself and laughing.

She turned to look at the box. There was a scrap of paper with this posy:

> "Pearls may be fair, but thou art fairer.
> Wear these for me, and I'll love the wearer."

She made a grimace and a grin. But she was drawn to the mirror again, to look at her ear-rings.

Whiston had made the fire burn, so he came to look for her. When she heard him, she started round quickly, guiltily. She was watching him with intent blue eyes when he appeared.

He did not see much, in his morning-drowsy warmth. He gave her, as ever, a feeling of warmth and slowness. His eyes were very blue, very kind, his manner simple.

"What ha' you got?" he asked.

"Valentines," she said briskly, ostentatiously turning to show him the silk handkerchief. She thrust it under his nose. "Smell how good," she said.

"Who's that from?" he replied, without smelling.

"It's a valentine," she cried. "How do I know who it's from?"

"I'll bet you know," he said.

"Ted! – I don't!" she cried, beginning to shake her head, then stopping because of the ear-rings.

He stood still a moment, displeased.

"They've no right to send you valentines, now," he said.

"Ted! – Why not? You're not jealous, are you? I haven't the least idea who it's from. Look – there's my initial" – she pointed with an emphatic finger at the heliotrope embroidery –

> "E for Elsie,
> Nice little gelsie,"

she sang.

"Get out," he said. "You know who it's from."

"Truth, I don't," she cried.

He looked round, and saw the white stocking lying on a chair.

"Is this another?" he said.

"No, that's a sample," she said. "There's only a comic." And she fetched in the long cartoon.

He stretched it out and looked at it solemnly.

"Fools!" he said, and went out of the room.

She flew upstairs and took off the ear-rings. When she returned, he was crouched before the fire blowing the coals. The skin of his face was flushed, and slightly pitted, as if he had had small-pox. But his neck was white and smooth and goodly. She hung her arms round his neck as he crouched there, and clung to him. He balanced on his toes.

"This fire's a slow-coach," he said.

"And who else is a slow-coach?" she said.

"One of us two, I know," he said, and he rose carefully. She remained clinging round his neck, so that she was lifted off her feet.

"Ha! – swing me," she cried.

He lowered his head, and she hung in the air, swinging from his neck, laughing. Then she slipped off.

"The kettle is singing," she sang, flying for the teapot. He bent down again to blow the fire. The veins in his neck stood out, his shirt collar seemed too tight.

> "Doctor Wyer,
> Blow the fire,
> Puff! puff! puff!"

she sang, laughing.

He smiled at her.

She was so glad because of her pearl ear-rings.

Over the breakfast she grew serious. He did not notice. She became portentous in her gravity. Almost it penetrated through his steady good-humour to irritate him.

"Teddy!" she said at last.

"What?" he asked.

"I told you a lie," she said, humbly tragic.

His soul stirred uneasily.

"Oh ay?" he said casually.

She was not satisfied. He ought to be more moved.

"Yes," she said.

He cut a piece of bread.

"Was it a good one?" he asked.

She was piqued. Then she considered – *was* it a good one? Then she laughed.

"No," she said, "it wasn't up to much."

"Ah!" he said easily, but with a steady strength of fondness for her in his tone. "Get it out then."

It became a little more difficult.

"You know that white stocking," she said earnestly. "I told you a lie. It wasn't a sample. It was a valentine."

A little frown came on his brow.

"Then what did you invent it as a sample for?" he said. But he knew this weakness of hers. The touch of anger in his voice frightened her.

"I was afraid you'd be cross," she said pathetically.

"I'll bet you were vastly afraid," he said.

"I *was*, Teddy."

There was a pause. He was resolving one or two things in his mind.

"And who sent it?" he asked.

"I can guess," she said, "though there wasn't a word with it – except –"

She ran to the sitting-room and returned with a slip of paper.

"Pearls may be fair, but thou art fairer.
Wear these for me, and I'll love the wearer."

He read it twice, then a dull red flush came on his face.

"And *who* do you guess it is?" he asked, with a ringing of anger in his voice.

"I suspect it's Sam Adams," she said, with a little virtuous indignation.

Whiston was silent for a moment.

"Fool!" he said. "An' what's it got to do with pearls? – and how can he say 'wear these for me' when there's only one? He hasn't got the brain to invent a proper verse."

He screwed the slip of paper into a ball and flung it into the fire.

"I suppose he thinks it'll make a pair with the one last year," she said.

"Why, did he send one then?"

"Yes. I thought you'd be wild if you knew."

His jaw set rather sullenly.

Presently he rose, and went to wash himself, rolling back his sleeves and pulling open his shirt at the breast. It was as if his fine, clear-cut temples and steady eyes were degraded by the lower, rather brutal part of his face. But she loved it. As she whisked about, clearing the table, she loved the way in which he stood washing himself. He was such a man. She liked to see his neck glistening with water as he swilled it. It amused her and pleased her and thrilled her. He was so sure, so permanent, he had her so utterly in his power. It gave her a delightful, mischievous sense of liberty. Within his grasp, she could dart about excitingly.

He turned round to her, his face red from the cold water, his eyes fresh and very blue.

"You haven't been seeing anything of him, have you?" he asked roughly.

"Yes," she answered, after a moment, as if caught guilty. "He got into the tram with me, and he asked me to drink a coffee and a Benedictine in the Royal."

"You've got it off fine and glib," he said sullenly. "And did you?"

"Yes," she replied, with the air of a traitor before the rack.

The blood came up into his neck and face, he stood motionless, dangerous.

"It was cold, and it was such fun to go into the Royal," she said.

"You'd go off with a nigger for a packet of chocolate," he said, in anger and contempt, and some bitterness. Queer how he drew away from her, cut her off from him.

"Ted – how beastly!" she cried. "You know quite well –" She caught her lip, flushed, and the tears came to her eyes.

He turned away, to put on his necktie. She went about her work, making a queer pathetic little mouth, down which occasionally dripped a tear.

He was ready to go. With his hat jammed down on his head, and his overcoat buttoned up to his chin, he came to kiss her. He would be miserable all the day if he went without. She allowed herself to be kissed. Her cheek was wet under his lips, and his heart burned. She hurt him so deeply. And she felt aggrieved, and did not quite forgive him.

In a moment she went upstairs to her ear-rings. Sweet they looked nestling in the little drawer – sweet! She examined them with voluptuous pleasure, she threaded them in her ears, she looked at herself, she posed and postured and smiled, and looked sad and tragic and winning and appealing, all in turn before the mirror. And she was happy, and very pretty.

She wore her ear-rings all morning, in the house. She was self-conscious, and quite brilliantly winsome, when the baker came, wondering if he would notice. All the tradesmen left her door with a glow in them, feeling elated, and unconsciously favouring the delightful little creature, though there had been nothing to notice in her behaviour.

She was stimulated all the day. She did not think about her husband. He was the permanent basis from which she took these giddy little flights into nowhere. At night, like chickens and curses, she would come home to him, to roost.

Meanwhile Whiston, a traveller and confidential support of a small firm, hastened about his work, his heart all the while anxious for her, yearning for surety, and kept tense by not getting it.

II

She had been a warehouse girl in Adams' lace factory before she was married. Sam Adams was her employer. He was a bachelor of forty, growing stout, a man well dressed and florid, with a large brown moustache and thin hair. From the rest of his well-groomed, showy appearance, it was evident his baldness was a chagrin to him. He had a good presence, and some Irish blood in his veins.

His fondness for the girls, or the fondness of the girls for him, was notorious. And Elsie, quick, pretty, almost witty little thing – she *seemed* witty, although, when her sayings were repeated, they were entirely trivial – she had a great attraction for him. He would come into the warehouse dressed in a rather sporting reefer coat, of fawn colour, and trousers of fine black-and-white check, a cap with a big peak and a scarlet carnation in his button-hole, to impress her. She was only half impressed. He was too loud for her good taste. Instinctively perceiving this, he sobered down to navy blue. Then a well-built man, florid, with large brown whiskers, smart navy blue suit, fashionable boots, and manly hat, he was the irreproachable. Elsie was impressed.

But meanwhile Whiston was courting her, and she made splendid little gestures, before her bedroom mirror, of the constant-and-true sort.

"True, true till death –"

That was her song. Whiston was made that way, so there was no need to take thought for him.

Every Christmas Sam Adams gave a party at his house, to which he invited his superior work-people – not factory hands and labourers, but those above. He was a generous man in his way, with a real warm feeling for giving pleasure.

Two years ago Elsie had attended this Christmas-party for the last time. Whiston had accompanied her. At that time he worked for Sam Adams.

She had been very proud of herself, in her close-fitting, full-skirted dress of blue silk. Whiston called for her. Then she tripped beside him, holding her large cashmere shawl across her breast. He strode with long strides, his trousers handsomely strapped under his boots, and her silk shoes bulging the pockets of his full-skirted overcoat.

They passed through the park gates, and her spirits rose. Above them the Castle Rock loomed grandly in the night, the naked trees stood still and dark in the frost, along the boulevard.

They were rather late. Agitated with anticipation, in the cloak-room she gave up her shawl, donned her silk shoes, and looked at herself in the mirror. The loose bunches of curls on either side her face danced prettily, her mouth smiled.

She hung a moment in the door of the brilliantly lighted room. Many people were moving within the blaze of lamps, under the crystal chandeliers, the full skirts of the women balancing and floating, the side-whiskers and white cravats of the men bowing above. Then she entered the light.

In an instant Sam Adams was coming forward, lifting both his arms in boisterous welcome. There was a constant red laugh on his face.

"Come late, would you," he shouted, "like royalty."

He seized her hands and led her forward. He opened his mouth wide when he spoke, and the effect of the warm, dark opening behind the brown whiskers was disturbing. But she was floating into the throng on his arm. He was very gallant.

"Now then," he said, taking her card to write down the dances, "I've got carte blanche,◇ haven't I?"

"Mr. Whiston doesn't dance," she said.

"I am a lucky man!" he said, scribbling his initials. "I was born with an *amourette*◇ in my mouth."

He wrote on, quietly. She blushed and laughed, not knowing what it meant.

"Why, what is that?" she said.

"It's you, even littler than you are, dressed in little wings," he said.

"I should have to be pretty small to get in your mouth," she said.

"You think you're too big, do you!" he said easily.

He handed her her card, with a bow.

"Now I'm set up, my darling, for this evening," he said.

Then, quick, always at his ease, he looked over the room. She waited in front of him. He was ready. Catching the eye of the band, he nodded. In a moment, the music began. He seemed to relax, giving himself up.

"Now then, Elsie," he said, with a curious caress in his voice that seemed to lap the outside of her body in a warm glow, delicious. She gave herself to it. She liked it.

He was an excellent dancer. He seemed to draw her close in to him by some male warmth of attraction, so that she became all soft and pliant to him, flowing to his form, whilst he united her with him and they lapsed along in one movement. She was just carried in a kind of strong, warm flood, her feet moved of themselves, and only the music threw her away from him, threw her back to him, to his clasp, in his strong form moving against her, rhythmically, deliciously.

When it was over, he was pleased and his eyes had a curious gleam which thrilled her and yet had nothing to do with her. Yet it held her. He did not speak to her. He only looked straight into her eyes with a curious, gleaming look that disturbed her fearfully and deliciously. But also there was in his look some of the automatic irony of the *roué*.° It left her partly cold. She was not carried away.

She went, driven by an opposite, heavier impulse to Whiston. He stood looking gloomy, trying to admit that she had a perfect right to enjoy herself apart from him. He received her with rather grudging kindliness.

"Aren't you going to play whist?" she asked.

"Ay," he said. "Directly."

"I do wish you could dance."

"Well, I can't," he said. "So you enjoy yourself."

"But I should enjoy it better if I could dance with you."

"Nay, you're all right," he said. "I'm not made that way."

"Then you ought to be!" she cried.

"Well, it's my fault, not yours. You enjoy yourself," he bade her. Which she proceeded to do, a little bit irked.

She went with anticipation to the arms of Sam Adams, when the time came to dance with him. It *was* so gratifying, irrespective of the man. And she felt a little grudge against Whiston, soon forgotten when her host was holding her near to him, in a delicious embrace. And she watched his eyes, to meet the gleam in them, which gratified her.

She was getting warmed right through, the glow was penetrating into her, driving away everything else. Only in her heart was a little tightness, like conscience.

When she got a chance, she escaped from the dancing-room to the card-room. There, in a cloud of smoke, she found Whiston playing cribbage. Radiant, roused, animated, she came up to him and greeted him. She was too strong, too vibrant a note in the quiet room. He lifted his head, and a frown knitted his gloomy forehead.

"Are you playing cribbage? Is it exciting? How are you getting on?" she chattered.

He looked at her. None of these questions needed answering, and he did not feel in touch with her. She turned to the cribbage-board.

"Are you white or red?" she asked.

"He's red," replied the partner.

"Then you're losing," she said, still to Whiston. And she lifted the red peg from the board. "One – two – three – four – five – six – seven – eight – Right up there you ought to jump –"

"Now put it back in its right place," said Whiston.

"Where was it?" she asked gaily, knowing her transgression. He took the little red peg away from her and stuck it in its hole.

The cards were shuffled.

"What a shame you're losing!" said Elsie.

"You'd better cut for him," said the partner.

She did so, hastily. The cards were dealt. She put her hand on his shoulder, looking at his cards.

"It's good," she cried, "isn't it?"

He did not answer, but threw down two cards. It moved him more strongly than was comfortable, to have her hand on his shoulder, her curls dangling and touching his ears, whilst she was roused to another man. It made the blood flame over him.

At that moment Sam Adams appeared, florid and boisterous, intoxicated more with himself, with the dancing, than with wine. In his eye the curious, impersonal light gleamed.

"I thought I should find you here, Elsie," he cried boisterously, a disturbing, high note in his voice.

"What made you think so?" she replied, the mischief rousing in her.

The florid, well-built man narrowed his eyes to a smile.

"I should never look for you among the ladies," he said, with a kind of intimate, animal call to her. He laughed, bowed, and offered her his arm.

"Madam, the music waits."

She went almost helplessly, carried along with him, unwilling, yet delighted.

That dance was an intoxication to her. After the first few steps, she felt herself slipping away from herself. She almost knew she was going, she did not even want to go. Yet she must have chosen to go. She lay in the arm of the steady, close man with whom she was dancing, and she seemed to swim away out of contact with the room, into him. She had passed into another, denser element of him, an essential privacy. The room was all vague around her, like an atmosphere, like under sea, with a flow of ghostly, dumb movements. But she herself was held real against her partner, and it seemed she was connected with him, as if the movements of his body and limbs were her own movements, yet not her own movements – and oh, delicious! He also was given up, oblivious, concentrated, into

21

the dance. His eye was unseeing. Only his large, voluptuous body gave off a subtle activity. His fingers seemed to search into her flesh. Every moment, and every moment, she felt she would give way utterly, and sink molten: the fusion point was coming when she would fuse down into perfect unconsciousness at his feet and knees. But he bore her round the room in the dance, and he seemed to sustain all her body with his limbs, his body, and his warmth seemed to come closer into her, nearer, till it would fuse right through her, and she would be as liquid to him, as an intoxication only.

It was exquisite. When it was over, she was dazed, and was scarcely breathing. She stood with him in the middle of the room as if she were alone in a remote place. He bent over her. She expected his lips on her bare shoulder, and waited. Yet they were not alone, they were not alone. It was cruel.

"'Twas good, wasn't it, my darling?" he said to her, low and delighted. There was a strange impersonality about his low, exultant call that appealed to her irresistibly. Yet why was she aware of some part shut off in her? She pressed his arm, and he led her towards the door.

She was not aware of what she was doing, only a little grain of resistant trouble was in her. The man, possessed, yet with a superficial presence of mind, made way to the dining-room, as if to give her refreshment, cunningly working to his own escape with her. He was molten hot, filmed over with presence of mind, and bottomed with cold disbelief.

In the dining-room was Whiston, carrying coffee to the plain, neglected ladies. Elsie saw him, but felt as if he could not see her. She was beyond his reach and ken. A sort of fusion existed between her and the large man at her side. She ate her custard, but an incomplete fusion all the while sustained and contained within the being of her employer.

But she was growing cooler. Whiston came up. She looked at him, and saw him with different eyes. She saw his slim, young man's figure real and enduring before her. That was he.

But she was in the spell with the other man, fused with him, and she could not be taken away.

"Have you finished your cribbage?" she asked, with hasty evasion of him.

"Yes," he replied. "Aren't you getting tired of dancing?"

"Not a bit," she said.

"Not she," said Adams heartily. "No girl with any spirit gets tired of dancing. – Have something else, Elsie. Come – sherry. Have a glass of sherry with us, Whiston."

Whilst they sipped the wine, Adams watched Whiston almost cunningly, to find his advantage.

"We'd better be getting back – there's the music," he said. "See the women get something to eat, Whiston, will you, there's a good chap."

And he began to draw away. Elsie was drifting helplessly with him. But Whiston put himself beside them, and went along with them. In silence they passed through to the dancing-room. There Adams hesitated, and looked round the room. It was as if he could not see.

A man came hurrying forward, claiming Elsie, and Adams went to his other partner. Whiston stood watching during the dance. She was conscious of him standing there observant of her, like a ghost, or a judgment, or a guardian angel. She was also conscious, much more intimately and impersonally, of the body of the other man moving somewhere in the room. She still belonged to him, but a feeling of distraction possessed her, and helplessness. Adams danced on, adhering to Elsie, waiting his time, with the persistence of cynicism.

The dance was over. Adams was detained. Elsie found herself beside Whiston. There was something shapely about him as he sat, about his knees and his distinct figure, that she clung to. It was as if he had enduring form. She put her hand on his knee.

"Are you enjoying yourself?" he asked.

"*Ever* so," she replied, with a fervent, yet detached tone.

"It's going on for one o'clock," he said.

"Is it?" she answered. It meant nothing to her.

"Should we be going?" he said.

She was silent. For the first time for an hour or more an inkling of her normal consciousness returned. She resented it.

"What for?" she said.

"I thought you might have had enough," he said.

A slight soberness came over her, an irritation at being frustrated of her illusion.

"Why?" she said.

"We've been here since nine," he said.

That was no answer, no reason. It conveyed nothing to her. She sat detached from him. Across the room Sam Adams glanced at her. She sat there exposed for him.

"You don't want to be too free with Sam Adams," said Whiston cautiously, suffering. "You know what he is."

"How, free?" she asked.

"Why – you don't want to have too much to do with him."

She sat silent. He was forcing her into consciousness of her position. But he could not get hold of her feelings, to change them. She had a curious, perverse desire that he should not.

"I like him," she said.

"What do you find to like in him?" he said, with a hot heart.

"I don't know – but I like him," she said.

She was immutable. He sat feeling heavy and dulled with rage. He was not clear as to what he felt. He sat there unliving whilst she danced. And she, distracted, lost to herself between the opposing forces of the two men, drifted. Between the dances, Whiston kept near to her. She was scarcely conscious. She glanced repeatedly at her card, to see when she would dance again with Adams, half in desire, half in dread. Sometimes she met his steady, glaucous eye as she passed him in the dance. Sometimes she saw the steadiness of his flank as he danced. And it was always as if she rested on his arm, were borne along, upborne by him, away from herself. And always there was present the other's antagonism. She was divided.

The time came for her to dance with Adams. Oh, the delicious closing of contact with him, of his limbs touching her limbs, his arm supporting her. She seemed to resolve. Whiston had not made himself real to her. He was only a heavy place in her consciousness.

But she breathed heavily, beginning to suffer from the closeness of strain. She was nervous. Adams also was constrained. A tightness, a tension was coming over them all. And he was exasperated, feeling something counteracting physical magnetism, feeling a will stronger with her than his own intervening in what was becoming a vital necessity to him.

Elsie was almost lost to her own control. As she went forward with him to take her place at the dance, she stooped for her pocket-handkerchief. The music sounded for quadrilles. Everybody was ready. Adams stood with his body near her, exerting his attraction over her. He was tense and fighting. She stooped for her pocket-handkerchief, and shook it as she rose. It shook out and fell from her hand. With agony, she saw she had taken a white stocking instead of a handkerchief. For a second it lay on the floor, a twist of white stocking. Then, in an instant, Adams picked it up, with a little, surprised laugh of triumph.

"That'll do for me," he whispered – seeming to take possession of her. And he stuffed the stocking in his trousers pocket, and quickly offered her his handkerchief.

The dance began. She felt weak and faint, as if her will were turned to water. A heavy sense of loss came over her. She could not help herself any more. But it was peace.

When the dance was over, Adams yielded her up. Whiston came to her.

"What was it as you dropped?" Whiston asked.

"I thought it was my handkerchief – I'd taken a stocking by mistake," she said, detached and muted.

"And he's got it?"

"Yes,"

"What does he mean by that?"

She lifted her shoulders.

"Are you going to let him keep it?" he asked.

"I don't let him."

There was a long pause.

"Am I to go and have it out with him?" he asked, his face flushed, his blue eyes going hard with opposition.

"No," she said, pale.

"Why?"

"No – I don't want you to say anything about it."

He sat exasperated and nonplussed.

"You'll let him keep it, then?" he asked.

She sat silent and made no form of answer.

"What do you mean by it?" he said, dark with fury. And he started up.

"No!" she cried. "Ted!" And she caught hold of him, sharply detaining him.

It made him black with rage.

"Why?" he said.

Then something about her mouth was pitiful to him. He did not understand, but he felt she must have her reasons.

"Then I'm not stopping here," he said. "Are you coming with me?"

She rose mutely, and they went out of the room. Adams had not noticed.

In a few moments they were in the street.

"What the hell do you mean?" he said, in a black fury.

She went at his side, in silence, neutral.

"That great hog, an' all," he added.

Then they went a long time in silence through the frozen, deserted darkness of the town. She felt she could not go indoors. They were drawing near her house.

"I don't want to go home," she suddenly cried in distress and anguish. "I don't want to go home."

He looked at her.

"Why don't you?" he said.

"I don't want to go home," was all she could sob.

He heard somebody coming.

"Well, we can walk a bit further," he said.

She was silent again. They passed out of the town into the fields. He held her by the arm – they could not speak.

"What's a-matter?" he asked at length, puzzled.

She began to cry again.

At last he took her in his arms, to soothe her. She sobbed by herself, almost unaware of him.

"Tell me what's a-matter, Elsie" he said. "Tell me what's a-matter – my dear – tell me, then –"

He kissed her wet face, and caressed her. She made no response. He was puzzled and tender and miserable.

At length she became quiet. Then he kissed her, and she put her arms round him, and clung to him very tight, as if for fear and anguish. He held her in his arms, wondering.

"Ted!" she whispered, frantic. "Ted!"

"What, my love?" he answered, becoming also afraid.

"Be good to me," she cried. "Don't be cruel to me."

"No, my pet," he said, amazed and grieved. "Why?"

"Oh, be good to me," she sobbed.

And he held her very safe, and his heart was white hot with love for her. His mind was amazed. He could only hold her against his chest that was white hot with love and belief in her. So she was restored at last.

III

She refused to go to her work at Adams' any more. Her father had to submit and she sent in her notice – she was not well.

Sam Adams was ironical. But he had a curious patience. He did not fight.

In a few weeks, she and Whiston were married. She loved him with passion and worship, a fierce little abandon of love that moved him to the depths of his being, and gave him a permanent surety and sense of realness in himself. He did not trouble about himself any more: he felt he was fulfilled and now he had only the many things in the world to busy himself about. Whatever troubled him, at the bottom was surety. He had found himself in this love.

They spoke once or twice of the white stocking.

"Ah!" Whiston exclaimed. "What does it matter?"

He was impatient and angry, and could not bear to consider the matter. So it was left unresolved.

She was quite happy at first, carried away by her adoration of her husband. Then gradually she got used to him. He always was the ground of her happiness, but she got used to him, as to the air she breathed. He never got used to her in the same way.

Inside of marriage she found her liberty. She was rid of the responsibility of herself. Her husband must look after that. She was free to get what she could out of her time.

So that, when, after some months, she met Sam Adams, she was not quite as unkind to him as she might have been. With a young wife's new and exciting knowledge of men, she perceived he was in love with her, she knew he had always kept an unsatisfied desire for her. And, sportive, she could not help playing a little with this, though she cared not one jot for the man himself.

When Valentine's day came, which was near the first anniversary of her wedding day, there arrived a white stocking with a little amethyst brooch. Luckily Whiston did not see it, so she said nothing of it to him. She had not the faintest intention of having anything to do with Sam Adams, but once a little brooch was in her possession, it was hers, and she did not trouble her head for a moment, how she had come by it. She kept it.

Now she had the pearl ear-rings. They were a more valuable and a more conspicuous present. She would have to ask her mother to give them to her, to explain their presence. She made a little plan in her head. And she was extraordinarily pleased. As for Sam Adams, even if he saw her wearing them, he would not give her away. What fun, if he saw her wearing his ear-rings! She would pretend she had inherited them from her grandmother, her mother's mother. She laughed to herself as she went down town in the afternoon, the pretty drops dangling in front of her curls. But she saw no one of importance.

Whiston came home tired and depressed. All day the male in him had been uneasy, and this had fatigued him. She was curiously against him, inclined, as she sometimes was nowadays, to make mock of him and jeer at him and cut him off. He did not understand this, and it angered him deeply. She was uneasy before him.

She knew he was in a state of suppressed irritation. The veins stood out on the backs of his hands, his brow was drawn stiffly. Yet she could not help goading him.

"What did you do wi' that white stocking?" he asked, out of a gloomy silence, his voice strong and brutal.

"I put it in a drawer – why?" she replied flippantly.

"Why didn't you put it on the fire back?" he said harshly. "What are you hoarding it up for?"

"I'm not hoarding it up," she said. "I've got a pair."

He relapsed into gloomy silence. She, unable to move him, ran away upstairs, leaving him smoking by the fire. Again she tried on the ear-rings. Then another little inspiration came to her. She drew on the white stockings, both of them.

Presently she came down in them. Her husband still sat immovable and glowering by the fire.

"Look!" she said. "They'll do beautifully."

And she picked up her skirts to her knees, and twisted round, looking at her pretty legs in the neat stockings.

He filled with unreasonable rage, and took the pipe from his mouth.

"Don't they look nice?" she said. "One from last year and one from this, they just do. Save you buying a pair."

And she looked over her shoulders at her pretty calves, and at the dangling frills of her knickers.

"Put your skirts down and don't make a fool of yourself," he said.

"Why a fool of myself?" she asked.

And she began to dance slowly round the room, kicking up her feet half reckless, half jeering, in a ballet-dancer's fashion. Almost fearfully, yet in defiance, she kicked up her legs at him, singing as she did so. She resented him.

"You little fool, ha' done with it," he said. "And you'll backfire° them stockings, I'm telling you." He was angry. His face flushed dark, he kept his head bent. She ceased to dance.

"I shan't," she said. "They'll come in very useful."

He lifted his head and watched her, with lighted, dangerous eyes.

"You'll put 'em on the fire back, I tell you," he said.

It was a war now. She bent forward, in a ballet-dancer's fashion, and put her tongue between her teeth.

"I shan't backfire them stockings," she sang, repeating his words, "I shan't, I shan't, I shan't."

And she danced round the room doing a high kick to the tune of her words. There was a real biting indifference in her behaviour.

"We'll see whether you will or not," he said, "trollops!° You'd like Sam Adams to know you was wearing 'em, wouldn't you? That's what would please you."

"Yes, I'd like him to see how nicely they fit me, he might give me some more then."

And she looked down at her pretty legs.

He knew somehow that she *would* like Sam Adams to see how pretty her legs looked in the white stockings. It made his anger go deep, almost to hatred.

"Yer nasty trolley,"◦ he cried. "Put yer petticoats down, and stop being so foul-minded."

"I'm not foul-minded," she said. "My legs are my own. And why shouldn't Sam Adams think they're nice!"

There was a pause. He watched her with eyes glittering to a point.

"Have you been havin' owt to do with him?" he asked.

"I've just spoken to him when I've seen him," she said. "He's not as bad as you would make out."

"Isn't he!" he cried, a certain wakefulness in his voice. "Them who has anything to do wi' him is too bad for me, I tell you."

"Why, what are you frightened of him for?" she mocked.

She was rousing all his uncontrollable anger. He sat glowering. Every one of her sentences stirred him up like a red-hot iron. Soon it would be too much. And she was afraid herself; but she was neither conquered nor convinced.

A curious little grin of hate came on his face. He had a long score against her.

"What am I frightened of him for?" he repeated automatically. "What am I frightened of him for? Why, for you, you stray-running little bitch."

She flushed. The insult went deep into her, right home.

"Well, if you're so dull –" she said, lowering her eyelids, and speaking coldly, haughtily.

"If I'm so dull I'll break your neck the first word you speak to him," he said, tense.

"Pf!" she sneered. "Do you think I'm frightened of you?" She spoke coldly, detached.

She was frightened, for all that, white round the mouth.

His heart was getting hotter.

"You *will* be frightened of me, the next time you have anything to do with him," he said.

"Do you think *you'd* ever be told – ha!"

Her jeering scorn made him go white hot, molten. He knew he was incoherent, scarcely responsible for what he might do. Slowly, unseeing, he rose and went out of doors, stifled, moved to kill her.

He stood leaning against the garden fence, unable either to see or hear. Below him, far off, fumed the lights of the town. He stood still, unconscious with a black storm of rage, his face lifted to the night.

Presently, still unconscious of what he was doing, he went indoors again. She stood, a small, stubborn figure with tight-pressed lips and big, sullen, childish eyes, watching him, white with fear. He went heavily across the floor and dropped into his chair.

There was a silence.

"*You're* not going to tell me everything I shall do, and everything I shan't," she broke out at last.

He lifted his head.

"I tell you *this*," he said, low and intense. "Have anything to do with Sam Adams, and I'll break your neck."

She laughed, shrill and false.

"How I hate your word 'break your neck'," she said, with a grimace of the mouth. "It sounds so common and beastly. Can't you say something else –"

There was a dead silence.

"And besides," she said, with a queer chirrup of mocking laughter, "what do you know about anything? He sent me an amethyst brooch and a pair of pearl ear-rings."

"He what?" said Whiston, in a suddenly normal voice. His eyes were fixed on her.

"Sent me a pair of pearl ear-rings, and an amethyst brooch," she repeated, mechanically, pale to the lips.

And her big, black, childish eyes watched him, fascinated, held in her spell.

He seemed to thrust his face and his eyes forward at her, as he rose slowly and came to her. She watched transfixed in terror. Her throat made a small sound, as she tried to scream.

Then, quick as lightning, the back of his hand struck her with a crash across the mouth, and she was flung back blinded against the wall. The shock shook a queer sound out of her. And then she saw him still coming on, his eyes holding her, his fist drawn back, advancing slowly. At any instant the blow might crash into her.

Mad with terror, she raised her hands with a queer clawing movement to cover her eyes and her temples, opening her mouth in a dumb shriek. There was no sound. But the sight of her slowly arrested him. He hung before her, looking at her fixedly, as she stood crouched against the wall with open, bleeding mouth, and wide-staring eyes, and two hands clawing over her temples. And his lust to see her bleed, to break her and destroy her, rose from an old source against her. It carried him. He wanted satisfaction.

But he had seen her standing there, a piteous, horrified thing, and he turned his face aside in shame and nausea. He went and sat heavily in his chair, and a curious ease, almost like sleep, came over his brain.

She walked away from the wall towards the fire, dizzy, white to the lips, mechanically wiping her small, bleeding mouth. He sat motionless. Then, gradually, her breath began to hiss, she shook, and was sobbing silently, in grief for herself. Without looking, he saw. It made his mad desire to destroy her come back.

At length he lifted his head. His eyes were glowing again, fixed on her.

"And what did he give them you for?" he asked, in a steady, unyielding voice.

Her crying dried up in a second. She also was tense.

33

"They came as valentines," she replied, still not subjugated, even if beaten.

"When, to-day?"

"The pearl ear-rings to-day – the amethyst brooch last year."

"You've had it a year?"

"Yes."

She felt that now nothing would prevent him if he rose to kill her. She could not prevent him any more. She was yielded up to him. They both trembled in the balance, unconscious.

"What have you had to do with him?" he asked, in a barren voice.

"I've not had anything to do with him," she quavered.

"You just kept 'em because they were jewellery?" he said.

A weariness came over him. What was the worth of speaking any more of it? He did not care any more. He was dreary and sick.

She began to cry again, but he took no notice. She kept wiping her mouth on her handkerchief. He could see it, the blood-mark. It made him only more sick and tired of the responsibility of it, the violence, the shame.

When she began to move about again, he raised his head once more from his dead, motionless position.

"Where are the things?" he said.

"They are upstairs," she quavered. She knew the passion had gone down in him.

"Bring them down," he said.

"I won't," she wept, with rage. "You're not going to bully me and hit me like that on the mouth."

And she sobbed again. He looked at her in contempt and compassion and in rising anger.

"Where are they?" he said.

"They're in the little drawer under the looking-glass," she sobbed.

He went slowly upstairs, struck a match, and found the trinkets. He brought them downstairs in his hand.

"These?" he said, looking at them as they lay in his palm.

She looked at them without answering. She was not interested in them any more.

He looked at the little jewels. They were pretty.

"It's none of their fault," he said to himself.

And he searched round slowly, persistently, for a box. He tied the things up and addressed them to Sam Adams. Then he went out in his slippers to post the little package.

When he came back she was still sitting crying.

"You'd better go to bed," he said.

She paid no attention. He sat by the fire. She still cried.

"I'm sleeping down here," he said. "Go you to bed."

In a few moments she lifted her tear-stained, swollen face and looked at him with eyes all forlorn and pathetic. A great flash of anguish went over his body. He went over, slowly, and very gently took her in his hands. She let herself be taken. Then as she lay against his shoulder, she sobbed aloud:

"I never meant –"

"My love – my little love –" he cried, in anguish of spirit, holding her in his arms.

Odour of Chrysanthemums

I

The small locomotive engine, Number 4, came clanking, stumbling down from Selston with seven full waggons. It appeared round the corner with loud threats of speed, but the colt that it startled from among the gorse, which still flickered indistinctly in the raw afternoon, outdistanced it at a canter. A woman, walking up the railway-line to Underwood, drew back into the hedge, held her basket aside, and watched the footplate of the engine advancing. The trucks thumped heavily past, one by one, with slow inevitable movement, as she stood insignificantly trapped between the jolting black waggons and the hedge; then they curved away towards the coppice where the withered oak-leaves dropped noiselessly, while the birds, pulling at the scarlet hips beside the track, made off into the dusk that had already crept into the spinney. In the open, the smoke from the engine sank and cleaved to the rough grass. The fields were dreary and forsaken, and in the marshy strip that led to the whimsey, a reedy pit-pond, the fowls had already abandoned their run among the alders, to roost in the tarred fowl-house. The pit-bank loomed up beyond the pond, flames like red sores licking its ashy sides, in the afternoon's stagnant light. Just beyond rose the tapering chimneys and the clumsy black headstocks of Brinsley Colliery. The two wheels were spinning fast up against the sky, and the winding-engine rapped out its little spasms. The miners were being turned up.

The engine whistled as it came into the wide bay of railway-lines beside the colliery, where rows of trucks stood in harbour. Miners, single, trailing, and in groups, passed like shadows diverging home. At the edge of the ribbed level of sidings squat a low cottage, three steps down from the cinder track. A large, bony vine clutched at the house, as if to claw down the tiled roof. Round the bricked yard grew a few wintry primroses. Beyond, the long garden sloped down to a bush-covered brook-course. There were some twiggy apple trees, winter-crack trees,° and ragged cabbages. Beside the path hung dishevelled pink chrysanthemums, like cloths hung on bushes. A woman came stooping out of the felt-covered fowl-house half-way down the garden. She closed and padlocked the door, then drew herself erect, having brushed some bits from her white apron.

She was a tall woman of imperious mien, handsome, with definite black eyebrows. Her smooth black hair was parted exactly. For a few moments she stood steadily watching the miners as they passed along the railway: then she turned towards the brook-course. Her face was calm and set, her mouth was closed with disillusionment. After a moment she called:

"John!" There was no answer. She waited, and then said distinctly:

"Where are you?"

"Here!" replied a child's sulky voice from among the bushes. The woman looked piercingly through the dusk.

"Are you at that brook?" she asked sternly.

For answer the child showed himself before the raspberry-canes that rose like whips. He was a small, sturdy boy of five. He stood quite still, defiantly.

"Oh!" said the mother, conciliated. "I thought you were down at that wet brook – and you remember what I told you –"

The boy did not move or answer.

"Come, come on in," she said more gently, "it's getting dark. There's your grandfather's engine coming down the line!"

The lad advanced slowly, with resentful, taciturn movement. He was dressed in trousers and waistcoat of cloth that was too thick and hard for the size of the garments. They were evidently cut down from a man's clothes.

As they went slowly towards the house he tore at the ragged wisps of chrysanthemums and dropped the petals in handfuls along the path.

"Don't do that – it *does* look nasty," said his mother. He refrained, and she, suddenly pitiful, broke off a twig with three or four wan flowers and held them against her face. When mother and son reached the yard her hand hesitated, and instead of laying the flower aside, she pushed it in her apron band. The mother and son stood at the foot of the three steps looking across the bay of lines at the passing-home of the miners. The trundle of the small train was imminent. Suddenly the engine loomed past the house and came to a stop opposite the gate.

The engine-driver, a short man with round grey beard, leaned out of the cab high above the woman.

"Have you got a cup of tea?" he said in a cheery, hearty fashion.

It was her father. She went in, saying she would mash.° Directly, she returned.

"I didn't come to see you on Sunday," began the little grey-bearded man.

"I didn't expect you," said his daughter.

The engine-driver winced; then, reassuming his cheery, airy manner, he said:

"Oh, have you heard then? Well – and what do you think –?"

"I think it is soon enough," she replied.

At her brief censure the little man made an impatient gesture, and said coaxingly, yet with dangerous coldness:

"Well, what's a man to do? It's no sort of life for a man of my years, to sit at my own hearth like a stranger. And if I'm going to marry again it may as well be soon as late – what does it matter to anybody?"

The woman did not reply, but turned and went into the house. The man in the engine-cab stood assertive, till she returned with a cup of tea and a piece of bread and butter on a plate. She went up the steps and stood near the footplate of the hissing engine.

"You needn't 'a brought me bread an' butter," said her father. "But a cup of tea" – he sipped appreciatively – "it's very nice." He sipped for a moment or two, then: "I hear as Walter's got another bout° on," he said.

"When hasn't he?" said the woman bitterly.

"I heered tell of him in the 'Lord Nelson' braggin' as he was going to spend that b— afore he went: half a sovereign that was."

"When?" asked the woman.

"A' Sat'day night – I know that's true."

"Very likely," she laughed bitterly. "He gives me twenty-three shillings."

"Ay, it's a nice thing, when a man can do nothing with his money but make a beast of himself!" said the grey-whiskered man. The woman turned her head away. Her father swallowed the last of his tea and handed her the cup.

"Ay," he sighed, wiping his mouth. "It's a settler,° it is –"

He put his hand on the lever. The little engine strained and groaned, and the train rumbled towards the crossing. The woman again looked across the metals. Darkness was settling over the spaces of the railway and trucks: the miners, in grey sombre groups, were still passing home. The winding-engine pulsed hurriedly, with brief pauses. Elizabeth Bates looked at the dreary flow of men, then she went indoors. Her husband did not come.

The kitchen was small and full of firelight; red coals piled glowing up the chimney mouth. All the life of the room seemed in the white warm hearth and the steel fender reflecting the red fire. The cloth was laid for tea; cups glinted in the shadow. At the back, where the lowest stair protruded into the room, the boy sat struggling with a knife and a piece of white wood. He was almost hidden in shadow, only his movement seemed visible. It was half past four. They had but to await the father's coming to begin tea. As the mother watched her son's sullen little struggle with the wood, she saw herself in his silence and pertinacity, she saw the father in her child's indifference to all but himself. She seemed to be occupied by her husband. He had probably gone past his home, slunk past his own door, to drink before he came in, while his dinner spoiled and wasted in waiting. She glanced at the clock, and took the potatoes to strain them in the yard. The garden and the fields beyond the brook were closed in uncertain darkness. When she rose with the saucepan, leaving the drain steaming into the night behind her, she saw the yellow lamps were lit along the highroad that went up the hill away beyond the space of the railway-lines and the field. Then again she watched the men trooping home, fewer now, and fewer.

Indoors the fire was sinking and the room was dark red. The woman put her saucepan on the hob, and set a batter pudding near the mouth of the oven. Then she stood unmoving. Directly, gratefully, came quick young steps to the door. Someone hung on the latch a moment, then a little girl entered, and began pulling off her outdoor things, dragging a mass of curls just ripening from gold to brown over her eyes with her hat.

Her mother chid her for coming late from school, and said she would have to keep her at home the dark winter days.

"Why, mother, it's hardly a bit dark. The lamp's not lighted, and my father's not home yet."

"No, he isn't. But it's a quarter to five! Did you see anything of him?"

The child became serious. She looked at her mother with large, wistful blue eyes.

"No, mother, I've never seen him. Why? Has he come up an' gone past to Old Brinsley? He hasn't, mother, 'cos I never saw him."

"He'd watch that," said the mother bitterly, "he'd take care as you didn't see him. But you may depend upon it, he's seated in the 'Prince o' Wales'. He wouldn't be this late."

The girl looked at her mother piteously.

"Let's have our teas, mother, should we?" said she. The mother called John to table.

She opened the door once more and leaned out to look across the darkness of the lines. All was deserted: she could not hear the winding-engines.

"Perhaps," she said to herself, "he's stopped to get some ripping° done."

They sat down to tea. John, at the end of the table near the door, was almost lost in the darkness. Their faces were hidden from each other.

The girl crouched against the fender slowly moving a thick piece of bread before the fire. The lad, his face a dusky mark on the shadow, sat watching her who was transfigured in the hot red glow.

"I do think it's beautiful to look in the fire," said the child.

"Do you?" said her mother. "Why?"

"It's so red, and full of little caves – and it feels so nice, and you can fair smell it."

"It'll want mending directly," replied her mother. "And then if your father comes he'll carry on and say there never is a fire when a man comes home sweating from the pit. – A public house is always warm enough."

There was silence till the boy said complainingly: "Make haste, our Annie."

"Well, I am doing! I can't make the fire do it no faster, can I?"

"She keeps waflin° it about so's to make 'er slow," grumbled the boy.

"Don't have such an evil imagination, child," replied the mother.

Soon the room was busy in the darkness with the crisp sound of crunching. The mother ate very little. She drank her tea determinedly, and sat thinking. When she rose her anger was evident in the stern unbending of her head. She looked at the pudding in the fender, and broke out:

"It *is* a scandalous thing as a man can't even come in to his dinner. If it's crozzled up° to a cinder I don't see why I should care. Past his very door he goes to get to a public house, and here I sit with his dinner waiting for him –"

She went out. As she dropped piece after piece of coal on the red fire, the shadows fell on the walls, till the room was almost in total darkness.

"I canna see," grumbled the invisible John. In spite of herself, the mother laughed.

"You know the way to your mouth," she said. She set the dustpan outside the door. When she came again like a shadow on the hearth, the lad repeated, complaining sulkily:

"I canna see."

"Good gracious!" cried the mother irritably, "you're as bad as your father if it's a bit dusk!"

Nevertheless she took a paper spill from a sheaf on the mantelpiece and proceeded to light the lamp that hung from the ceiling in the middle of the room. As she reached up her figure displayed itself just rounding with maternity.

"Oh mother –!" exclaimed the girl.

"What?" said the woman, suspended in the act of putting the lamp-glass over the flame. The copper reflector shone handsomely on her, as she stood with uplifted arm, turning her face to her daughter.

"You've got a flower in your apron!" said the child, in a little rapture at this unusual event.

"Goodness me!" exclaimed the woman, relieved. "One would think the house was afire." She replaced the glass and waited a moment before turning up the wick. A pale shadow was seen floating weirdly on the floor.

"Let me smell!" said the child, still rapturously, coming forward and putting her face to her mother's waist.

"Go along, silly!" said the mother, turning up the lamp. The light revealed their suspense, so that the woman felt it almost unbearable. Annie was still bending at her waist. Irritably, the mother took the flowers from out of her apron band.

"Oh mother – don't take them out!" cried Annie, catching her hand, and trying to replace the sprig.

"Such nonsense!" said the mother, turning away. The child put the pale chrysanthemums to her lips, murmuring:

"Don't they smell beautiful!"

Her mother gave a short laugh.

"No," she said. "Not to me. It was chrysanthemums when I married him, and chrysanthemums when you were born, and the first time they ever brought him home drunk he'd got brown chrysanthemums in his button-hole."

She looked at the children. Their eyes and their parted lips were wondering. The mother sat rocking in silence for some time. Then she looked at the clock.

"Twenty minutes to six!" In a tone of fine bitter carelessness she continued: "Eh, he'll not come now till they bring him. There he'll stick! But he needn't come rolling in here in his pit-dirt, for *I* won't wash him. He can lie on the floor – Eh, what a fool I've been, what a fool! And this is what I came here for, to this dirty hole, rats and all, for him to slink past his very door. Twice last week – he's begun now –"

She silenced herself, and rose to clear the table.

While, for an hour or more, the children played subduedly, intent, fertile of invention, united in fear of their mother's wrath and in dread of their father's homecoming, Mrs. Bates sat in her rocking-chair making a 'singlet' of thick, cream coloured flannel, which gave a dull wounded sound as she tore off the grey edge. She worked at her sewing with energy, listening to the children, and her anger wearied itself, lay down to rest, opening its eyes from time to time and steadily watching, its ears raised to listen. Sometimes, even her anger quailed and shrank, and the mother suspended her sewing, tracing the footsteps that thudded along the sleepers outside; she would lift her head sharply to bid the children "hush," but she recovered herself in time, and the footsteps went past the gate, and the children were not flung out of their play-world.

But at last Annie sighed, and gave in. She glanced at her waggon of slippers, and loathed the game. She turned plaintively to her mother:

"Mother! –" – but she was inarticulate.

John crept out like a frog from under the sofa. His mother glanced up.

"Yes," she said, "just look at those shirt sleeves."

The boy held them out to survey them, saying nothing. Then somebody called in a hoarse voice away down the line, and suspense bristled in the room, till two people had gone by outside, talking.

"It is time for bed," said the mother.

"My father hasn't come," wailed Annie plaintively.

But her mother was primed with courage:

"Never mind. They'll bring him when he does come – like a log." She meant there would be no scene. "And he may sleep on the floor till he wakes himself. I know he'll not go to work tomorrow after this!"

The children had their hands and faces wiped with the flannel. They were very quiet. When they had put on their nightdresses, they said their prayers, the boy mumbling. The mother looked down at them, at the brown silken bush of intertwining curls in the nape of the girl's neck, at the little black head of the lad, and her heart burst with anger at their father, who caused all three such distress. The children hid their faces in her skirts, for comfort.

When Mrs. Bates came down, the room was strangely empty, with a tension of expectancy. She took up her sewing and stitched for some time without raising her head. Meantime her anger was tinged with fear.

II

The clock struck eight and she rose suddenly, dropping her sewing on her chair. She went to the stairfoot door, opened it, listening. The children were evidently asleep. She went out, locking the door behind her.

Something scuffled down the yard, and she started, though she knew it was only the rats, with which the place was overrun. The night was very dark. In the great bay of railway-lines bulked with trucks there was no trace of light, only away back she could see a few yellow lamps at the pit-top, and the red smear of the burning pit-bank on the night. She hurried along the edge of the track, then, crossing the converging lines, came to the stile by the white gates, whence she emerged on the road. Then the fear which had led her shrank. People were walking up to New Brinsley; she saw the lights in the houses; twenty yards further on were the broad windows of the "Prince of Wales", very warm and bright, and the loud voices of men could be heard distinctly. What a fool she had been to imagine that anything had happened to him! He was merely drinking over there at the "Prince of Wales". She faltered. She had never yet been to fetch him, and she never would go. Yet, while she was out, she must get some satisfaction. So she continued her walk towards the long straggling line of houses standing blank on the highway. She entered a passage between the dwellings.

"Mr. Rigley? – Yes! Did you want him? No, he's not in at this minute."

The raw-boned woman leaned forward from her dark scullery and peered at the other, upon whom fell a dim light through the blind of the kitchen window.

"Is it Mrs. Bates?" she asked in a tone tinged with respect.

"Yes. I wondered if your Master was at home. Mine hasn't come yet."

"'Asn't 'e! Oh, Jack's been 'ome an 'ad 'is dinner an' gone out. E's just gone for 'alf an 'our afore bed-time. Did you call at th' 'Prince of Wales'?"

"No –"

"No, you didn't like –! It's not very nice." The other woman was indulgent. There was an awkward pause. "Jack never said nothink about – about your Mester," she added.

"No! – I expect he's stuck in there!"

Elizabeth Bates said this bitterly, and with recklessness. She knew that the woman across the yard was standing at her door listening, but she did not care. As she turned away,

"Stop a minute! I'll just go an' ask Jack if 'e knows anythink," said Mrs. Rigley.

"Oh, no – I wouldn't like to put –!"

"Yes, I will, if you'll just step inside an' see as th' childer doesn't come downstairs and set theirselves afire."

Elizabeth Bates, murmuring a remonstrance, stepped inside. The other woman apologised for the state of the room.

The kitchen needed apology. There were little frocks and trousers and childish undergarments on the squab and on the floor, and a litter of playthings everywhere. On the black American cloth of the table were pieces of bread and cake, crusts, slops, and a teapot with cold tea.

"Eh, ours is just as bad," said Elizabeth Bates. Mrs. Rigley put a shawl over her head and hurried out, saying:

"I shanna be a minute."

The other sat noting with faint disapproval the general untidiness of the room. Then she fell to counting the shoes of various sizes scattered over the floor. There were twelve. She sighed and said to herself, "No wonder!" glancing at the litter. There came the scratching of two pairs of feet across the yard, and the Rigleys entered. Elizabeth Bates rose. Rigley was a big man, with very large bones. His head looked particularly bony.

Across his temple was a blue scar, caused by a wound got in the pit, a wound in which the coal-dust remained blue like tattooing.

"'Asna 'e come whoam yit?" asked the man, without any form of greeting, but with deference and sympathy. "I couldna say wheer he is – 'e's non ower theer!" – he jerked his head to signify the "Prince of Wales".

"'E's 'appen gone up to th' 'Yew'," said Mrs. Rigley.

There was another pause. Rigley had evidently something to get off his mind:

"Ah left 'im finishin' a stint," he began. "Loose-a'◊ 'ad bin gone about ten minutes when we com'n away, an' I shouted, 'Are ter comin', Walt?' an' 'e said, 'Go on, Ah shanna be but a'ef a minnit,' so we com'n ter th' bottom, me an' Bower, thinkin' as 'e wor just behint us. Ah'd a ta'en a hoath as 'e wor just behint – an' 'ud come up i' th' next bantle –"◊

He stood perplexed, as if answering a charge of desertion of his mate. Elizabeth Bates, now again certain of disaster, hastened to reassure him:

"I expect 'e's gone to th' 'Yew Tree', as you say. It's not the first time. – I've fretted myself into a fever before now. He'll come home when they carry him."

"Ay, isn't it a bit too bad!" deplored the other woman.

"I'll just step up to Dick's an' see if 'e *is* theer," offered the man, afraid of appearing alarmed, afraid of taking liberties.

"Oh, I wouldn't think of bothering you that far," said Elizabeth Bates, with emphasis. But he knew she was glad of his offer.

As they stumbled up the entry, Elizabeth Bates heard Rigley's wife run across the yard and open her neighbour's door. At this suddenly all the blood in her body seemed to switch away from her heart.

"Mind!" warned Rigley. "Ah've said many a time as Ah'd fill up them ruts in this entry, sumb'dy 'll be breakin' their legs yit."

She recovered herself and walked quickly along with the miner.

"I don't like leaving the children in bed, and nobody in the house," she said.

"No, you dunna!" he replied, courteously. They were soon at the gate of the cottage.

"Well, I shanna be many minnits. Dunna you be frettin' now, 'e'll be a' right," said the butty.°

"Thank you very much, Mr. Rigley," she replied.

"You're welcome!" he stammered, moving away. "I shanna be many minnits."

The house was quiet. Elizabeth Bates took off her hat and shawl, and rolled back the rug. She was in a hurry to tidy the house. Somebody would be coming, she knew. When she had finished, she sat down. It was a few minutes past nine. She was startled by the rapid chuff of the winding-engine at the pit, and the sharp whirr of the brakes on the rope as it descended. Again she felt the painful sweep of her blood, and she put her hand to her side, saying aloud, "Good gracious! – it's only the nine o'clock deputy going down," rebuking herself.

She sat still, listening. Half an hour of this, and she was wearied out.

"What am I working myself up like this for?" she said pitiably to herself, "I s'll only be doing myself some damage."

She took out her sewing again.

At a quarter to ten there were footsteps. One person! She watched for the door to open. It was an elderly woman, in a black bonnet and a black woollen shawl – his mother. She was about sixty years old, pale, with blue eyes, and her face all wrinkled and lamentable. She shut the door and turned to her daughter-in-law peevishly.

"Eh, Lizzie, whatever shall we do, whatever shall we do!" she cried.

Elizabeth drew back a little, sharply.

"What is it, mother?" she said.

The elder woman seated herself on the sofa.

"I don't know, child, I can't tell you!" – she shook her head slowly. Elizabeth sat watching her, anxious and vexed.

"I don't know," replied the grandmother, sighing very deeply. "There's no end to my troubles, there isn't. The things I've gone through, I'm sure it's enough –!" She wept without wiping her eyes, the tears running.

"But mother," interrupted Elizabeth, "what do you mean? What is it?"

The grandmother slowly wiped her eyes. The fountains of her tears were stopped by Elizabeth's directness. She wiped her eyes slowly.

"Poor child! eh, you poor thing!" she moaned. "I don't know what we're going to do, I don't – and you as you are – it's a thing, it is indeed!"

Elizabeth waited.

"Is he dead?" she asked, and at the words her heart swung violently, though she felt a slight flush of shame at the ultimate extravagance of the question. Her words sufficiently frightened the old lady, almost brought her to herself.

"Don't say so, Elizabeth! We'll hope it's not as bad as that; no, may the Lord spare us that, Elizabeth. Jack Rigley came just as I was sittin' down to a glass afore going to bed, an' 'e said, ''Appen you'll go down th' line, Mrs. Bates. Walt's had an accident. 'Appen you'll go an' sit wi' 'er till we can get him home.' I hadn't time to ask him a word, afore he was gone. An' I put my bonnet on an' come straight down, Lizzie. I thought to myself, 'Eh, that poor blessed child, if anybody should come an' tell her of a sudden, there's no knowin' what'll 'appen to 'er.' You mustn't let it upset you, Lizzie – or you know what to expect. How long is it, six months – or is it five, Lizzie? Ay!" – the old woman shook her head – "time slips on, it slips on! Ay!"

Elizabeth's thoughts were busy elsewhere. If he was killed – would she be able to manage on the little pension and what she could earn? – she counted up rapidly. If he was hurt – they wouldn't take him to the hospital – how tiresome he would be to nurse! – but perhaps she'd get him away from the drink and his hateful ways. She would – while he was ill. The tears offered to come to her eyes at the picture. But what sentimental luxury was this she was beginning? – She turned to consider the children. At any rate she was absolutely necessary for them. They were her business.

"Ay!" repeated the old woman, "it seems but a week or two since he brought me his first wages. Ay – he was a good lad, Elizabeth, he was, in his way. I don't know why he got to be such a trouble, I don't. He was a happy lad at home, only full of spirits. But there's no mistake he's been a handful o' trouble, a handful o' trouble, he has! I hope the Lord'll spare him to mend his ways, I hope so, I hope so. You've had a sight o' trouble with him, Elizabeth, you have indeed. But he was a jolly enough lad wi' me, he was, I can assure you. I don't know how it is…"

The old woman continued to muse aloud, a monotonous irritating sound, while Elizabeth thought concentratedly, startled once, when she heard the winding-engine chuff quickly and the brakes skirr with a shriek. Then she heard the engine more slowly, and the brakes made no sound. The old woman did not notice. Elizabeth waited in suspense. The mother-in-law talked, with lapses into silence.

"But he wasn't your son, Lizzie – an' it makes a difference. Whatever he was, I remember him when he was little, an' I learned to understand him and to make allowances. You've got to make allowances for them –"

It was half past ten, and the old woman was saying: "But it's trouble from beginning to end; you're never too old for trouble, never too old for that –" when the gate banged back, and there were heavy feet on the steps.

"I'll go, Lizzie, let me go," cried the old woman, rising. But Elizabeth was at the door. It was a man in pit-clothes.

"They're bringin' 'im, Missis," he said. Elizabeth's heart halted a moment. Then it surged on again, almost suffocating her.

"Is he – is it bad?" she asked.

The man turned away, looking at the darkness:

"The doctor says 'e'd been dead hours. 'E saw 'im i' th' lamp cabin."

The old woman, who stood just behind Elizabeth, dropped into a chair, and folded her hands, crying: "Oh, my boy, my boy!"

"Hush!" said Elizabeth, with a sharp twitch of a frown. "Be still, mother, don't waken th' children: I wouldn't have them down for anything!"

The old woman moaned softly, rocking herself. The man was drawing away. Elizabeth took a step forward.

"How was it?" she asked.

"Well, I couldn't say for sure," the man replied, very ill at ease. "'E wor finishin' a stint, an' th' butties 'ad gone, an' a lot o' stuff come down atop 'n 'im."

"And crushed him?" cried the widow, with a shudder.

"No," said the man, "it fell at th' back of 'im. 'E wor under th' face, an' it niver touched 'im. It shut 'im in. It seems 'e wor smothered."

Elizabeth shrank back. She heard the old woman behind her cry:

"What? – what did 'e say it was?"

The man replied, more loudly: "'E wor smothered!"

Then the old woman wailed aloud, and this relieved Elizabeth.

"Oh, mother," she said, putting her hand on the old woman, "don't waken th' children, don't waken th' children."

She wept a little, unknowing, while the old mother rocked herself and moaned. Elizabeth remembered that they were bringing him home, and she must be ready. "They'll lay him in the parlour," she said to herself, standing a moment pale and perplexed.

Then she lighted a candle and went into the tiny room. The air was cold and damp, but she could not make a fire, there was no fireplace. She set down the candle and looked round. The candle-light glittered on the lustre-glasses, on the two vases that held some of the pink chrysanthemums, and on the dark mahogany. There was a cold, deathly smell of chrysanthemums in the room. Elizabeth stood looking at the flowers. She turned away, and calculated whether there would be room to lay him on the floor, between the couch and the chiffonier. She pushed the chairs aside. There would be room to lay him down and to step round him. Then she fetched the old red table-cloth, and another old cloth, spreading them down to save her bit of carpet. She shivered on leaving the parlour; so, from the dresser drawer she took a clean shirt and put it at the fire to air. All the time her mother-in-law was rocking herself in the chair and moaning.

"You'll have to move from there, mother," said Elizabeth. "They'll be bringing him in. Come in the rocker."

The old mother rose mechanically, and seated herself by the fire, continuing to lament. Elizabeth went into the pantry for another candle, and there, in the little pent-house under the naked tiles, she heard them coming. She stood still in the pantry doorway, listening. She heard them pass the end of the house, and come awkwardly down the three steps, a jumble of shuffling footsteps and muttering voices. The old woman was silent. The men were in the yard.

Then Elizabeth heard Matthews, the manager of the pit, say: "You go in first, Jim. Mind!"

The door came open, and the two women saw a collier backing into the room, holding one end of a stretcher, on which they could see the nailed pit-boots of the dead man. The two carriers halted, the man at the head stooping to the lintel of the door.

"Wheer will you have him?" asked the manager, a short, white-bearded man.

Elizabeth roused herself and came away from the pantry, carrying the unlighted candle.

"In the parlour," she said.

"In there Jim!" pointed the manager, and the carriers backed round into the tiny room. The coat with which they had covered the body fell off as they awkwardly turned through the two doorways, and the women saw their man, naked to the waist, lying stripped for work. The old woman began to moan in a low voice of horror.

"Lay th' stretcher at th' side," snapped the manager, "an' put '*im* on th' cloths. Mind now, mind! Look you now – !"

One of the men had knocked off a vase of chrysanthemums. He stared awkwardly, then they set down the stretcher. Elizabeth did not look at her husband. As soon as she could get in the room, she went and picked up the broken vase, and the flowers.

"Wait a minute!" she said.

The three men waited in silence while she mopped up the water with a duster.

"Eh, what a job, what a job, to be sure!" the manager was saying, rubbing his brow with trouble and perplexity. "Never knew such a thing in my life, never! He'd no business to ha' been left. I never knew such a thing in my life! Fell over him clean as a whistle, an' shut him in. Not four foot of space, there wasn't – yet it scarce bruised him."

He looked down at the dead man, lying prone, half naked, all grimed with coal-dust.

"'Sphyxiated,' the doctor said. It *is* the most terrible job I've ever known. Seems as if it was done o' purpose. Clean over him, an' shut 'im in, like a mouse-trap" – he made a sharp, descending gesture with his hand.

The colliers standing by jerked aside their heads in hopeless comment.

The horror of the thing bristled upon them all.

Then they heard the girl's voice upstairs calling shrilly: "Mother, mother – who is it? Mother! – who is it?"

Elizabeth hurried to the foot of the stairs and opened the door:

"Go to sleep!" she commanded sharply. "What are you shouting about? Go to sleep at once – there's nothing –"

Then she began to mount the stairs. They could hear her on the boards, and on the plaster floor of the little bedroom. They could hear her distinctly:

"What's the matter now? – what's the matter with you, silly thing?" – her voice was much agitated, with an unreal gentleness.

"I thought it was some men come," said the plaintive voice of the child. "Has he come?"

"Yes, they've brought him. There's nothing to make a fuss about. Go to sleep now, like a good child."

They could hear her voice in the bedroom, they waited whilst she covered the children under the bedclothes.

"Is he drunk?" the girl asked, timidly, faintly.

"No! No – he's not! He – he's asleep."

"Is he asleep downstairs?"

"Yes...and don't make a noise."

There was silence for a moment, then the men heard the frightened child again:

"What's that noise?"

"It's nothing, I tell you, what are you bothering for?"

The noise was the grandmother moaning. She was oblivious of everything, sitting on her chair rocking and moaning. The manager put his hand on her arm and bade her "Sh – sh!!"

The old woman opened her eyes and looked at him. She was shocked by this interruption, and seemed to wonder.

"What time is it?" – the plaintive thin voice of the child, sinking back unhappily into sleep, asked this last question.

"Ten o'clock," answered the mother more softly. Then she must have bent down and kissed the children.

Matthews beckoned the men to come away. They put on their caps and took up the stretcher. Stepping over the body, they tiptoed out of the house. None of them spoke till they were far from the wakeful children.

When Elizabeth came down she found her mother alone on the parlour floor, leaning over the dead man, the tears dropping on him.

"We must lay him out," the wife said. She put on the kettle, then returned and kneeling at the feet, began to unfasten the knotted leather laces. The room was clammy and dim with only one candle, so that she had to bend her face almost to the floor. At last she got off the heavy boots, and put them away.

"You must help me now," she whispered to the old woman. Together they stripped the man.

When they arose, saw him lying in the naïve dignity of death, the women stood arrested in fear and respect. For a few moments they remained still, looking down, the old mother whimpering. Elizabeth felt countermanded. She saw him, how utterly inviolable he lay in himself. She had nothing to do with him. She could not accept it. Stooping, she laid her hand on him, in claim. He was still warm, for the mine was hot where he had died. His mother had his face between her hands, and was murmuring incoherently. The old tears fell in succession as drops from wet leaves; the mother was not weeping, merely her tears flowed. Elizabeth embraced the body of her husband, with cheek and lips. She seemed to be listening, inquiring, trying to get some connection. But she could not. She was driven away. He was impregnable.

She rose, went into the kitchen, where she poured warm water into a bowl, brought soap and flannel and a soft towel.

"I must wash him," she said. Then the old mother rose stiffly, and watched Elizabeth as she carefully washed his face, carefully brushing the big blonde moustache from his mouth with the flannel. She was afraid with a bottomless fear, so she ministered to him. The old woman, jealous, said:

"Let me wipe him!" – and she kneeled on the other side, slowly drying as Elizabeth washed, her big black bonnet sometimes brushing the dark head of her daughter. They worked thus in silence for a long time. They never forgot it was death, and the touch of the man's dead body gave them strange emotions, different in each of the women; a great dread possessed them both, the mother felt the lie was given to her womb, she was denied; the wife felt the utter isolation of the human soul, the child within her was a weight apart from her.

At last it was finished. He was a man of handsome body, and his face showed no traces of drink. He was blonde, full-fleshed, with fine limbs. But he was dead.

"Bless him," whispered his mother, looking always at his face, and speaking out of sheer terror. "The dear lad – bless him!" She spoke in a faint, sibilant ecstasy of fear and mother love.

Elizabeth sank down again to the floor, and put her face against his neck, and trembled and shuddered. But she had to draw away again. He was dead, and her living flesh had no place against his. A great dread and weariness held her: she was so unavailing. Her life was gone like this.

"White as milk he is, clear as a twelvemonth baby, bless him, the darling!" the old mother murmured to herself. "Not a mark on him, clear and clean and white, as beautiful as ever a child was made," she murmured with pride. Elizabeth kept her face hidden.

"He went peaceful, Lizzie – peaceful as sleep. Isn't he beautiful, the lamb? Ay – he must ha' made his peace, Lizzie. 'Appen he made it all right, Lizzie, shut in there. He'd have time. He wouldn't look like this if he hadn't made his peace. The lamb, the dear lamb. Eh, but he had a hearty laugh. I loved to hear it. He had the heartiest laugh, Lizzie, as a lad –"

Elizabeth looked up. The man's mouth was fallen back, slightly open, under the cover of the moustache. The eyes, half shut, did not show glazed in the obscurity. Life with its smoky burning gone from him, had left him apart and utterly alien to her. And she knew what a stranger he was to her. In her womb was ice of fear, because of this separate stranger with whom she had been living as one flesh. Was this what it all meant – utter, intact separateness, obscured by heat of living? In dread she turned her face away. The fact was too deadly.

There had been nothing between them, and yet they had come together, exchanging their nakedness repeatedly. Each time he had taken her, they had been two isolated beings, far apart as now. He was no more responsible than she. The child was like ice in her womb. For as she looked at the dead man, her mind, cold and detached, said clearly: "Who am I? What have I been doing? I have been fighting a husband who did not exist. *He* existed all the time. What wrong have I done? What was that I have been living with? There lies the reality, this man." – And her soul died in her for fear: she knew she had never seen him, he had never seen her, they had met in the dark and had fought in the dark, not knowing whom they met nor whom they fought. And now she saw, and turned silent in seeing. For she had been wrong. She had said he was something he was not; she had felt familiar with him. Whereas he was apart all the while, living as she never lived, feeling as she never felt.

In fear and shame she looked at his naked body, that she had known falsely. And he was the father of her children. Her soul was torn from her body and stood apart. She looked at his naked body and was ashamed, as if she had denied it. After all, it was itself. It seemed awful to her. She looked at his face, and she turned her own face to the wall. For his look was other than hers, his way was not her way. She had denied him what he was – she saw it now. She had refused him as himself. – And this had been her life, and his life. – She was grateful to death, which restored the truth. And she knew she was not dead.

And all the while her heart was bursting with grief and pity for him. What had he suffered? What stretch of horror for this helpless man! She was rigid with agony. She had not been able to help him. He had been cruelly injured, this naked man, this other being, and she could make no reparation. There were the children – but the children belonged to life. This dead man had nothing to do with them. He and she were only channels through which life had flowed to issue in the children. She was a mother – but how awful she knew it now to have been a wife. And he, dead now, how awful he must have felt it to be a husband. She felt that in the next world he would be a stranger to her. If they met there, in the beyond, they would only be ashamed of what had been before. The children had come, for some mysterious reason, out of both of them. But the children did not unite them. Now he was dead, she knew how eternally he was apart from her, how eternally he had nothing more to do with her. She saw this episode of her life closed. They had denied each other in life. Now he had withdrawn. An anguish came over her. It was finished then: it had become hopeless between them long before he died. Yet he had been her husband. But how little!

"Have you got his shirt, 'Lizabeth?"

Elizabeth turned without answering, though she strove to weep and behave as her mother-in-law expected. But she could not, she was silenced. She went into the kitchen and returned with the garment.

"It is aired," she said, grasping the cotton shirt here and there to try. She was almost ashamed to handle him; what right had she or anyone to lay hands on him; but her touch was humble on his body. It was hard work to clothe him. He was so heavy and inert. A terrible dread gripped her all the while: that he could be so heavy and utterly inert, unresponsive, apart.

The horror of the distance between them was almost too much for her – it was so infinite a gap she must look across.

At last it was finished. They covered him with a sheet and left him lying, with his face bound. And she fastened the door of the little parlour, lest the children should see what was lying there. Then, with peace sunk heavy on her heart, she went about making tidy the kitchen. She knew she submitted to life, which was her immediate master. But from death, her ultimate master, she winced with fear and shame.

Daughters of the Vicar

1

Mr. Lindley was first vicar of Aldecross. The cottages of this tiny hamlet had nestled in peace since their beginning, and the country folk had crossed the lanes and farm-lands, two or three miles, to the parish church at Greymeed, on the bright Sunday mornings.

But when the pits were sunk, blank rows of dwellings started up beside the high-roads, and a new population, skimmed from the floating scum of workmen, was filled in, the cottages and the country people almost obliterated.

To suit the convenience of these new collier-inhabitants, a church must be built at Aldecross. There was not too much money. And so the little building crouched like a humped stone-and-mortar mouse, with two little turrets at the west corners for ears, in the fields near the cottages and the apple-trees, as far as possible from the dwellings down the high road. It had an uncertain, timid look about it. And so they planted big-leaved ivy, to hide its shrinking newness. So that now the little church stands buried in its greenery, stranded and sleeping among the fields, while the brick houses elbow nearer and nearer, threatening to crush it down. It is already obsolete.

The Reverend Ernest Lindley, aged twenty-seven, and newly married, came from his curacy in Suffolk to take charge of his church. He was just an ordinary young man, who had been to Cambridge and taken orders. His wife was a self-assured young woman, daughter of a Cambridgeshire rector. Her father had spent the whole of his thousand a year, so that Mrs. Lindley had nothing of her own. Thus, the young married people came to Aldecross to live on a stipend of about a hundred and twenty pounds, and to keep up a superior position.

They were not very well received by the new, raw, disaffected population of colliers. Being accustomed to farm labourers, Mr. Lindley had considered himself as belonging indisputably to the upper or ordering classes. He had to be humble to the county families, but still, he was of their kind, whilst the common people were something different. He had no doubts of himself.

He found, however, that the collier population refused to accept this arrangement. They had no use for him in their lives, and they told him so, callously. The women merely said, "they were throng,"° or else, "Oh, it's no good you coming here, we're chapel."° The men were quite good-humoured so long as he did not touch them too nigh, they were cheerfully contemptuous of him, with a preconceived contempt he was powerless against.

At last, passing from indignation to silent resentment, even, if he dared have acknowledged it, to conscious hatred of the majority of his flock, and unconscious hatred of himself, he confined his activities to a narrow round of cottages, and he had to submit. He had no particular character, having always depended on his position in society to give him position among men. Now he was so poor, he had no social standing even among the common vulgar tradespeople of the district, and he had not the nature nor the wish to make his society agreeable to them, nor the strength to impose himself where he would have liked to be recognized. He dragged on, pale and miserable and neutral.

At first his wife raged with mortification. She took on airs and used a high hand. But her income was too small, the wrestling with tradesmen's bills was too pitiful, she only met with general, callous ridicule when she tried to be impressive.

Wounded to the quick of her pride, she found herself isolated in an indifferent, callous population. She raged indoors and out. But soon she learned that she must pay too heavily for her outdoor rages, and then she only raged within the walls of the rectory. There her feeling was so strong, that she frightened herself. She saw herself hating her husband, and she knew that, unless she were careful, she would smash her form of life and bring catastrophe upon him and upon herself. So in very fear, she went quiet. She hid, bitter and beaten by fear, behind the only shelter she had in the world, her gloomy, poor parsonage.

Children were born one every year; almost mechanically, she continued to perform her maternal duty, which was forced upon her. Gradually, broken by the suppressing of her violent anger and misery and disgust, she became an invalid and took to her couch.

The children grew up healthy, but unwarmed and rather rigid. Their father and mother educated them at home, made them very proud and very genteel, put them definitely and cruelly in the upper classes, apart from the vulgar around them. So they lived quite isolated. They were good-looking, and had that curiously clean, semi-transparent look of the genteel, isolated poor.

Gradually Mr. and Mrs. Lindley lost all hold on life, and spent their hours, weeks and years merely haggling to make ends meet, and bitterly repressing and pruning their children into gentility, urging them to ambition, weighting them with duty. On Sunday morning the whole family, except the mother, went down the lane to church, the long-legged girls in skimpy frocks, the boys in black coats and long, grey, unfitting trousers. They passed by their father's parishioners with mute clear faces, childish mouths closed in pride that was like a doom to them, and childish eyes already unseeing. Miss Mary, the eldest, was the leader. She was a long, slim thing with a fine profile and a proud, pure look of submission to a high fate. Miss Louisa, the second, was short and plump and obstinate looking. She had more enemies than ideals. She looked after the lesser children, Miss Mary after the elder. The collier children watched this pale, distinguished procession of the vicar's family pass mutely by, and they were impressed by the air of gentility and distance, they made mock of the trousers of the small sons, they felt inferior in themselves, and hate stirred their hearts.

In her time, Miss Mary received as governess a few little daughters of tradesmen; Miss Louisa managed the house and went among her father's church-goers, giving lessons on the piano to the colliers' daughters at thirteen shillings for twenty-six lessons.

2

One winter morning, when his daughter Mary was about twenty years old, Mr. Lindley, a thin unobtrusive figure in his black overcoat and his wideawake,° went down into Aldecross with a packet of white papers under his arm. He was delivering the parish almanack.

A rather pale, neutral man of middle age, he waited while the train thumped over the level crossing, going up to the pit which rattled busily just along the line. A wooden-legged man hobbled to open the gate, Mr. Lindley passed on. Just at his left hand, below the road and the railway, was the red roof of a cottage, showing through the bare twigs of apple trees. Mr. Lindley passed round the low wall, and descended the worn steps that led from the highway down to the cottage which crouched darkly and quietly away below the rumble of passing trains and the clank of coal carts, in a quiet little under-world of its own. Snowdrops with tight-shut buds were hanging very still under the bare currant bushes.

The clergyman was just going to knock when he heard a clinking noise, and turning saw through the open door of a black shed just behind him an elderly woman in a black lace cap stooping among reddish big cans, pouring a very bright

64

liquid into a tundish.° There was a smell of paraffin. The woman put down her can, took the tundish and laid it on a shelf, then rose with a tin bottle. Her eyes met those of the clergyman.

"Oh is it you, Mr. Lin'ley!" she said, in a complaining tone. "Go in."

The minister entered the house. In the hot kitchen sat a big elderly man with a great grey beard, taking snuff. He grunted in a deep, muttering voice, telling the minister to sit down, and then took no more notice of him, but stared vacantly into the fire. Mr. Lindley waited.

The woman came in, the ribbons of her black lace cap, or bonnet, hanging on her shawl. She was of medium stature, everything about her was tidy. She went up a step out of the kitchen, carrying the paraffin tin. Feet were heard entering the room up the step. It was a little haberdashery shop, with parcels on the shelves of the walls, a big, old-fashioned sewing-machine with tailor's work lying round it, in the open space. The woman went behind the counter, gave the child, who had entered, the paraffin bottle, and took from her a jug.

"My mother says shall yer put it down," said the child, and she was gone. The woman wrote in a book, then came into the kitchen with her jug. The husband, a very large man, rose and brought more coal to the already hot fire. He moved slowly and sluggishly. Already he was going dead; being a tailor, his large form had become an encumbrance to him. In his youth he had been a great dancer and boxer. Now he was taciturn, and inert. The minister had nothing to say, so he sought for his phrases. But John Durant took no notice, existing silent and dull.

Mrs. Durant spread the cloth. Her husband poured himself beer into a mug, and began to smoke and drink.

"Shall you have some?" he growled through his beard at the clergyman, looking slowly from the man to the jug, capable of this one idea.

"No, thank you," replied Mr. Lindley, though he would have liked some beer. He must set the example in a drinking parish.

"We need a drop to keep us going," said Mrs. Durant.

She had rather a complaining manner. The clergyman sat on uncomfortably while she laid the table for the half-past ten lunch. Her husband drew up to eat. She remained in her little round arm-chair by the fire.

She was a woman who would have liked to be easy in her life, but to whose lot had fallen a rough and turbulent family, and a slothful husband who did not care what became of himself or anybody. So, her rather good-looking square face was peevish, she had that air of having been compelled all her life to serve unwillingly, and to control where she did not want to control. There was about her too that masterful *aplomb* of a woman who has brought up and ruled her sons: but even them she had ruled unwillingly. She had enjoyed managing her little haberdashery shop, riding in the carrier's cart to Nottingham, going through the big warehouses to buy her goods. But the fret of managing her sons she did not like. Only she loved her youngest boy, because he was her last, and she saw herself free.

This was one of the houses the clergyman visited occasionally. Mrs. Durant, as part of her regulation, had brought up all her sons in the church. Not that she had any religion. Only, it was what she was used to. Mr. Durant was without religion. He read the fervently evangelical *Life* of John Wesley° with a curious pleasure, getting from it a satisfaction as from the warmth of the fire, or a glass of brandy. But he cared no more about John Wesley, in fact, than about John Milton, of whom he had never heard.

Mrs. Durant took her chair to the table.

"I don't feel like eating," she sighed.

"Why – aren't you well?" asked the clergyman, patronising.

"It isn't that," she sighed. She sat with shut, straight mouth. "I don't know what's going to become of us."

But the clergyman had ground himself down so long, that he could not easily sympathise.

"Have you any trouble?" he asked.

"Ay, have I any trouble!" cried the elderly woman. "I shall end my days in the workhouse."

The minister waited unmoved. What could she know of poverty, in her little house of plenty.

"I hope not," he said.

"And the one lad as I wanted to keep by me –" she lamented.

The minister listened without sympathy, quite neutral.

"And the lad as would have been a support to my old age. What is going to become of us?" she said.

The clergyman, justly, did not believe in the cry of poverty, but wondered what had become of the son.

"Has anything happened to Alfred?" he asked.

"We've got word he's gone for a Queen's sailor," she said sharply.

"He has joined the navy!" exclaimed Mr. Lindley. "I think he could scarcely have done better – to serve his Queen and country on the sea –"

"He is wanted to serve *me*," she cried. "And I wanted my lad at home."

Alfred was her baby, her last, whom she had allowed herself the luxury of spoiling.

"You will miss him," said Mr. Lindley, "that is certain. But this is no regrettable step for him to have taken – on the contrary."

"That's easy for you to say, Mr. Lindley," she replied tartly. "Do you think I want my lad climbing ropes at another man's bidding, like a monkey –"

"There is no *dishonour*, surely, in serving in the navy?"

"Dishonour this dishonour that," cried the angry old woman. "He goes and makes a slave of himself, and he'll rue it."

Her angry, scornful impatience nettled the clergyman, and silenced him for some moments.

"I do not see," he retorted at last, white at the gills and inadequate, "that the Queen's service is any more to be called slavery than working in a mine."

"At home he was at home, and his own master. *I* know he'll find a difference."

"It may be the making of him," said the clergyman. "It will take him away from bad companionship and drink."

Some of the Durants' sons were notorious drinkers, and Alfred was not quite steady.

"And why indeed shouldn't he have his glass," cried the mother. "He picks no man's pocket to pay for it."

The clergyman stiffened at what he thought was an allusion to his own profession, and his unpaid bills.

"With all due consideration, I am glad to hear he has joined the navy," he said.

"Me with my old age coming on, and his father working very little. I'd thank you to be glad about something else besides that, Mr. Lindley. –"

The woman began to cry. Her husband, quite impassive, finished his lunch of meat pie, and drank some beer. Then he turned to the fire, as if there were no-one in the room but himself.

"I shall respect all men who serve God and their Country on the sea, Mrs. Durant," said the clergyman, stubbornly.

"That is very well, when they are not your sons who are doing the dirty work. – It makes a difference," she replied tartly.

"I should be proud if one of my sons were to enter the navy."

"Ay – well – we're not all of us made alike –"

The minister rose. He put down a large folded paper.

"I've brought the almanack," he said.

Mrs. Durant unfolded it.

"I do like a bit of colour in things," she said, petulantly.

The clergyman did not reply.

"There's that envelope for the organist's fund –" said the old woman, and rising, she took the thing from the mantelpiece, went into the shop, and returned sealing it up.

"Which is all I can afford," she said.

Mr. Lindley took his departure, in his pocket the envelope containing Mrs. Durant's offering for Miss Louisa's services. He went from door to door delivering the almanacks, in dull routine. Jaded with the monotony of the business, and with the repeated effort of greeting half-known people, he felt barren and rather irritable. At last he returned home.

In the dining room was a small fire. Mrs. Lindley, grown very stout, lay on her couch. The vicar carved the cold mutton, Miss Louisa, short and plump and rather flushed, came in from the kitchen, Miss Mary, dark, with a beautiful white brow and grey eyes, served the vegetables, the children chattered a little, but not exuberantly. The very air seemed starved.

"I went to the Durants," said the vicar, as he served out the small portions of mutton. "It appears Alfred has run away to join the navy."

"Do him good," came the rough voice of the invalid. Miss Louisa, attending to the youngest child, looked up in protest.

"Why has he done that?" asked Mary's low, musical voice.

"He wanted some excitement, I suppose," said the vicar. "Shall we say grace?"

The children were arranged, all bent their heads, grace was pronounced. At the last word every face was being raised, to go on with the interesting subject.

"He's just done the right thing, for once," came the rather deep voice of the mother. "Save him from becoming a drunken sot, like the rest of them."

"They're not *all* drunken, mama," said Miss Louisa, stubbornly.

"It's no fault of their upbringing if they're not. Walter Durant is a standing disgrace."

"As I told Mrs. Durant," said the vicar, eating hungrily, "it is the best thing he could have done. It will take him away from temptation during the most dangerous years of his life – how old is he – nineteen –?"

"Twenty," said Miss Louisa.

"Twenty!" repeated the vicar. "It will give him wholesome discipline and set before him some sort of standard of duty and honour – nothing could have been better for him. But –"

"We shall miss him from the choir," cried Miss Louisa, as if taking opposite sides to her parents.

"That is as it may be," said the vicar. "I prefer to know he is safe in the navy, than running the risk of getting into bad ways here."

"Was he getting into bad ways?" asked the stubborn Miss Louisa.

"You know, Louisa, he wasn't quite what he used to be," said Miss Mary gently and steadily. Miss Louisa shut her rather heavy jaw sulkily. She wanted to deny it, but she knew it was true.

For her he had been a laughing, warm lad, with something kindly and something rich about him. It had made her feel warm. It seemed the days would be colder since he had gone.

"Quite the best thing he could do," said the mother with emphasis.

"I think so," said the vicar. "But his mother was almost abusive because I suggested it."

He spoke in an injured tone.

"What does *she* care for her children's welfare," said the invalid. "Their wages is all her concern."

"I suppose she wanted him at home with her," said Miss Louisa.

"Yes, she did – at the expense of his learning to be a drunkard like the rest of them," retorted her mother.

"George Durant doesn't drink," defended her daughter.

"Because he got burned so badly when he was nineteen – in the pit – and that frightened him. The navy is a better remedy than that, at least."

"Certainly," said the vicar. "Certainly."

And to this Miss Louisa agreed. Yet she could not but feel angry that he had gone away for so many years. She herself was only nineteen.

3

It happened when Miss Mary was twenty three years old, Mr. Lindley was very ill. The family was exceedingly poor at the time, such a lot of money was needed, so little was forthcoming. Neither Miss Mary nor Miss Louisa had suitors. What chance had they? They met no eligible young men in Aldecross. And what they earned was a mere drop in a void. The girls' hearts were chilled and hardened with fear of this perpetual cold penury, this narrow struggle, this horrible nothingness of their lives.

A clergyman had to be found for the church work. It so happened the son of an old friend of Mr. Lindley's was waiting three months before taking up his duties. He would come and officiate, for nothing. The young clergyman was keenly expected. He was not more than twenty seven, a Master of Arts of Oxford, had written his thesis on Roman Law. He came of an old Cambridgeshire family, had some private means, was going to take a church in Northamptonshire with a good stipend, and was not married. Mrs. Lindley incurred new debts, and scarcely regretted her husband's illness.

But when Mr. Massey came, there was a shock of disappointment in the house. They had expected a young man with a pipe and a deep voice, but with better manners than Sidney, the eldest of the Lindleys. There arrived instead a small, chétif° man, scarcely larger than a boy of twelve, spectacled, timid in the extreme, without a word to utter at first; yet with a certain inhuman self-sureness.

"What a little abortion!" was Mrs. Lindley's exclamation to herself on first seeing him, in his buttoned-up clerical coat. And for the first time for many days, she was profoundly thankful to God: that all her children were decent specimens.

He had not normal powers of perception. They soon saw that he lacked the full range of human feelings, had rather a strong, philosophical mind, from which he lived. His body was almost unthinkable, in intellect he was something definite. The conversation at once took a balanced, abstract tone when he participated. There was no spontaneous exclamation, no violent assertion or expression of personal conviction, but all cold, reasonable assertion. This was very hard on Mrs. Lindley. The little man would look at her, after one of her pronouncements, and then give, in his thin voice, his own calculated version, so that she felt as if she were tumbling into thin air through a hole in the flimsy floor on which their conversation stood. It was she who felt a fool. Soon she was reduced to a hardy silence.

Still, at the back of her mind, she remembered that he was an unattached gentleman, who would shortly have an income altogether of six or seven hundred a year. What did the man matter, if there were pecuniary ease! The man was a trifle thrown in. After twenty two years her sentimentality was ground away, and only the millstone of poverty mattered to her. So she supported the little man as a representative of a decent income.

His most irritating habit was that of a sneering little giggle, all on his own, which came when he perceived or related some illogical absurdity on the part of another person. It was the only form of humour he had. Stupidity in thinking seemed to him exquisitely funny. But any novel was unintelligibly meaningless and dull, and to an Irish sort of humour he listened curiously, examining it like mathematics, or else simply not hearing. In normal human relationship he was not there. Quite unable to take part in simple everyday talk, he padded silently round the house, or sat in the dining room looking nervously from side to side, always apart in a cold, rarefied little world of his own. Sometimes he made an ironic remark, that did not seem humanly relevant, or he gave his little laugh, like a sneer. He had to defend himself and his own insufficiency. And he answered questions grudgingly, with a yes or no, because he did not see their import, and was nervous. It seemed to Miss Louisa he scarcely distinguished one person from another, but that he liked to be near to her, or to Mary, for some sort of contact which stimulated him unknown.

Apart from all this, he was the most admirable workman. He was unremittingly shy, but perfect in his sense of duty: as far as he could conceive Christianity, he was a perfect Christian. Nothing that he realised he could do for anyone did he leave undone, although he was so incapable of coming into contact with another being, that he could not proffer help. Now he attended assiduously to the sick man, investigated all the affairs of the parish or the church which Mr. Lindley had in control, straightened out accounts, made lists of the sick and needy, padded round with help and to see what he could do. He heard of Mrs. Lindley's anxiety about her sons, and began to investigate means of sending them to Cambridge. His kindness almost frightened Miss Mary. She honoured it so, and yet she shrank from it. For in it all Mr. Massey seemed to have no sense of any person, any human being whom he was helping: he only realised a kind of mathematical working out, solving of given situations, a calculated well-doing. And it was as if he had accepted the Christian tenets as axioms. His religion consisted in what his scrupulous, abstract mind approved of.

Seeing his acts, Miss Mary must respect and honour him. In consequence she must serve him. To this she had to force herself, shuddering and yet desirous, but he did not perceive it. She accompanied him on his visiting in the parish, and whilst she was cold with admiration for him, often she was touched with pity for the little padding figure with bent shoulders, buttoned up to the chin in his overcoat. She was a handsome, calm girl, tall, with a beautiful repose. Her clothes were poor, and she wore a black silk scarf, having no furs. But she was a lady. As the people saw her walking down Aldecross beside Mr. Massey, they said:

"My word, Miss Mary's got a catch. Did ever you see such a measley little shrimp!"

She knew they were talking so, and it made her heart grow hot against them, and she drew herself as it were protectively towards the little man beside her. At any rate, she could see and give honour to his genuine goodness.

He could not walk fast, or far.

"You have not been well?" she asked, in her dignified way.

"I have an internal trouble."

He was not aware of her slight shudder. There was silence, whilst she bowed to recover her composure, to resume her gentle manner towards him.

He was fond of Miss Mary. She had made it a rule of hospitality that he should always be escorted by herself or by her sister on his visits in the parish, which were not many. But some mornings she was engaged. Then Miss Louisa took her place. It was no good Miss Louisa's trying to adopt to Mr. Massey an attitude of queenly service. She was unable to regard him save with aversion. When she saw him from behind, thin and bentshouldered, looking like a sickly lad of thirteen, she disliked him exceedingly, and felt a desire to put him out of existence. And yet a deeper justice in Mary made Louisa humble before her sister.

They were going to see Mr. Durant, who was paralysed and not expected to live. Miss Louisa was crudely ashamed at being admitted to the cottage in company with the little clergyman.

Mrs. Durant was, however, much quieter in the face of her real trouble.

"How is Mr. Durant?" asked Louisa.

"He is no different – and we don't expect him to be," was the reply. The little clergyman stood looking on.

They went upstairs. The three stood for some time looking at the bed, at the grey head of the old man on the pillow, the grey beard over the sheet. Miss Louisa was shocked and afraid.

"It is so dreadful," she said, with a shudder.

"It is how I always thought it would be," replied Mrs. Durant.

Then Miss Louisa was afraid of her. The two women were uneasy, waiting for Mr. Massey to say something. He stood, small and bent, too nervous to speak.

"Has he any understanding?" he asked at length.

"Maybe," said Mrs. Durant. "Can you hear, John?" she asked loudly. The dull blue eye of the inert man looked at her feebly.

"Yes, he understands," said Mrs. Durant to Mr. Massey. Except for the dull look in his eyes, the sick man lay as if dead. The three stood in silence. Miss Louisa was obstinate but heavy-hearted under the load of unlivingness. It was Mr. Massey who kept her there in discipline. His non-human will dominated them all.

Then they heard a sound below, a man's footsteps, and a man's voice called subduedly:

"Are you upstairs mother?"

Mrs. Durant started and moved to the door. But already a quick firm step was running up the stairs.

"I'm a bit early, mother," a troubled voice said, and on the landing they saw the form of the sailor. His mother came and clung to him. She was suddenly aware that she needed something to hold on to. He put his arms round her, and bent over her, kissing her.

"He's not gone, mother?" he asked anxiously, struggling to control his voice.

Miss Louisa looked away from the mother and son who stood together in the gloom on the landing. She could not bear it that she and Mr. Massey should be there. The latter stood nervously, as if ill at ease before the emotion that was running. He was a witness, nervous, unwilling, but dispassionate. To Miss Louisa's hot heart it seemed all, all wrong that they should be there.

Mrs. Durant entered the bedroom, her face wet.

"There's Miss Louisa and the vicar," she said, out of voice and quavering.

Her son, red faced and slender, drew himself up to salute. But Miss Louisa held out her hand. Then she saw his hazel eyes recognise her for a moment, and his small, white teeth showed in a glimpse of the greeting she used to love. She was covered with confusion. He went round to the bed; his boots clicked on the plaster floor, he bowed his head with dignity.

"How are you, Dad?" he said, laying his hand on the sheet, faltering. But the old man stared fixedly and unseeing. The son stood perfectly still for a few moments, then slowly recoiled. Miss Louisa saw the fine outline of his breast, under the blue sailor's blouse, as his chest began to heave.

"He doesn't know me," he said, turning to his mother. He gradually went white.

"No my boy!" cried the mother, pitiful, lifting her face. And suddenly she put her face against his shoulder, he was stooping down to her, holding her against him, and she cried aloud for a moment or two. Miss Louisa saw his sides heaving, and heard the sharp hiss of his breath. She turned away, tears streaming down her face. The father lay inert upon the white bed. Mr. Massey looked queer and obliterated, so little now that the sailor with his sun-burned skin was in the room. He stood waiting. Miss Louisa wanted to die, she wanted to have done. She dared not turn round again to look.

"Shall I offer a prayer?" came the frail voice of the clergyman, and all knelt down.

Miss Louisa was frightened of the inert man upon the bed. Then she felt a flash of fear of Mr. Massey, hearing his thin, detached voice. And then, calmed, she looked up. On the far side of the bed were the heads of the mother and son, the one in the black lace cap, with the small white nape of the neck beneath, the other, with brown, sun scorched hair too close and wiry to allow of a parting, and neck tanned firm, bowed as if unwillingly. The great grey beard of the old man did not move, the prayer continued. Mr. Massey prayed with a pure lucidity, that they all might conform to the higher will. He was like something that dominated the bowed heads, something dispassionate that governed them inexorably. Miss Louisa was afraid of him. And she was bound, during the course of the prayer, to have a little reverence for him. It was like a foretaste of inexorable, cold death, a taste of pure justice.

That evening she talked to Mary of the visit. Her heart, her veins were possessed by the thought of Alfred Durant as he held his mother in his arms; then the break in his voice, as she remembered it again and again, was like a flame through her; and she wanted to see his face more distinctly in her mind, ruddy with the sun, and his golden-brown eyes, kind and careless, strained now with a natural fear, the fine nose tanned hard by the sun, the mouth that could not help smiling at her. And it went through her with pride, to think of his figure, a straight, fine jet of life.

"He is a handsome lad," she said to Miss Mary, as if he had not been a year older than herself. Underneath was the deeper dread, almost hatred, of the inhuman being of Mr. Massey. She felt she must protect herself and Alfred from him.

"When I felt Mr. Massey there," she said, "I almost hated him. What right had he to be there!"

"Surely he has all right," said Miss Mary after a pause. "He is *really* a Christian."

"He seems to me nearly an imbecile," said Miss Louisa.

Miss Mary, quiet and beautiful, was silent for a moment.

"Oh no," she said. "Not *imbecile* –"

"Well then – he reminds me of a six months child – or a five months child – as if he didn't have time to get developed enough before he was born."

"Yes," said Miss Mary slowly. "There is something lacking. But there is something wonderful in him: and he is really *good* –"

"Yes," said Miss Louisa. "It doesn't seem right that he should be. What right has *that* to be called goodness!"

"But it *is* goodness," persisted Mary. Then she added, with a laugh: "And come, you wouldn't deny that as well."

There was a doggedness in her voice. She went about very quietly. In her soul, she knew what was going to happen. She knew that Mr. Massey was stronger than she, and that she must submit to what he was. Her physical self was prouder, stronger than he, her physical self disliked and despised him. But she was in the grip of his moral, mental being. And she felt the days allotted out to her. And her family watched.

4

A few days after, old Mr. Durant died. Miss Louisa saw Alfred once more, but he was stiff before her now, treating her not like a person, but as if she were some sort of will in command and he a separate, distinct will waiting in front of her. She had never felt such utter steel-plate separation from anyone. It puzzled her and frightened her. What had become of him? And she hated the military discipline – she was antagonistic to it. Now he was not himself. He was the will which obeys set over against the will which commands. She hesitated over accepting this. He had put himself out of her range. He had ranked himself inferior, subordinate to her. And that was how he would get away from her, that was how he would avoid all connection with her: by fronting her impersonally from the opposite camp, by taking up the abstract position of an inferior.

She went brooding steadily and sullenly over this, brooding and brooding. Her fierce, obstinate heart could not give way. It clung to its own rights. Sometimes she dismissed him. Why should he, her inferior, trouble her?

Then she relapsed to him, and almost hated him. It was his way of getting out of it. She felt the cowardice of it, his calmly placing her in a superior class, and placing himself inaccessibly apart, in an inferior, as if she, the sensient° woman who was fond of him, did not count. But she was not going to submit. Dogged in her heart she held on to him.

5

In six months' time Miss Mary had married Mr. Massey. There had been no love-making, nobody had made any remark. But everybody was tense and callous with expectation. When one day Mr. Massey asked for Mary's hand, Mr. Lindley started and trembled from the thin, abstract voice of the little man. Mr. Massey was very nervous, but so curiously absolute.

"I shall be very glad," said the vicar, "but of course the decision lies with Mary herself." And his still feeble hand shook as he moved a Bible on his desk.

The small man, keeping fixedly to his idea, padded out of the room to find Miss Mary. He sat a long time by her, while she made some conversation, before he had readiness to speak. She was afraid of what was coming, and sat stiff in apprehension. She felt as if her body would rise and fling him aside. But her spirit quivered and waited. Almost in expectation she waited, almost wanting him. And then she knew he would speak.

"I have already asked Mr. Lindley," said the clergyman, while suddenly she looked with aversion at his little knees, "if he would consent to my proposal." He was aware of his own disadvantage, but his will was set.

She went cold as she sat, and impervious, almost as if she had become stone. He waited a moment nervously. He would not persuade her. He himself never even heard persuasion, but pursued his own course. He looked at her, sure of himself, unsure of her, and said:

"Will you become my wife, Mary?"

Still her heart was hard and cold. She sat proudly.

"I should like to speak to Mama first," she said.

"Very well," replied Mr. Massey.

And in a moment he padded away.

Mary went to her mother. She was cold and reserved.

"Mr. Massey has asked me to marry him, Mama," she said. Mrs. Lindley went on staring at her book. She was cramped in her feeling.

"Well, and what did you say?"

They were both keeping calm and cold.

"I said I would speak to you before answering him."

This was equivalent to a question. Mrs. Lindley did not want to reply to it. She shifted her heavy form irritably on the couch. Miss Mary sat calm and straight, with closed mouth.

"Your father thinks it would not be a bad match," said the mother, as if casually.

Nothing more was said. Everybody remained cold and shut-off. Miss Mary did not speak to Miss Louisa, the Reverend Ernest Lindley kept out of sight.

At evening Miss Mary accepted Mr. Massey.

"Yes, I will marry you," she said, with even a little movement of tenderness towards him. He was embarrassed, but satisfied. She could see him making some movement towards her, could feel the male in him, something cold and triumphant, asserting itself. She sat rigid, and waited.

When Miss Louisa knew, she was silent with bitter anger against everybody, even against Mary. She felt her faith wounded. Did the real things to her not matter after all? She wanted to get away. She thought of Mr. Massey. He had some curious power, some unanswerable right. He was a will that they could not controvert. – Suddenly a flush started in her. If he had come to her she would have flipped him out of the room. He was never going to touch *her*. And she was glad. She was glad that her blood would rise and exterminate the little man, if he came too near to her, no matter how her judgment was paralysed by him, no matter how he moved in abstract goodness. She thought she was perverse to be glad, but glad she was. "I would just flip him out of the room," she said, and she derived great satisfaction from the open statement. Nevertheless, perhaps she ought still to feel that Mary, on her plane, was a higher being than herself. But then Mary was Mary, and she was Louisa, and that also was inalterable.

Mary, in marrying him, tried to become a pure reason such as he was, without feeling or impulse. She shut herself up, she shut herself rigid against the agonies of shame and the terror of violation which came at first. She *would* not feel, and she *would* not feel. She was a pure will acquiescing to him. She elected a certain kind of fate. She would be good and purely just, she would live in a higher freedom than she had ever known, she would be free of mundane care, she was a pure will towards right. She had sold herself, but had a new freedom. She had got rid of her body. She had sold a lower thing, her body, for a higher thing, her freedom from material things. She considered that she paid for all she got from her husband. So, in a kind of independence, she moved proud and free. She had paid with her body: that was henceforward out of consideration. She was glad to be rid of it. She had bought her position in the world – that henceforth was taken for granted. There remained only the direction of her activity towards charity and high-minded living.

She could scarcely bear other people to be present with her and her husband. Her private life was her shame. But then, she could keep it hidden. She lived almost isolated in the rectory of the tiny village miles from the railway. She suffered as if it were an insult to her own flesh, seeing the repulsion which some people felt for her husband, or the special manner they had of treating him, as if he were a 'case'. But most people were uneasy before him, which restored her pride.

If she had let herself, she would have hated him, hated his padding round the house, his thin voice devoid of human-understanding, his bent little shoulders and rather incomplete face that reminded her of an abortion. But rigorously she kept to her position. She took care of him and was just to him. There was also a deep, craven fear of him, something slave-like.

There was not much fault to be found with his behaviour. He was scrupulously just and kind according to his lights. But the male in him was cold and self-complete, and utterly domineering. Weak, insufficient little thing as he was, she had not expected this of him. It was something in the bargain she had not understood. It made her hold her head, to keep still. She knew, vaguely, that she was murdering herself. After all, her body was not quite so easy to get rid of. And this manner of disposing of it – ah, sometimes she felt she must rise and bring about death, lift her hand for utter denial of everything, by a general destruction.

He was almost unaware of the conditions about him. He did not fuss in the domestic way, she did as she liked in the house. Indeed, she was a great deal free of him. He would sit obliterated for hours. He was kind, and almost anxiously considerate. But when he considered he was right, his will was just blindly male, like a cold machine. And on most points he was logically right, or he had with him the right of the creed they both accepted. It was so. There was nothing for her to go against.

Then she found herself with child, and felt for the first time horror, afraid before God and man. This also she had to go through – it was the right. When the child arrived, it was a bonny, healthy lad. Her heart hurt in her body, as she took the baby between her hands. The flesh that was trampled and silent in her must speak again in the boy. After all, she had to live – it was not so simple after all. Nothing was finished completely. She looked and looked at the baby, and almost hated it, and suffered an anguish of love for it. She hated it because it made her live again in the flesh, when she *could* not live in the flesh, she could not. She wanted to trample her flesh down, down, extinct, to live in the mind. And now there was this child. It was too cruel, too racking. For she must love the child. Her purpose was broken in two again. She had to become amorphous, purposeless, without real being. As a mother, she was a fragmentary, ignoble thing.

Mr. Massey, blind to everything else in the way of human feeling, became obsessed by the idea of his child. When it arrived, suddenly it filled the whole world of feeling for him. It was his obsession, his terror was for its safety and well-being. It was something new, as if he himself had been born a naked infant, conscious of his own exposure, and full of apprehension. He who had never been aware of any-one else, all his life, now was aware of nothing but the child. Not that he ever played with it, or kissed it, or tended it. He did nothing for it. But it dominated him, it filled, and at the same time emptied his mind. The world was all baby for him.

This his wife must also bear, his question: "What is the reason that he cries?" – his reminder, at the first sound: "Mary, that is the child," – his restlessness if the feeding time were five minutes past. She had bargained for this – now she must stand by her bargain.

6

Miss Louisa, at home in the dingy vicarage, had suffered a great deal over her sister's wedding. Having once begun to cry out against it, during the engagement, she had been silenced by

Mary's quiet: "I don't agree with you about him, Louisa, I *want* to marry him." Then Miss Louisa had been angry deep in her heart, and therefore silent. This dangerous state started the change in her. Her own revulsion made her recoil from the hitherto undoubted Mary.

"I'd beg the streets barefoot first," said Miss Louisa, thinking of Mr. Massey.

But evidently Mary could perform a different heroism. So she, Louisa the practical, suddenly felt that Mary, her ideal, was questionable after all. How could she be pure – one cannot be dirty in act and spiritual in being. Louisa distrusted Mary's high spirituality. It was no longer genuine for her. And if Mary were spiritual and misguided, why did not her father protect her? Because of the money. He disliked the whole affair, but he backed away, because of the money. And the mother frankly did not care: her daughters could do as they liked. Her mother's pronouncement:

"Whatever happens to *him*, Mary is safe for life," – so evidently and shallowly a calculation, incensed Louisa.

"I'd rather be safe in the workhouse," she cried.

"Your father will see to that," replied her mother brutally. This speech, in its indirectness, so injured Miss Louisa that she hated her mother deep, deep in her heart, and almost hated herself. It was a long time resolving itself out, this hate. But it worked and worked, and at last the young woman said:

"They are wrong – they are all wrong. They have ground out their souls for what isn't worth anything, and there isn't a grain of love in them anywhere. And I *will* have love. They want us to deny it. They've never found it, so they want to say it doesn't exist. But I *will* have it. I *will* love – it is my birthright. I will love the man I marry – that is all I care about."

So Miss Louisa stood isolated from everybody. She and Mary had parted over Mr. Massey. In Louisa's eyes, Mary was degraded, married to Mr. Massey. She could not bear to think of her lofty, spiritual sister degraded in the body like this. Mary was wrong, wrong, wrong: she was not superior, she was flawed, incomplete. The two sisters stood apart. They still loved each other, they would love each other as long as they lived. But they had parted ways. A new solitariness came over the obstinate Louisa, and her heavy jaw set stubbornly. She was going on her own way. But which way? She was quite alone, with a blank world before her? How could she be said to have any way. Yet she had her fixed will to love, to have the man she loved.

7

When her boy was three years old, Mary had another baby, a girl. The three years had gone by monotonously. They might have been an eternity, they might have been brief as a sleep. She did not know. Only, there was always a weight on top of her, something that pressed down her life. The only thing that had happened was that Mr. Massey had had an operation. He was always exceedingly fragile. His wife had soon learned to attend to him mechanically, as part of her duty.

But this third year, after the baby girl had been born, Mary felt oppressed and depressed. Christmas drew near: the gloomy, unleavened Christmas of the rectory, where all the days were of the same dark fabric. And Mary was afraid. It was as if the darkness were coming upon her.

"Edward, I should like to go home for Christmas," she said, and a certain terror filled her as she spoke.

"But you can't leave baby," said her husband, blinking.

"We can all go."

He thought, and stared in his collective fashion.

"Why do you wish to go?" he asked.

"Because I need a change. A change would do me good, and it would be good for the milk."

He heard the will in his wife's voice, and was at a loss. Her language was unintelligible to him. But somehow he felt that

Mary was set upon it. And while she was breeding, either about to have a child, or nursing, he regarded her as a special sort of being.

"Wouldn't it hurt baby to take her by the train?" he said.

"No," replied the mother, "why should it."

They went. When they were in the train, it began to snow. From the window of his first-class carriage the little clergyman watched the big flakes sweep by, like a blind drawn across the country. He was obsessed by thought of the baby, and afraid of the draughts of the carriage.

"Sit right in the corner," he said to his wife, "and hold baby close back."

She moved at his bidding, and stared out of the window. His eternal presence was like an iron weight on her brain. But she was going partially to escape for a few days.

"Sit on the other side, Jack," said the father. "It is less draughty. Come to this window."

He watched the boy in anxiety. But his children were the only beings in the world who took not the slightest notice of him.

"Look, mother, look!" cried the boy. "They fly right at my face" – he meant the snowflakes.

"Come into this corner," repeated his father, out of another world.

"He's jumped on this one's back, mother, an' they're riding to the bottom!" cried the boy, jumping with glee.

"Tell him to come on this side," the little man bade his wife.

"Jack, kneel on this cushion," said the mother, putting her white hand on the place.

The boy slid over in silence to the place she indicated, waited still for a moment, then almost deliberately, stridently cried:

"Look at all those in the corner, mother, making a heap," and he pointed to the cluster of snowflakes with finger pressed dramatically on the pane, and he turned to his mother a bit ostentatiously.

"All in a heap!" she said.

He had seen her face, and had her response, and he was somewhat assured. Vaguely uneasy, he was reassured if he could win her attention.

They arrived at the vicarage at half-past two, not having had lunch.

"How are you, Edward?" said Mr. Lindley, trying on his side to be fatherly. But he was always in a false position with his son-in-law, frustrated before him, therefore, as much as possible, he shut his eyes and ears to him. The vicar was looking thin and pale and ill-nourished. He had gone quite grey. He was, however, still haughty, but, since the growing-up of his children, it was a brittle haughtiness, that might break at any moment and leave the vicar only an impoverished, pitiable figure. Mrs. Lindley took all the notice of her daughter, and of the children. She ignored her son-in-law. Miss Louisa was clucking and laughing and rejoicing over the baby. Mr. Massey stood aside, a bent, persistent little figure.

"Oh a pretty! – a little pretty! – oh a cold little pretty come in a railway-train!" Miss Louisa was cooing to the infant, crouching on the hearthrug opening the white woollen wraps and exposing the child to the fireglow.

"Mary," said the little clergyman. "I think it would be better to give baby a warm bath. She may take a cold."

"I think it is not necessary," said the mother, coming and closing her hand judiciously over the rosy feet and hands of the mite. "She is not chilly."

"Not a bit," cried Miss Louisa. "She's not caught cold."

"I'll go and bring her flannels," said Mr. Massey, with one idea.

"I can bath her in the kitchen then," said Mary, in an altered, cold tone.

"You can't, the girl is scrubbing there," said Miss Louisa. "Besides, she doesn't want a bath at this time of day."

"She'd better have one," said Mary, quietly, out of submission. Miss Louisa's gorge rose, and she was silent. When the little man padded down with the flannels on his arm, Mrs. Lindley asked:

"Hadn't *you* better take a hot bath Edward?"

But the sarcasm was lost on the little clergyman. He was absorbed in the preparations round the baby.

The room was dull and threadbare, and the snow outside seemed fairy-land by comparison, so white on the lawn and tufted on the bushes. Indoors the heavy pictures hung obscurely on the walls, everything was dingy with gloom.

Except in the fireglow, where they had laid the bath on the hearth! Mrs. Massey, her black hair always smoothly coiled and queenly, kneeled by the bath, wearing a rubber apron, and holding the kicking child. Her husband stood holding the towels and the flannels to warm. Louisa, too cross to share in the joy of the baby's bath, was laying the table. The boy was hanging on the door-knob, wrestling with it to get out. His father looked round.

"Come away from the door, Jack" he said, ineffectually. Jack tugged harder at the knob as if he did not hear. Mr. Massey blinked at him.

"He must come away from the door, Mary," he said. "There will be a draught if it is opened."

"Jack, come away from the door, dear," said the mother, dexterously turning the shiny wet baby onto her towelled knee, then glancing round, "Go and tell Auntie Louisa about the train."

Louisa, also afraid to open the door, was watching the scene on the hearth. Mr. Massey stood holding the baby's flannel, as if assisting at some ceremonial. If everybody had not been subduedly angry, it would have been ridiculous.

"I want to see out of the window," Jack cried. His father turned hastily.

"Do *you* mind lifting him onto a chair, Louisa," said Mary hastily. The father was too delicate.

When the baby was flannelled, Mr. Massey went upstairs and returned with four pillows, which he set in the fender to warm. Then he stood watching the mother feed her child, obsessed by the idea of his infant.

Louisa went on with her preparations for the meal. She could not have told why she was so sullenly angry. Mrs. Lindley, as usual, lay silently watching.

Mary carried her child upstairs, followed by her husband with the pillows. After a while he came down again.

"What is Mary doing? Why doesn't she come down to eat?" asked Mrs. Lindley.

"She is staying with baby. The room is rather cold. I will ask the girl to put in a fire."

He was going absorbedly to the door.

"But Mary has had nothing to eat. It is *she* who will catch cold," said the mother, exasperated.

Mr. Massey seemed as if he did not hear. Yet he looked at his mother-in-law, and answered:

"I will take her something."

He went out. Mrs. Lindley shifted on her couch with anger. Miss Louisa glowered. But no one said anything, because of the money that came to the vicarage from Mr. Massey.

Louisa went upstairs. Her sister was sitting by the bed, reading a scrap of paper.

"Won't you come down and eat?" the younger asked.

"In a moment or two," Mary replied, in a quiet, reserved voice, that forbade anyone to approach her.

It was this that made Miss Louisa most furious. She went downstairs, and announced to her mother:

"I am going out. I may not be home to tea."

8

No one remarked on her exit. She put on her fur hat, that the village people knew so well, and the old norfolk jacket. Louisa was short and plump and plain. She had her mother's heavy jaw, her father's proud brow, and her own grey, brooding eyes that were very beautiful when she smiled. It was true, as the people said, that she looked sulky. Her chief attraction was her glistening, heavy, deep-blonde hair, which shone and gleamed with a richness that was not entirely foreign to her.

"Where am I going?" she said to herself, when she got outside in the snow. She did not hesitate, however, but, by mechanical walking, found herself descending the hill towards Old Aldecross. In the valley that was black with trees, the colliery breathed in stertorous pants, sending out high conical columns of steam that remained upright, whiter than the snow on the hills, yet shadowy, in the dead air. Louisa would not acknowledge to herself whither she was making her way, till she came to the railway crossing. Then the bunches of snow in the twigs of the apple tree that leaned towards the fence told her she must go and see Mrs. Durant. The tree was in Mrs. Durant's garden.

Alfred was now at home again, living with his mother in the cottage below the road. From the highway hedge, by the railroad crossing, the snowy garden sheered down steeply, like the side of a hole, then dropped straight in a wall. In this depth the house was snug, its chimney just level with the road. Miss Louisa descended the stone stairs, and stood below in the little back yard, in the dimness and the semi-secrecy. A big tree leaned overhead, above the paraffin hut. Louisa felt secure from all the world down there. She knocked at the open door, then looked round. The tongue of garden narrowing in from the quarry bed was white with snow: she thought of the thick fringes of snowdrops it would show beneath the currant bushes in a month's time. The ragged fringe of pinks hanging over from the garden brim behind her was whitened now with snow-flakes, that in summer held white blossom to Louisa's face. It was pleasant, she thought, to gather flowers that stooped to one's face from above.

She knocked again. Peeping in, she saw the scarlet glow of the kitchen, red firelight falling on the brick floor and on the bright chintz cushions. It was alive and bright as a peepshow. She crossed the scullery, where still an almanack hung. There was no one about. "Mrs. Durant," called Louisa softly. "Mrs. Durant!"

She went up the brick step into the front room, that still had its little shop counter and its bundles of goods, and she called from the stairfoot. Then she knew Mrs. Durant was out.

She went into the yard, to follow the old woman's footsteps up the garden path.

She emerged from the bushes and raspberry canes. There was the whole quarry bed, a wide garden white and dimmed, brindled with dark bushes, lying half submerged. On the left, overhead, the little colliery train rumbled. Right away at the back was a mass of trees.

Louisa followed the open path, looking from right to left, and then she gave a cry of concern. The old woman was sitting rocking slightly among the ragged snowy cabbages. Louisa ran to her, found her whimpering with little, involuntary cries.

"Whatever have you done?" cried Louisa, kneeling in the snow.

"I've – I've – I was pulling a brussel-sprout stalk – and – Oh –h! – something tore inside me, I've had a pain –" the old woman wept from shock and suffering, gasping between her whimpers – "I've had a pain there – a long time – and now – Oh – Oh!" She panted, pressed her hand on her side, leaned as if she would faint, looking yellow against the snow. Louisa supported her.

"Do you think you could walk now," she asked.

"Yes," gasped the old woman.

Louisa helped her to her feet.

"Get the cabbage – I want it for Alfred's dinner," panted Mrs. Durant. Louisa picked up the stalk of brussel-sprouts, and with difficulty got the old woman indoors. She gave her brandy, laid her on the couch, saying:

"I'm going to send for a doctor – wait just a minute."

The young woman ran up the steps to the public house a few yards away. The landlady was astonished to see Miss Louisa.

"Will you send for the doctor at once to Mrs. Durant," she said, with some of her father in her commanding tone.

"Is somethink the matter –?" fluttered the landlady in concern. Louisa, glancing out up the road, saw the grocer's cart driving to Eastwood. She ran and stopped the man, and told him.

Mrs. Durant lay on the sofa, her face turned away, when the young woman came back.

"Let me put you to bed," Louisa said. Mrs. Durant did not resist.

Louisa knew the ways of the working people. In the bottom drawer of the dresser she found dusters and flannels. With the old pitflannel she snatched out the oven shelves, wrapped them up, and put them in the bed. From the son's bed she took a blanket, and, running down, set it before the fire. Having undressed the little old woman, Louisa carried her upstairs.

"You'll drop me, you'll drop me," cried Mrs. Durant.

Louisa did not answer, but bore her burden quickly. She could not light a fire, because there was no fireplace in the bedroom. And the floor was plaster. So she fetched the lamp, and stood it lighted in one corner.

"It will air the room," she said.

"Yes," moaned the old woman.

Louisa ran with more hot flannels, replacing those from the oven shelves. Then she made a bran bag,* and laid it on the woman's side. There was a big lump on the side of the abdomen.

"I've felt it coming a long time," moaned the old lady, when the pain was easier, "but I've not said anything; I didn't want to upset our Alfred."

Louisa did not see why "our Alfred" should be spared.

"What time is it?" came the plaintive voice.

"A quarter to four."

"Oh!" wailed the old lady, "he'll be here in half an hour, and no dinner ready for him."

"Let me do it?" said Louisa, gently.

"There's that cabbage – and you'll find the meat in the pantry – and there's an apple pie you can hot up. But *don't you* do it –!"

"Who will, then?" asked Louisa.

"I don't know," moaned the sick woman, unable to consider. Louisa did it.

The doctor came and gave serious examination. He looked very grave.

"What is it doctor?" asked the old lady, looking up at him with old, pathetic eyes in which already hope was dead.

"I think you've torn the skin in which a tumour hangs," he replied.

"Ay!" she murmured, and she turned away.

"You see, she may die any minute – and it *may* be swaled away," ⋄ said the old doctor to Louisa.

The young woman went upstairs again.

"He says the lump may be swaled away, and you may get quite well again," she said.

"Ay!" murmured the old lady. It did not deceive her. Presently she asked:

"Is there a good fire?"

"I think so," answered Louisa.

"He'll want a good fire," the mother said. Louisa attended to it.

Since the death of Durant, the widow had come to church occasionally, and Louisa had been friendly to her. In the girl's heart the purpose was fixed. No man had affected her as Alfred Durant had done, and to that she kept. In her heart, she adhered to him. A natural sympathy existed between her and his rather hard, materialistic mother.

Alfred was the most lovable of the old woman's sons. He had grown up like the rest, however, headstrong and blind to everything but his own will. Like the other boys, he had insisted on going into the pit as soon as he left school, because that was the only way speedily to become a man, level with all the other men. This was a great chagrin to his mother, who would have liked to have this last of her sons a gentleman.

But still he remained constant to her. His feeling for her was deep and unexpressed. He noticed when she was tired, or when she had a new cap. And he bought little things for her occasionally. She was not wise enough to see how much he lived by her.

At the bottom he did not satisfy her, he did not seem manly enough. He liked to read books occasionally, and better still he liked to play the piccolo. It amused her to see his head nod over the instrument as he made an effort to get the right note. It made her fond of him, with tenderness, almost pity, but not with respect. She wanted a man to be fixed, going his own way without knowledge of women. Whereas she knew Alfred depended on her. He sang in the choir because he liked singing. In the summer he worked in the garden, attended to the fowls and pigs. He kept pigeons. He played on Saturdays in the cricket or football team. But to her he did not seem the man, the independent man her other boys had been. He was her baby – and whilst she loved him for it, she was a little bit contemptuous of him.

There grew up a little hostility between them. Then he began to drink, as the others had done; but not in their blind, oblivious way. He was a little self-conscious over it. She saw this, and she pitied it in him. She loved him most, but she was not satisfied with him because he was not free of her. He could not quite go his own way.

Then at twenty he ran away and served his time in the navy. This had made a man of him. He had hated it bitterly, the service, the subordination. For years he fought with himself under the military discipline, for his own self-respect, struggling through blind anger and shame and a cramping sense of inferiority. Out of humiliation and self-hatred, he rose into a sort of inner freedom. And his love for his mother, whom he idealised, remained the fact of hope and of belief.

He came home again, nearly thirty years old but naïve and inexperienced as a boy, only with a silence about him that was new: a sort of dumb humility before life, a fear of living. He was almost quite chaste. A strong sensitiveness had kept him from women. Sexual talk was all very well among men, but somehow it had no application to living women. There were two things for him, the *idea* of women, with which he sometimes debauched himself, and real women, before whom he felt a deep uneasiness, and a need to draw away. He shrank and defended himself from the approach of any woman. And then he felt ashamed. In his innermost soul he felt he was not a man, he was less than the normal man. In Genoa he went with an under officer to a drinking house where the cheaper sort of girl came in to look for lovers. He sat there with his glass, the girls looked at him, but they never came to him. He knew that if they did come he could only pay for food and drink for them, because he felt a pity for them, and was anxious lest they lacked good necessities. He could not have gone with one of them: he knew it, and was ashamed, looking with curious envy at the swaggering, easy-passionate Italian whose body went to a woman by instinctive impersonal attraction. They were men, he was not a man. He sat feeling short, feeling like a leper. And he went away imagining sexual scenes between himself and a woman, walking wrapt in this indulgence. But when the ready woman presented herself, the very fact that she was a palpable woman made it impossible for him to touch her. And this incapacity was like a core of rottenness in him.

So several times he went, drunk, with his companions, to the licensed prostitute houses abroad. But the sordid insignificance of the experience appalled him. It had not been anything really: it meant nothing. He felt as if he were, not physically, but spiritually impotent: not actually impotent, but intrinsically so.

He came home with this secret, never changing burden of his unknown, unbestowed self torturing him. His navy training left him in perfect physical condition. He was sensible of, and proud of his body. He bathed and used dumb-bells, and kept himself fit. He played cricket and football. He read books and began to hold fixed ideas which he got from the Fabians. He played his piccolo, and was considered an expert. But at the bottom of his soul was always this canker of shame and incompleteness: he was miserable beneath all his healthy cheerfulness, he was uneasy and felt despicable among all his confidence and superiority of ideas. He would have changed with any mere brute, just to be free of himself, to be free of this shame of self-consciousness. He saw some collier lurching straight forward without misgiving, pursuing his own satisfactions, and he envied him. Anything, he would have given anything for this spontaneity and this blind stupidity which went to its own satisfaction direct.

9

He was not unhappy in the pit. He was admired by the men, and well enough liked. It was only he himself who felt the difference between himself and the others. He seemed to hide his own stigma. But he was never sure that the others did not really despise him for a ninny, as being less a man than they were. Only he pretended to be more manly, and was surprised by the ease with which they were deceived. And, being naturally cheerful, he was happy at work. He was sure of himself there. Naked to the waist, hot and grimy with labour, they squatted on their heels for a few minutes and talked, seeing each other dimly by the light of the safety lamps, while the black coal rose jutting round them, and the props of wood stood like little pillars in the low, black, very dark temple. Then the pony came, and the gang-lad◇ with a message from Number 7, or a bottle of water from the horse-trough or some news of the world above. The day passed pleasantly enough. There was an ease, a go-as-you-please about the day underground, a delightful camaraderie of men shut off alone from the rest of the world, in a dangerous place, and a variety of labour, holing, loading, timbering, and a glamour of mystery and adventure in the atmosphere, that made the pit not unattractive to him when he had again got over his anguish of desire for the open air and the sea.

This day there was much to do and Durant was not in humour to talk. He went on working in silence through the afternoon.

"Loose-all"◇ came, and they tramped to the bottom. The whitewashed underground-office shone brightly. Men were putting out their lamps. They sat in dozens round the bottom of the shaft, down which black, heavy drops of water fell continuously into the sumph.◇ The electric lights shone away down the main underground road.

"Is it raining?" asked Durant.

"Snowing," said an old man, and the younger was pleased. He liked to go up when it was snowing.

"It'll just come right for Christmas?" said the old man.

"Ay," replied Durant.

"A green Christmas, a fat churchyard,"◇ said the other sententiously.

Durant laughed, showing his small, rather pointed teeth.

The cage came down, a dozen men lined on. Durant noticed tufts of snow on the perforated, arched roof of the chair,° and he was pleased. He wondered how it liked its excursion underground. But already it was getting soppy with black water.

He liked things about him. There was a little smile on his face. But underlying it was the curious consciousness he felt in himself.

The upper world came almost with a flash, because of the glimmer of snow. Hurrying along the bank, giving up his lamp at the office, he smiled to feel the open about him again, all glimmering round him with snow. The hills on either hand were pale blue in the dusk, and the hedges looked savage and dark. The snow was trampled between the railway lines, but far ahead, beyond the black figures of miners moving home, it became smooth again, spreading right up to the dark wall of the coppice.

To the west there was a pinkness, and a big star hovered half revealed. Below, the lights of the pit came out crisp and yellow among the darkness of the buildings, and the lights of Old Aldecross twinkled in rows down the bluish twilight.

Durant walked glad with life among the miners, who were all talking animatedly because of the snow. He liked their company, he liked the white dusky world. It gave him a little thrill to stop at the garden gate, and see the light of home down below, shining on the silent blue snow.

10

By the big gate of the railway, in the fence, was a little latch gate, that he kept locked. As he unfastened it, he watched the kitchen light that shone onto the bushes and the snow outside. It was a candle burning till night set in, he thought to himself. He slid down the steep path to the level below. He liked making the first marks in the smooth snow. Then he came through the bushes to the house. The two women heard his heavy boots ring outside on the scraper, and his voice as he opened the door:

"How much worth of oil do you reckon to save by that candle, mother?" He liked a good light from the lamp.

He had just put down his bottle and snap-bag° and was hanging his coat behind the scullery door, when Miss Louisa came upon him. He was startled, but he smiled.

His eyes began to laugh – then his face went suddenly straight, and he was afraid.

"Your mother's had an accident," she said.

"How!" he exclaimed.

"In the garden," she answered. He hesitated with his coat in his hands. Then he hung it up and turned to the kitchen.

"Is she in bed?" he asked.

"Yes," said Miss Louisa, who found it hard to deceive him. He was silent. He went into the kitchen, sat down heavily in his father's old chair, and began to pull off his boots. His head was small, rather finely shapen. His brown hair, close and crisp, would look jolly whatever happened. He wore heavy, moleskin trousers that gave off the stale, exhausted scent of the pit. Having put on his slippers, he carried his boots into the scullery.

"What is it?" he asked, afraid.

"Something internal," she replied.

He went upstairs. His mother kept herself calm for his coming. Louisa felt his tread shake the plaster floor of the bedroom above.

"What have you done?" he asked.

"It's nothing, my lad," said the old woman, rather hard. "It's nothing. You needn't fret, my boy, it's nothing more the matter with me than I had yesterday, or last week. The doctor said I'd done nothing serious."

"What were you doing?" asked her son.

"I was pulling up a cabbage, and I suppose I pulled too hard; for, oh – there was such a pain –"

Her son looked at her quickly. She hardened herself.

"But who doesn't have a sudden pain sometimes, my boy. We all do."

"And what's it done?"

"I don't know," she said, "but I don't suppose it's anything."

The big lamp in the corner was screened with a dark green screen, so that he could scarcely see her face. He was strung tight with apprehension, and many emotions. Then his brow knitted.

"What did you go pulling your inside out at cabbages for!" he asked, "and the ground frozen? You'd go on dragging and dragging, if you killed yourself."

"Somebody's got to get them," she said.

"You needn't do yourself harm."

But they had reached futility.

Miss Louisa could hear plainly downstairs. Her heart sank. It seemed so hopeless between them.

"Are you sure it's nothing much, mother?" he asked, appealing, after a little silence.

"Ay, it's nothing," said the old woman, rather bitter.

"I don't want you to – to – be badly – you know."

"Go an' get your dinner," she said. She knew she was going to die: moreover the pain was torture just then. "They're only cosseting me up a bit because I'm an old woman. Miss Louisa's *very* good – and she'll have got your dinner ready, so you'd better go and eat it."

He felt stupid and ashamed. His mother put him off. He had to turn away. The pain burned in his bowels. He went downstairs. The mother was glad he was gone, so that she could moan with pain.

He had resumed the old habit of eating before he washed himself. Miss Louisa served his dinner. It was strange and exciting to her. She was strung up tense, trying to understand him and his mother. She watched him as he sat. He was turned away from his food, looking in the fire. Her soul watched him, trying to see what he was. His black face and arms were uncouth, he was foreign. His face was masked black with coal-dust. She could not see him, she could not know him. The brown eyebrows, the steady eyes, the coarse, small moustache above the closed mouth – these were the only familiar indications. What was he, as he sat there in his pit dirt? She could not see him, and it hurt her.

She ran upstairs, presently coming down with the flannels and the bran bag, to heat them, because the pain was on again.

He was half way through his dinner. He put down the fork, suddenly nauseated.

"They will soothe the wrench," she said. He watched, useless and left out.

"Is she bad?" he asked.

"I think she is," she answered.

It was useless for him to stir or comment. Louisa was busy. She went upstairs. The poor old woman was in a white, cold sweat of pain. Louisa's face was sullen with suffering as she went about to relieve her. Then she sat and waited. The pain passed gradually, the old woman sank into a state of coma. Louisa still sat silent by the bed. She heard the sound of water downstairs. Then came the voice of the old mother, faint but unrelaxing:

"Alfred's washing himself – he'll want his back washing."

Louisa listened anxiously, wondering what the sick woman wanted.

"He can't bear if his back isn't washed –" the old woman persisted, in a cruel attention to his needs. Louisa rose and wiped the sweat from the yellowish brow.

"I will go down," she said soothingly.

"If you would," murmured the sick woman.

Louisa waited a moment. Mrs. Durant closed her eyes, having discharged her duty. The young woman went downstairs. Herself, or the man, what did they matter? Only the suffering woman must be considered.

Alfred was kneeling on the hearthrug, stripped to the waist, washing himself in a large panchion of earthenware. He did so every evening, when he had eaten his dinner; his brothers had done so before him. But Miss Louisa was strange in the house.

He was mechanically rubbing the white lather on his head, with a repeated, unconscious movement, his hand every now and then passing over his neck. Louisa watched. She had to brace herself to this also. He bent his head into the water, washed it free of soap, and pressed the water out of his eyes.

"Your mother said you would want your back washing," she said.

Curious how it hurt her to take part in their fixed routine of life! Louisa felt the almost repulsive intimacy being forced upon her. It was all so common, so like herding. She lost her own distinctness.

He ducked his face round, looking up at her in what was a very comical way. She had to harden herself.

"How funny he looks with his face upside down," she thought. After all, there was a difference between her and the common people. The water in which his arms were plunged was quite black, the soap-froth was darkish. She could scarcely conceive him as human. Mechanically, under the influence of habit, he groped in the black water, fished out the soap and flannel, and handed them backwards to Louisa. Then he remained rigid and submissive, his two arms thrust straight in the panchion, supporting the weight of his shoulders. His skin was beautifully white and unblemished, of an opaque, solid whiteness. Gradually Louisa saw it: this also was what he was. It fascinated her. Her feeling of separateness passed away: she ceased to draw back from contact with him and his mother. There was this living centre. Her heart ran hot. She had reached some goal in this beautiful, clear, male body. She loved him in a white, impersonal heat. But the sun-burnt, reddish neck and ears: they were more personal, more curious. A tenderness rose in her, she loved even his queer ears. A person – an intimate being he was to her. She put down the towel and went upstairs again, troubled in her heart. She had only seen one human being in her life – and that was Mary. All the rest were strangers. Now her soul was going to open, she was going to see another. She felt strange and pregnant.

"He'll be more comfortable," murmured the sick woman abstractedly, as Louisa entered the room. The latter did not answer. Her own heart was heavy with its own responsibility. Mrs. Durant lay silent awhile, then she murmured plaintively:

"You mustn't mind, Miss Louisa."

"Why should I?" replied Louisa, deeply moved.

"It's what we're used to," said the old woman.

And Louisa felt herself excluded again from their life. She sat in pain, with the tears of disappointment distilling in her heart. Was that all?

Alfred came upstairs. He was clean, and in his shirt sleeves. He looked a workman now. Louisa felt that she and he were foreigners, moving in different lives. It dulled her again. Oh, if she could only find some fixed relations, something sure and abiding.

"How do you feel?" he said to his mother.

"It's a bit better," she replied wearily, impersonally. This strange putting herself aside, this abstracting herself and answering him only what she thought good for him to hear, made the relations between mother and son poignant and cramping to Miss Louisa. It made the man so ineffectual, so nothing. Louisa groped as if she had lost him. The mother was real and positive – he was not very actual. It puzzled and chilled the young woman.

"I'd better fetch Mrs. Harrison?" he said, waiting for his mother to decide.

"I suppose we shall have to have somebody," she replied.

Miss Louisa stood by, afraid to interfere in their business. They did not include her in their lives, they felt she had nothing to do with them, except as a help from outside. She was quite external to them. She felt hurt and powerless against this unconscious difference. But something patient and unyielding in her made her say:

"I will stay and do the nursing: you can't be left."

The other two were shy, and at a loss for an answer.

"Wes'll manage to get somebody," said the old woman wearily. She did not care very much what happened, now.

"I will stay until tomorrow, in any case," said Louisa. "Then we can see."

"I'm sure you've no right to trouble yourself," moaned the old woman. But she must leave herself in any hands.

Miss Louisa felt glad that she was admitted, even in an official capacity. She wanted to share their lives. At home they would need her, now Mary had come. But they must manage without her.

"I must write a note to the vicarage," she said.

Alfred Durant looked at her inquiringly, for her service. He had always that intelligent readiness to serve, since he had been in the navy. But there was a simple independence in his willingness, which she loved. She felt nevertheless it was hard to get at him. He was so deferential, quick to take the slightest suggestion of an order from her, implicitly, that she could not get at the man in him.

He looked at her very keenly. She noticed his eyes were golden brown, with a very small pupil, the kind of eyes that can see a long way off. He stood alert, at military attention. His face was still rather weather-reddened.

"Do you want pen and paper?" he asked, with deferential suggestion to a superior, which was more difficult for her than reserve.

"Yes, please," she said.

He turned and went downstairs. He seemed to her so self-contained, so utterly sure in his movement. How was she to approach him? For he would take not one step towards her. He would only put himself entirely and impersonally at her service, glad to serve her, but keeping himself quite removed from her. She could see he felt real joy in doing anything for her, but any recognition would confuse him and hurt him. Strange, it was to her, to have a man going about the house in his shirt sleeves, his waistcoat unbuttoned, his throat bare, waiting on her. He moved well, as if he had plenty of life to spare. She was attracted by his completeness. And yet, when all was ready, and there was nothing more for him to do, she quivered, meeting his questioning look.

As she sat writing, he placed another candle near her. The rather dense light fell in two places on the overfoldings of her hair till it glistened heavy and bright, like a dense golden plumage folded up. Then the nape of her neck was very white, with fine down and pointed wisps of gold. He watched it as it were a vision, losing himself. She was all that was beyond him, of revelation and exquisiteness. All that was ideal and beyond him, she was that – and he was lost to himself in looking at her. She had no connection with him. He did not approach her. She was there like a wonderful distance. But it was a treat, having her in the house. Even with this anguish for his mother tightening about him, he was sensible of the wonder of living this evening. The candles glistened on her hair, and seemed to fascinate him. He felt a little awe of her, and a sense of uplifting, that he and she and his mother should be together for a time, in the strange, unknown atmosphere. And, when he got out of the house, he was afraid. He saw the stars above ringing with fine brightness, the snow beneath just visible, and a new night was gathering round him. He was afraid almost with obliteration. What was this new night ringing about him, and what was he? He could not recognise himself nor any of his surroundings. He was afraid to think of his mother. And yet his chest was conscious of her, and of what was happening to her. He could not escape from her, she carried him with her into an unformed, unknown chaos.

11

He went up the road in an agony, not knowing what it was all about, but feeling as if red hot iron were gripped round his chest. Without thinking, he shook two or three tears onto the snow. Yet in his mind he did not believe his mother would die. He was in the grip of some greater consciousness. As he sat in the hall of the Vicarage, waiting whilst Mary put things for Louisa into a bag, he wondered why he had been so upset. He felt abashed and humbled by the big house, he felt again as if he were one of the rank and file. When Miss Mary spoke to him, he almost saluted.

"An honest man," thought Mary. And the patronage was applied as salve to her own sickness. She had station, so she could patronise: it was almost all that was left to her. But she could not have lived without having a certain position. She could never have trusted herself outside of a definite place, nor respected herself except as a woman of superior class.

As Alfred came to the latch gate, he felt the grief at his heart again, and saw the new heavens. He stood a moment looking northward to the Plough clambering up the night, and at the far glimmer of snow in distant fields. Then his grief came on like physical pain. He held tight to the gate, biting his mouth, whispering 'Mother!' It was a fierce, cutting, physical pain of grief, that came on in bouts, as his mother's pain came on in bouts, and was so acute he could scarcely keep erect. He did not know where it came from, the pain, nor why. It had nothing to do with his thoughts. Almost it had nothing to do with him. Only it gripped him and he must submit. The whole tide of his soul, gathering in its unknown towards this expansion into death, carried him with it helplessly, all the fritter of his thought and consciousness caught up as nothing, the heave passing on towards its breaking, taking him further than he had ever been. When the young man had regained himself, he went indoors, and there he was almost gay. It seemed to excite him. He felt in high spirits: he made whimsical fun of things. He sat on one side of his mother's bed, Louisa on the other, and a certain gaiety seized them all. But the night and the dread was coming on.

Alfred kissed his mother and went to bed. When he was half undressed, the knowledge of his mother came upon him, and the suffering seized him in its grip like two hands, in agony. He lay on the bed screwed up tight. It lasted so long, and exhausted him so much, that he fell asleep, without having the energy to get up and finish undressing. He awoke after midnight to find himself stone cold. He undressed and got into bed, and was soon asleep again.

At a quarter to six he woke, and instantly remembered. Having pulled on his trousers and lighted a candle, he went into his mother's room. He put his hand before the candle flame so that no light fell on the bed.

"Mother!" he whispered.

"Yes," was the reply.

There was a hesitation.

"Should I go to work?"

He waited, his heart was beating heavily.

"I think I'd go, my lad."

His heart went down in a kind of despair.

"You want me to?"

He let his hand down from the candle flame. The light fell on the bed. There he saw Louisa lying looking up at him. Her eyes were upon him. She quickly shut her eyes and half buried her face in the pillow, her back turned to him. He saw the rough hair like bright vapour about her round head, and the two plaits flung coiled among the bedclothes. It gave him a shock. He stood almost himself, determined. Louisa cowered down.

He looked, and met his mother's eyes. Then he gave way again, and ceased to be sure, ceased to be himself.

"Yes, go to work, my boy," said the mother.

"All right," replied he, kissing her. His heart was down at despair, and bitter. He went away.

"Alfred!" cried his mother faintly.

He came back with beating heart.

"What mother?"

"You'll always do what's right, Alfred?" the mother asked, beside herself in terror now he was leaving her. He was too terrified and bewildered to know what she meant.

"Yes," he said.

She turned her cheek to him. He kissed her, then went away, in bitter despair. He went to work.

12

By mid day his mother was dead. The word met him at the pit-mouth. As he had known, inwardly, it was not a shock to him, and yet he trembled. He went home calmly, feeling only heavy in his breathing.

Miss Louisa was still at the house. She had seen to everything possible. Very succinctly, she informed him of what he needed to know. But there was one point of anxiety for her.

"You *did* half expect it – it's not come as a blow to you?" she asked, looking up at him. Her eyes were dark and calm and searching. She too felt lost. He was so dark and inchoate.

"I suppose – yes," he said stupidly.

He looked aside, unable to endure her eyes on him.

"I could not bear to think – you might not have guessed," she said.

He did not answer.

He felt it a great strain to have her near him at this time. He wanted to be alone. As soon as the relatives began to arrive, Louisa departed, and came no more. While everything was arranging, and a crowd was in the house, whilst he had business to settle, he went well enough, with only those uncontrollable paroxysms of grief. Before the rest, he was superficial. By himself, he endured the fierce, almost insane bursts of grief which passed again and left him calm, almost clear, just wondering. He had not known before that everything could break down, that he himself could break down, and all be a great chaos, very vast and wonderful. It seemed as if life in him had burst its bounds, and he was lost in a great, bewildering flood, immense and unpeopled. He himself was broken and spilled out amid it all. He could only breathe panting in silence. Then the anguish came on again.

When all the people had gone from the Quarry Cottage, leaving the young man alone with an elderly housekeeper, then the long trial began. The snow had thawed and frozen, a fresh fall had whitened the grey, this then began to thaw. The world was a place of loose grey slosh. Alfred had nothing to do in the evenings. He was a man whose life had been filled up with small activities. Without knowing it, he had been centralised, polarised in his mother. It was she who had kept him. Even now, when the old housekeeper had left him, he might still have gone on in his old way. But the force and balance of his life was lacking. He sat pretending to read, all the time holding his fists clenched and holding himself in, enduring he did not know what. He walked the black and soddened miles of field paths, till he was tired out: but all this was only running away from whence he must return. At work he was all right: if it had been summer he might have escaped by working in the garden till bed-time. But now, there was no escape, no relief, no help. He, perhaps, was made for action rather than for understanding; for doing rather than for being. He was shocked out of his activities, like a swimmer who forgets to swim.

For a week, he had the force to endure this suffocation and struggle, then he began to get exhausted, and knew he must come out. The instinct of self preservation became strongest.

But then was the question: where was he to go? The public-house really meant nothing to him, it was no good going there. He began to think of emigration. In another country he would be all right. He wrote to the emigration offices.

On the Sunday after the funeral, when all the Durant people had attended church, Alfred had seen Miss Louisa, impassive and reserved, sitting with Miss Mary, who was proud and very distant, and with the other Lindleys, who were people removed. Alfred saw them as people remote. He did not think about it. They had nothing to do with his life. After service Louisa had come to him and shaken hands.

"My sister would like you to come to supper one evening, if you would be so good."

He looked at Miss Mary, who bowed. Out of kindness, Mary had proposed this to Louisa, disapproving of herself even as she did so. But she did not examine herself closely.

"Yes," said Durant awkwardly. "I'll come if you want me." But he vaguely felt that it was misplaced.

"You'll come tomorrow evening, then, about half-past six."

He went. Miss Louisa was very kind to him. There could be no music, because of the babies. He sat with his fists clenched on his thighs, very quiet and unmoved, lapsing, among all those people, into a kind of muse or daze. There was nothing between him and them. They knew it as well as he. But he remained very steady in himself, and the evening passed slowly. Mrs. Lindley called him 'young man'.

"Will you sit here, young man?"

He sat there. One name was as good as another. What had they to do with him?

Mr. Lindley kept a special tone for him, kind, indulgent, but patronising. Durant took it all without criticism or offence, just submitting. But he did not want to eat – that troubled him, to have to eat in their presence. He knew he was out of place. But it was his duty to stay yet awhile. He answered precisely, in monosyllables.

When he left he winced with confusion. He was glad it was finished. He got away as quickly as possible. And he wanted still more intensely to go right away, to Canada.

Miss Louisa suffered in her soul, indignant with all of them, with him too, but quite unable to say why she was indignant.

13

Two evenings after, Louisa tapped at the door of the Quarry Cottage at half-past six. He had finished dinner, the woman had washed up and gone away, but still he sat in his pit dirt. He was going later to the New Inn. He had begun to go there because he must go somewhere. The mere contact with other men was necessary to him, the noise, the warmth, the forgetful flight of the hours. But still he did not move. He sat alone in the empty house till it began to grow on him like something unnatural.

He was in his pit dirt when he opened the door.

"I have been wanting to call – I thought I would," she said, and she went to the sofa. He wondered why she wouldn't use his mother's round arm-chair. Yet something stirred in him, like anger, when the housekeeper placed herself in it.

"I ought to have been washed by now," he said, glancing at the clock, which was adorned with butterflies and cherries, and the name of "T. Brooks, Mansfield". He laid his black hands along his mottled dirty arms. Louisa looked at him. There was the reserve, and the simple neutrality towards her, which she dreaded in him. It made it impossible for her to approach him.

"I'm afraid," she said, "that I wasn't kind in asking you to supper."

"I'm not used to it," he said, smiling with his mouth, showing the interspaced white teeth. His eyes, however, were steady and unseeing.

"It's not *that*," she said hastily. Her repose was exquisite, and her dark grey eyes rich with understanding. He felt afraid of her as she sat there, as he began to grow conscious of her.

"How do you get on alone?" she asked.

He glanced away to the fire.

"Oh –" he answered, shifting uneasily, not finishing his answer.

Her face settled heavily.

"How close it is in this room. You have such immense fires. I will take off my coat," she said.

He watched her take off her hat and coat. She wore a cream cashmere blouse embroidered with gold silk. It seemed to him a very fine garment, fitting her throat and wrists close. It gave him a feeling of pleasure and cleanness and relief from himself.

"What were you thinking about that you didn't get washed?" she asked, half intimately. He laughed, turning aside his head. The whites of his eyes showed very distinct in his black face.

"Oh," he said, "I couldn't tell you."

There was a pause.

"Are you going to keep this house on?" she asked.

He stirred in his chair, under the question.

"I hardly know," he said. "I'm very likely going to Canada."

Her spirit became very quiet and attentive.

"What for?" she asked.

Again he shifted restlessly on his seat.

"Well" – he said slowly – "to try the life."

"But which life?"

"There's various things – farming or lumbering or mining. I don't mind much what it is."

"And is that what you want?"

He did not think in these times, so he could not answer.

"I don't know," he said, "till I've tried."

She saw him drawing away from her for ever.

112

"Aren't you sorry to leave this house and garden?" she asked.

"I don't know," he answered reluctantly. "I suppose our Fred would come in – that's what he's wanting."

"You don't want to settle down?" she asked.

He was leaning forward on the arms of his chair. He turned to her. Her face was pale and set. It looked heavy and impassive, her hair shone richer as she grew white. She was to him something steady and immovable and eternal presented to him. His heart was hot in an anguish of suspense. Sharp twitches of fear and pain were in his limbs. He turned his whole body away from her. The silence was unendurable. He could not bear her to sit there any more. It made his heart go hot and stifled in his breast.

"Were you going out tonight?" she asked.

"Only to the New Inn," he said.

Again there was silence.

She reached for her hat. Nothing else was suggested to her. She *had* to go. He sat waiting for her to be gone, for relief. And she knew that if she went out of that house as she was, she went out a failure. Yet she continued to pin on her hat; in a moment she would have to go. Something was carrying her.

Then suddenly a sharp pang, like lightning, seared her from head to foot, and she was beyond herself.

"Do you want me to go?" she asked, controlled, yet speaking out of a fiery anguish, as if the words were spoken from her without her intervention.

He went white under his dirt.

"Why?" he asked, turning to her in fear, compelled.

"Do you want me to go?" she repeated.

"Why?" he asked again.

"Because I wanted to stay with you," she said, suffocated, with her lungs full of fire.

His face worked, he hung forward a little, suspended, staring straight into her eyes, in torment, in an agony of chaos, unable to collect himself. And as if turned to stone, she looked back into his eyes. Their souls were exposed bare for a few moments. It was agony. They could not bear it. He dropped his head, whilst his body jerked with little sharp twitchings.

She turned away for her coat. Her soul had gone dead in her. Her hands trembled, but she could not feel any more. She drew on her coat. There was a cruel suspense in the room. The moment had come for her to go. He lifted his head. His eyes were like agate, expressionless, save for the black points of torture. They held her, she had no will, no life any more. She felt broken.

"Don't you want me?" she said helplessly.

A spasm of torture crossed his eyes, which held her fixed.

"I – I –" he began, but he could not speak. Something drew him from his chair to her. She stood motionless, spellbound, like a creature given up as prey. He put his hand tentatively, uncertainly, on her arm. The expression of his face was strange and inhuman. She stood utterly motionless. Then clumsily he put his arms round her, and took her, cruelly, blindly, straining her till she nearly lost consciousness, till he himself had almost fallen.

Then, gradually, as he held her gripped, and his brain reeled round, and he felt himself falling, falling from himself, and whilst she, yielded up, swooned to a kind of death of herself, a moment of utter darkness came over him, and they began to wake up again as if from a long sleep. He was himself.

After a while his arms slackened, she loosened herself a little, and put her arms round him, as he held her. So they held each other close, and hid each against the other for assurance, helpless in speech. And it was ever her hands that trembled more closely upon him, drawing him nearer into her, with love.

And at last she drew back her face and looked up at him, her eyes wet, and shining with light. His heart, which saw, was silent with fear. He was with her. She saw his face all sombre and inscrutable, and he seemed eternal to her. And all the echo of pain came back into the rarity of bliss, and all her tears came up.

"I love you," she said, her lips drawn to sobbing. He put down his head against her, unable to hear her, unable to bear the sudden coming of the peace and passion that almost broke his heart. They stood together in silence whilst the thing moved away a little.

At last she wanted to see him. She looked up. His eyes were strange and glowing, with a tiny black pupil. Strange, they were, and powerful over her. And his mouth came to hers, and slowly her eyelids closed, as his mouth sought hers closer and closer, and took possession of her.

They were silent for a long time, too much mixed up with passion and grief and death to do anything but hold each other in pain and kiss with long, hurting kisses wherein fear was transfused into desire. At last she disengaged herself. He felt as if his heart were hurt, but glad, and he scarcely dared look at her.

"I'm glad," she said also.

He held her hands in passionate gratitude and desire. He had not yet the presence of mind to say anything. He was dazed with relief.

"I ought to go," she said.

He looked at her. He could not grasp the thought of her going, he knew he could never be separated from her any more. Yet he dared not assert himself. He held her hands tight.

"Your face is black," she said.

He laughed.

"Yours is a bit smudged," he said.

They were afraid of each other, afraid to talk. He could only keep her near to him. After a while she wanted to wash her face. He brought her some warm water, standing by and watching her. There was something he wanted to say, that he dared not. He watched her wiping her face, and making tidy her hair.

"They'll see your blouse is dirty," he said.

She looked at her sleeves and laughed for joy.

He was sharp with pride.

"What shall you do?" he asked.

"How?" she said.

He was awkward at a reply.

"About me," he said.

"What do you want me to do?" she laughed.

He put his hand out slowly to her. What did it matter!

"But make yourself clean," she said.

14

As they went up the hill, the night seemed dense with the unknown. They kept close together, feeling as if the darkness were alive and full of knowledge, all around them. In silence they walked up the hill. At first the street lamps went their way. Several people passed them. He was more shy than she, and would have let her go had she loosened in the least. But she held firm.

Then they came into the true darkness, between the fields. They did not want to speak, feeling closer together in silence. So they arrived at the Vicarage gate. They stood under the naked horse chestnut tree.

"I wish you didn't have to go," he said.

She laughed a quick little laugh.

"Come tomorrow," she said, in a low tone, "and ask father."

She felt his hand close on hers.

She gave the same sorrowful little laugh of sympathy. Then she kissed him, sending him home.

At home, the old grief came on in another paroxysm, obliterating Louisa, obliterating even his mother for whom the stress was, raging like a burst of fever in a wound. But something was sound in his heart.

15

The next evening he dressed to go to the Vicarage, feeling it was to be done, not imagining what it would be like. He would not take this seriously. He was sure of Louisa, and this marriage was like fate to him. It filled him also with a blessed feeling of fatality. He was not responsible, neither had her people anything really to do with it.

They ushered him into the little study, which was fireless. By and by the vicar came in. His voice was cold and hostile as he said:

"What can I do for you, young man?"

He knew already, without asking.

Durant looked up at him, again like a sailor before a superior. He had the subordinate manner. Yet his spirit was clear.

"I wanted, Mr. Lindley –" he began respectfully, then all the colour suddenly left his face. It seemed now a violation to say what he had to say. What was he doing there? But he stood on, because it had to be done. He held firmly to his own independence and self-respect. He must not be indecisive. He must put himself aside: the matter was bigger than just his personal self. He must not feel. This was his highest duty.

"You wanted –" said the vicar.

Durant's mouth was dry, but he answered with steadiness:

"Miss Louisa – Louisa – promised to marry me –"

"You asked Miss Louisa if she would marry you – yes –," corrected the vicar. Durant reflected he hadn't asked her this:

"If she would marry me, sir. I hope you – don't mind."

He smiled. He was a good-looking man, and the vicar could not help seeing it.

"And my daughter was willing to marry you?" said Mr. Lindley.

"Yes," said Durant seriously. It was pain to him, nevertheless. He felt the natural hostility between himself and the elder man.

"Will you come this way," said the vicar. He led into the dining room, where were Mary, Louisa, and Mrs. Lindley. Mr. Massey sat in a corner with a lamp.

"This young man has come on your account, Louisa?" said Mr. Lindley.

"Yes," said Louisa, her eyes on Durant, who stood erect, in discipline. He dared not look at her, but he was aware of her.

"You don't want to marry a collier, you little fool," cried Mrs. Lindley harshly. She lay obese and helpless upon the couch, swathed in a loose, dove-grey gown.

"Oh, hush, mother," cried Mary, with quiet intensity and pride.

"What means have you to support a wife?" demanded the vicar's wife roughly.

"I!" Durant replied, starting. "I think I can earn enough."

"Well, and how much?" came the rough voice.

"Seven and six a day," replied the young man.

"And will it get to be any more?"

"I hope so."

"And are you going to live in that poky little house?"

"I think so," said Durant, "if it's all right."

He took small offence, only was upset, because they would not think him good enough. He knew that, in their sense, he was not.

"Then she's a fool, I tell you, if she marries you," cried the mother roughly, casting her decision.

"After all, mama, it is Louisa's affair," said Mary distinctly, "and we must remember –"

"As she makes her bed, she must lie – but she'll repent it," interrupted Mrs. Lindley.

"And after all," said Mr. Lindley, "Louisa cannot quite hold herself free to act entirely without consideration for her family."

"What do you want, papa?" asked Louisa sharply.

"I mean that if you marry this man, it will make my position very difficult for me, particularly if you stay in this parish. If you were moving quite away, it would be simpler. But living here in a collier's cottage, under my nose, as it were – it would be almost unseemly. I have my position to maintain, and a position which may not be taken lightly."

"Come over here, young man," cried the mother, in her rough voice, "and let us look at you."

Durant, flushing, went over and stood – not quite at attention, so that he did not know what to do with his hands. Miss Louisa was angry to see him standing there, obedient and acquiescent. He ought to show himself a man.

"Can't you take her away and live out of sight," said the mother. "You'd both of you be better off."

"Yes, we can go away," he said.

"Do you want to?" asked Miss Mary clearly.

He faced round. Mary looked very stately and impressive. He flushed.

"I do if it's going to be a trouble to anybody," he said.

"For yourself, you would rather stay?" said Mary.

"It's my home," he said, "and that's the house I was born in."

"Then" – Mary turned clearly to her parents, "I really don't see how you can make the conditions, papa. He has his own rights, and if Louisa wants to marry him –"

"Louisa, Louisa!" cried the father impatiently. "I cannot understand why Louisa should not behave in the normal way. I cannot see why she should only think of herself, and leave her family out of count. The thing is enough in itself, and she ought to try to ameliorate it as much as possible. And if –"

"But I love the man, papa," said Louisa.

"And I hope you love your parents, and I hope you want to spare them as much of the – the loss of prestige, as possible."

"We *can* go away to live," said Louisa, her face breaking to tears. At last she was really hurt.

"Oh, yes, easily," Durant replied hastily, pale, distressed.

There was dead silence in the room.

"I think it would really be better," murmured the vicar, mollified.

"Very likely it would," said the rough-voiced invalid.

"Though I think we ought to apologise for asking such a thing," said Mary haughtily.

"No," said Durant. "It will be best all round." He was glad there was no more bother.

"And shall we put up the banns here or go to the registrar?" he asked clearly, like a challenge.

"We will go to the registrar," replied Louisa decidedly.

Again there was a dead silence in the room.

"Well, if you will have your own way, you must go your own way," said the mother emphatically.

All the time Mr. Massey had sat obscure and unnoticed in a corner of the room. At this juncture he got up, saying:

"There is baby, Mary."

Mary rose and went out of the room, stately; her little husband padded after her. Durant watched the fragile, small man go, wondering.

"And where," asked the vicar, almost genial, "do you think you will go when you are married?"

Durant started.

"I was thinking of emigrating," he said.

"To Canada? or where?"

"I think to Canada."

"Yes, that would be very good."

Again there was a pause.

"We shan't see much of you then, as a son-in-law," said the mother, roughly but amicably.

"Not much," he said.

Then he took his leave. Louisa went with him to the gate. She stood before him in distress.

"You won't mind them, will you?" she said humbly.

"I don't mind them, if they don't mind me!" he said. Then he stooped and kissed her.

"Let us be married soon," she murmured, in tears.

"All right," he said. "I'll go tomorrow to Barford."

The Prussian Officer

They had marched more than thirty kilometres since dawn, along the white, hot road, where occasional thickets of trees threw a moment of shade, then out into the glare again. On either hand, the valley, wide and shallow, glistered with heat; dark green patches of rye, pale young corn, fallow and meadow and black pine-woods spread in a dull, hot diagram under a glistening sky. But right in front the mountains ranged across, pale blue and very still, the snow gleaming gently out of the deep atmosphere. And towards the mountains, on and on, the regiment marched between the rye-fields and the meadows, between the scraggy fruit-trees set regularly on either side the highroad. The burnished, dark green rye threw off a suffocating heat, the mountains drew gradually nearer and more distinct. While the feet of the soldiers grew hotter, sweat ran through their hair under their helmets, and their knapsacks could burn no more in contact with their shoulders, but seemed instead to give off a cold, prickly sensation.

He walked on and on in silence, staring at the mountains ahead, that rose sheer out of the land, and stood fold behind fold, half earth, half heaven, the heaven, the barrier with slits of soft snow in the pale, bluish peaks.

He could now walk almost without pain. At the start, he had determined not to limp. It had made him sick to take the first steps, and during the first mile or so, he had compressed his breath, and the cold drops of sweat had stood on his forehead. But he had walked it off. What were they after all but bruises! He had looked at them, as he was getting up: deep bruises on the backs of his thighs. And since he had made his first step in the morning, he had been conscious of them, till now he had a tight, hot place in his chest, with suppressing the pain, and holding himself in. There seemed no air when he breathed. But he walked almost lightly.

The captain's hand had trembled in taking his coffee at dawn: his orderly saw it again. And he saw the fine figure of the captain wheeling on horseback at the farm-house ahead, a handsome figure in pale blue uniform with facings of scarlet, and the metal gleaming on the black helmet and the sword scabbard, and dark streaks of sweat coming on the silky bay horse. The orderly felt he was connected with that figure moving so suddenly on horseback: he followed it like a shadow, mute and inevitable and damned by it. And the officer was always aware of the tramp of the company behind, the march of his orderly among the men.

The captain was a tall man of about forty, grey at the temples. He had a handsome, finely-knit figure, and was one of the best horsemen in the West. His orderly, having to rub him down, admired the amazing riding-muscles of his loins.

For the rest, the orderly scarcely noticed the officer any more than he noticed himself. It was rarely he saw his master's face: he did not look at it. The captain had reddish-brown, stiff hair, that he wore short upon his skull. His moustache also was cut short and bristly over a full, brutal mouth. His face was rather rugged, the cheeks thin. Perhaps the man was the more handsome for the deep lines in his face, the irritable tension of his brow, which gave him the look of a man who fights with life. His fair eyebrows stood bushy over light blue eyes that were always flashing with cold fire.

He was a Prussian aristocrat, haughty and overbearing. But his mother had been a Polish Countess. Having made too many gambling debts when he was young, he had ruined his prospects in the army, and remained an infantry captain. He had never married: his position did not allow it, and no woman had ever moved him to it. His time he spent riding –

occasionally he rode one of his own horses at the races – and at the officers' club. Now and then he took himself a mistress. But after such an event, he returned to duty with his brow still more tense, his eyes still more hostile and irritable. With the men, however, he was merely impersonal, though a devil when roused, so that on the whole they feared him but had no great aversion from him. They accepted him as the inevitable.

To his orderly he was at first cold and just and indifferent: he did not fuss over trifles. So that his servant knew practically nothing about him, except just what orders he would give, and how he wanted them obeyed. That was quite simple. Then the change gradually came.

The orderly was a youth of about twenty-two, of medium height, and well-built. He had strong, heavy limbs, was swarthy, with a soft, black, young moustache. There was something altogether warm and young about him. He had firmly marked eyebrows over dark, expressionless eyes, that seemed never to have thought, only to have received life direct through his senses, and acted straight from instinct.

Gradually the officer had become aware of his servant's young, vigorous, unconscious presence about him. He could not get away from the sense of the youth's person, while he was in attendance. It was like a warm flame upon the older man's tense, rigid body, that had become almost unliving, fixed. There was something so free and self-contained about him, and something in the young fellow's movement, that made the officer aware of him. And this irritated the Prussian. He did not choose to be touched into life by his servant. He might easily have changed his man, but he did not. He now very rarely looked direct at his orderly, but kept his face averted, as if to avoid seeing him. And yet as the young soldier moved unthinking about the apartment, the elder watched him, and would notice the movement of his strong young shoulders under the blue cloth, the bend of his neck. And it irritated him. To see the soldier's young, brown, shapely peasants' hands grasp the loaf or the wine-bottle sent a flash of hate or of anger through the elder man's blood. It was not that the youth was clumsy: it was rather the blind, instinctive sureness of movement of an unhampered young animal that irritated the officer to such a degree.

Once, when a bottle of wine had gone over, and the red gushed out onto the table-cloth, the officer had started up with an oath, and his eyes, bluey like fire, had held those of the confused youth for a moment. It was a shock for the young soldier. He felt something sink deeper, deeper into his soul, where nothing had ever gone before. It left him rather blank and wondering. Some of his natural completeness in himself was gone, a little uneasiness took its place. And from that time an undiscovered feeling had held between the two men.

Henceforward the orderly was afraid of really meeting his master. His subconsciousness remembered those steely blue eyes and the harsh brows, and did not intend to meet them again. So he always stared past his master, and avoided him. Also, in a little anxiety, he waited for the three months to have gone, when his time would be up. He began to feel a constraint in the captain's presence, and the soldier even more than the officer wanted to be left alone in his neutrality as servant.

He had served the captain for more than a year, and knew his duty. This he performed easily, as if it were natural to him. The officer and his commands he took for granted, as he took the sun and the rain, and he served as a matter of course. It did not implicate him personally.

But now if he were going to be forced into a personal interchange with his master, he would be like a wild thing caught, he felt he must get away.

But the influence of the young soldier's being had penetrated through the officer's stiffened discipline, and perturbed the man in him. He, however, was a gentleman, with long fine hands and cultivated movements, and was not going to allow such a thing as the stirring of his innate self. He was a man of

126

passionate temper, who had always kept himself suppressed. Occasionally there had been a duel, an outburst before the soldiers. He knew himself to be always on the point of breaking out. But he kept himself hard to the idea of the Service. Whereas the young soldier seemed to live out his warm, full nature, to give it off in his very movements, which had a certain zest, such as wild animals have in free movement. And this irritated the officer more and more.

In spite of himself, the captain could not regain his neutrality of feeling towards his orderly. Nor could he leave the man alone. In spite of himself, he watched him, gave him sharp orders, tried to take up as much of his time as possible. Sometimes he flew into a rage with the young soldier, and bullied him. Then the orderly shut himself off, as it were out of earshot, and waited with sullen, flushed face, for the end of the noise. The words never pierced to his intelligence, he made himself, protectively, impervious to the feelings of his master.

He had a scar on his left thumb, a deep seam going across the knuckle. The officer had long suffered from it, and wanted to do something to it. Still it was there, ugly and brutal on the young, brown hand. At last the captain's reserve gave way. One day, as the orderly was smoothing out the table-cloth, the officer pinned down his thumb with a pencil, asking:

"How did you come by that?"

The young man winced and drew back at attention.

"A wood-axe, Herr Hauptmann," he answered.

The officer waited for further explanation. None came. The orderly went about his duties. The elder man was sullenly angry. His servant avoided him. And the next day he had to use all his will-power to avoid seeing the scarred thumb. He wanted to get hold of it and –. A hot flame ran in his blood.

He knew his servant would soon be free, and would be glad. As yet, the soldier had held himself off from the elder man. The captain grew madly irritable. He could not rest when the soldier was away, and when he was present, he glared at him with tormented eyes. He hated those fine black brows over the unmeaning dark eyes, he was infuriated by the free movement of the handsome limbs, which no military discipline could make stiff. And he became harsh and cruelly bullying, using contempt and satire. The young soldier only grew more mute and expressionless.

"What cattle were you bred by, that you can't keep straight eyes. Look me in the eyes when I speak to you."

And the soldier turned his dark eyes to the other's face, but there was no sight in them: he stared with the slightest possible cast,◇ holding back his sight, perceiving the blue of his master's eyes, but receiving no look from them. And the elder man went pale, and his reddish eyebrows twitched. He gave his order, barrenly.

Once he flung a heavy military glove into the young soldier's face. Then he had the satisfaction of seeing the black eyes flare up into his own, like a blaze when straw is thrown on a fire. And he had laughed with a little tremor and a sneer.

But there were only two months more. The youth instinctively tried to keep himself intact: he tried to serve the officer as if the latter were an abstract authority, and not a man. All his instinct was to avoid personal contact, even definite hate. But in spite of himself the hate grew, responsive to the officer's passion. However, he put it in the background. When he had left the army he could dare acknowledge it. By nature he was active, and had many friends. He thought what amazing good fellows they were. But, without knowing it, he was alone. Now this solitariness was intensified. It would carry him through his term. But the officer seemed to be going irritably insane, and the youth was deeply frightened.

The soldier had a sweetheart, a girl from the mountains, independent and primitive. The two walked together, rather silently. He went with her, not to talk, but to have his arm round her, and for the physical contact. This eased him, made it easier for him to ignore the captain; for he could rest with her held fast against his chest. And she, in some unspoken fashion, was there for him. They loved each other.

The captain perceived it, and was mad with irritation. He kept the young man engaged all the evenings long, and took pleasure in the dark look that came on his face. Occasionally, the eyes of the two men met, those of the younger sullen and dark, doggedly unalterable, those of the elder sneering with restless contempt.

The officer tried hard not to admit the passion that had got hold of him. He would not know that his feeling for his orderly was anything but that of a man incensed by his stupid, *perverse* servant. So, keeping quite justified and conventional in his consciousness, he let the other thing run on. His nerves, however, were suffering. At last he slung the end of a belt in his servant's face. When he saw the youth start back, the pain-tears in his eyes and the blood on his mouth, he had felt at once a thrill of deep pleasure, and of shame. *violence*

But this, he acknowledged to himself was a thing he had never done before. The fellow was too exasperating. His own nerves must be going to pieces. He went away for some days with a woman.

It was a mockery of pleasure. He simply did not want the woman. But he stayed on for his time. At the end of it, he came back in an agony of irritation, torment, and misery. He rode all the evening, then came straight in to supper. His orderly was out. The officer sat with his long, fine hands lying on the table, perfectly still, and all his blood seemed to be corroding.

At last his servant entered. He watched the strong, easy young figure, the fine eyebrows, the thick black hair. In a week's time the youth had got back his old well-being. The hands of the officer twitched, and seemed to be full of mad flame. The young man stood at attention, unmoving, shut off.

The meal went in silence. But the orderly seemed eager. He made a clatter with the dishes.

"Are you in a hurry?" asked the officer, watching the intent, warm face of his servant. The other did not reply.

"Will you answer my question?" said the captain.

"Yes Sir," replied the orderly, standing with his pile of deep army-plates. The captain waited, looked at him, then asked again:

"Are you in a hurry?"

"Yes Sir," came the answer, that sent a flash through the listener.

"For what?"

"I was going out Sir."

"I want you this evening."

There was a moment's hesitation. The officer had a curious stiffness of countenance.

"Yes Sir," replied the servant, in his throat.

"I want you tomorrow evening also – in fact you may consider your evenings occupied, unless I give you leave."

The mouth with the young moustache set close.

"Yes Sir," answered the orderly, loosening his lips for a moment.

He again turned to the door.

"And why have you a piece of pencil in your ear?"

The orderly hesitated, then continued on his way without answering. He set the plates in a pile outside the door, took the stump of pencil from his ear, and put it in his pocket. He had been copying a verse for his sweetheart's birthday-card. He returned to finish clearing the table. The officer's eyes were dancing, he had a little, eager smile.

"Why have you a piece of pencil in your ear?" he asked.

The orderly took his hands full of dishes. His master was standing near the great green stove, a little smile on his face, his chin thrust forward. When the young soldier saw him his heart suddenly ran hot. He felt blind. Instead of answering, he turned dazedly to the door. As he was crouching to set down the dishes, he was pitched forward by a kick from behind. The

130

pots went in a stream down the stairs, he clung to the pillar of the banisters. And as he was rising he was kicked heavily again, and again, so that he clung sickly to the post for some moments. His master had gone swiftly into the room and closed the door. The maid-servant downstairs looked up the staircase and made a mocking face at the crockery disaster.

The officer's heart was plunging. He poured himself a glass of wine, part of which he spilled on the floor, and gulped the remainder, leaning against the cool, green stove. He heard his man collecting the dishes from the stairs. Pale, as if intoxicated, he waited. The servant entered again. The captain's heart gave a pang, as of pleasure, seeing the young fellow bewildered and uncertain on his feet, with pain.

"Schöner!"* he said.   *The servant's name means handsome*

The soldier was a little slower in coming to attention.

"Yes Sir!"

The youth stood before him, with pathetic young moustache, and fine eyebrows very distinct on his forehead of dark marble.

"I asked you a question."

"Yes Sir."

The officer's tone bit like acid.

"Why had you a pencil in your ear?"

Again the servant's heart ran hot, and he could not breathe. With dark, strained eyes, he looked at the officer, as if fascinated. And he stood there sturdily planted, unconscious. The dithering smile came into the captain's eyes, and he lifted his foot.

"I – I forgot it – Sir," panted the soldier, his dark eyes fixed on the other man's dancing blue ones.

"What was it doing there?"

He saw the young man's breast heaving as he made an effort for words.

"I had been writing."

"Writing what?"

Again the soldier looked him up and down. The officer could hear him panting. The smile came into the blue eyes. The soldier worked his dry throat, but could not speak. Suddenly the smile lit like a flame on the officer's face, and a kick came heavily against the orderly's thigh. The youth moved a pace sideways. His face went dead, with two black, staring eyes.

"Well?" said the officer.

The orderly's mouth had gone dry, and his tongue rubbed in it as on dry brown paper. He worked his throat. The officer raised his foot. The servant went stiff.

"Some poetry, Sir," came the crackling, unrecognisable sound of his voice.

"Poetry, what poetry?" asked the captain, with a sickly smile.

Again there was the working in the throat. The captain's heart had suddenly gone down heavily, and he stood sick and tired.

"For my girl, Sir," he heard the dry, inhuman sound.

"Oh!" he said, turning away. "Clear the table."

'Click!' – went the soldier's throat; then again, 'click!'; and then the half articulate:

"Yes Sir."

The young soldier was gone, looking old, and walking heavily. The officer, left alone, held himself rigid, to prevent himself from thinking. His instinct warned him that he must not think. Deep inside him was the intense gratification of his passion, still working powerfully. Then there was a counteraction, a horrible breaking down of something inside him, a whole agony of reaction. He stood there for an hour motionless, a chaos of sensations, but rigid with a will to keep blank his consciousness, to prevent his mind grasping. And he held himself so until the worst of the stress had passed, when he began to drink, drank himself to an intoxication, till he slept obliterated. When he woke in the morning he was shaken to the base of his nature. But he had fought off the realisation of what he had done. He had prevented his mind from taking it in, had suppressed it along with his instincts, and the conscious man had nothing to do with it. He felt only as after a bout of intoxication, weak, but the affair itself all dim and not to be recovered. Of the drunkenness of his passion he successfully refused remembrance. And when his orderly appeared with coffee, the officer assumed the same self he had had the morning before. He refused the event of the past night – denied it had ever been – and was successful in his denial. He had not done any such thing – not he himself. Whatever there might be lay at the door of a stupid, insubordinate servant.

The orderly had gone about in a stupor all the evening. He drank some beer because he was parched, but not much, the alcohol made his feeling come back, and he could not bear it. He was dulled, as if nine-tenths of the ordinary man in him were inert. He crawled about disfigured. Still, when he thought of the kicks, he went sick, and when he thought of the threats of more kicking, in the room afterwards, his heart went hot and faint, and he panted, remembering the one that had come. He had been forced to say 'For my girl'. He was much too done even to want to cry. His mouth hung slightly open, like an idiot's. He felt vacant, and wasted. So, he wandered at his work, painfully, and very slowly and clumsily, fumbling blindly with the brushes, and finding it difficult, when he sat down, to summon the energy to move again. His limbs, his jaw were slack and nerveless. But he was very tired. He got to bed at last and slept inert, relaxed, in a sleep that was rather stupor than slumber, a dead night of stupefaction shot through with gleams of anguish.

In the morning were the manoeuvres. But he woke even before the bugle sounded. The painful ache in his chest, the dryness of his throat, the awful steady feeling of misery made his eyes come awake and dreary at once. He knew without thinking, what had happened. And he knew that the day had come again, when he must go on with his round. The last bit of darkness was being pushed out of the room. He would have to move his inert body and go on. He was so young, and had known so little trouble, that he was bewildered. He only wished it would stay night, so that he could lie still, covered up by the darkness. And yet nothing would prevent the day from coming, nothing would save him from having to get up, and saddle the captain's horse, and make the captain's coffee. It was there, inevitable. And then, he thought, it was impossible. Yet they would not leave him free. He must go and take the coffee to the captain. He was too stunned to understand it. He only knew it was inevitable – inevitable, however long he lay inert.

At last, after heaving at himself, for he seemed to be a mass of inertia, he got up. But he had to force every one of his movements from behind, with his will. He felt lost, and dazed, and helpless. Then he clutched hold of the bed, the pain was so keen. And looking at his thighs, he saw the darker bruises on his swarthy flesh and he knew that, if he pressed one of his fingers on one of the bruises, he should faint. But he did not want to faint – he did not want anybody to know. No one should ever know. It was between him and the captain. There were only the two people in the world now – himself and the captain.

Slowly, economically, he got dressed and forced himself to walk. Everything was obscure, except just what he had his hands on. But he managed to get through his work. The very pain revived his dulled senses. The worst remained yet. He took the tray and went up to the captain's room. The officer, pale and heavy, sat at the table. The orderly, as he saluted, felt himself put out of existence. He stood still for a moment submitting to his own nullification – then he gathered himself, seemed to regain himself, and then the captain began to grow vague, unreal, and the younger soldier's heart beat up. He clung to this sensation – that the captain did not exist, so that he himself might live. But when he saw his officer's hand tremble as he took the coffee, he felt everything falling shattered. And he went away, feeling as if he himself were coming to pieces, disintegrated. And when the captain was there on horseback, giving orders, while he himself stood, with rifle and knapsack, sick with pain, he felt as if he must shut his eyes – as if he must shut his eyes on everything. It was only the long agony of marching with a parched throat that filled him with one single, sleep-heavy intention: to save himself.

2

He was getting used even to his parched throat. That the snowy peaks were radiant among the sky, that the whitey-green glacier river twisted through its pale shoals, in the valley below, seemed almost supernatural. But he was going mad with fever and thirst. He plodded on, uncomplaining. He did not want to speak, not to anybody. There were two gulls, like flakes of water and snow, over the river. The scent of green rye soaked in sunshine came like a sickness. And the march continued, monotonously, almost like a bad sleep.

At the next farm-house, which stood low and broad near the highroad, tubs of water had been put out. The soldiers clustered round to drink. They took off their helmets, and the steam mounted from their wet hair. The captain sat on horseback, watching. He needed to see his orderly. His helmet threw a dark shadow over his light, fierce eyes, but his moustache and mouth and chin were distinct in the sunshine. The orderly must move under the presence of the figure of the horseman. It was not that he was afraid, or cowed. It was as if he were disembowelled, made empty, like an empty shell. He felt himself as nothing, a shadow creeping under the sunshine. And, thirsty as he was, he could scarcely drink, feeling the captain near him. He would not take off his helmet to wipe his wet hair. He wanted to stay in shadow, not to be forced into consciousness. Starting, he saw the light heel of the officer prick

135

the belly of the horse; the captain cantered away, and he himself could relapse into vacancy.

Nothing, however, could give him back his living place in the hot, bright morning. He felt like a gap among it all. Whereas the captain was prouder, overriding. A hot flash went through the young servant's body. The captain was firmer and prouder with life, he himself was empty as a shadow. Again the flash went through him, dazing him out. But his heart ran a little firmer.

The company turned up the hill, to make a loop for the return. Below, from among the trees, the farm-bell clanged. He saw the laborers mowing barefoot at the thick grass leave off their work and go downhill, their scythes hanging over their shoulders, like long, bright claws curving down behind them. They seemed like dream-people, as if they had no relation to himself. He felt as in a blackish dream: as if all the other things were there and had form, but he himself was only a consciousness, a gap that could think and perceive.

The soldiers were tramping silently up the glaring hillside. Gradually his head began to revolve slowly, rhythmically. Sometimes it was dark before his eyes, as if he saw this world through a smoked glass, frail shadows and unreal. It gave him a pain in his head to walk.

The air was too scented, it gave no breath. All the lush green-stuff seemed to be issuing its sap, till the air was deathly, sickly with the smell of greenness. There was the perfume of clover, like pure honey and bees. Then there grew a faint acrid tang – they were near the beeches; and then a queer clattering noise, and a suffocating, hideous smell: they were passing a flock of sheep, a shepherd in a black smock, holding his hook. Why should the sheep huddle together under this fierce sun? He felt that the shepherd could not see him, though he could see the shepherd.

At last there was the halt. They stacked rifles in a conical stack, put down their kit in a scattered circle around it, and dispersed a little, sitting on a small knoll high on the hillside. The chatter began. The soldiers were steaming with heat, but were lively. He sat still, seeing the blue mountains rise upon the land, twenty kilometres away. There was a blue fold in the ranges, then out of that, at the foot, the broad pale bed of the river, stretches of whitey-green water between pinkish-grey shoals among the dark pine-woods. There it was, spread out a long way off. And it seemed to come downhill, the river. There was a raft being steered, a mile away. It was a strange country. Nearer, a red-roofed, broad farm with white base and square dots of windows crouched beside the wall of beech-foliage on the wood's edge. There were long strips of rye and clover and pale green corn. And just at his feet, below the knoll, was a darkish bog, where globe flowers stood breathless still on their slim stalks. And some of the pale gold bubbles were burst, and a broken fragment hung in the air. He thought he was going to sleep.

Suddenly something moved into this coloured mirage before his eyes. The captain, a small, light blue and scarlet figure, was trotting evenly between the strips of corn, along the level brow of the hill. And the man making flag-signals was coming on. – Proud and sure moved the horseman figure, the quick, bright thing in which was concentrated all the light of this morning, which for the rest lay a fragile, shining shadow. Submissive, apathetic, the young soldier sat and stared. But as the horse slowed to a walk, coming up the last steep path, the great flash flared over the body and soul of the orderly. He sat waiting. The back of his head felt as if it were weighted with a heavy piece of fire. He did not want to eat. His hands trembled slightly as he moved them. Meanwhile the officer on horseback was approaching slowly and proudly. The tension grew in the orderly's soul. Then again, seeing the captain ease himself on the saddle, the flash blazed through him.

The captain looked at the patch of light blue and scarlet, and dark heads, scattered closely on the hillside. It pleased him.

disassociate

The command pleased him. And he was feeling proud. His orderly was among them in common subjection. The officer rose a little on his stirrups to look. The young soldier sat with averted, dumb face. The captain relaxed on his seat. His slim legged, beautiful horse, brown as a beech nut, walked proudly uphill. The captain passed into the zone of the company's atmosphere: a hot smell of men, of sweat, of leather. He knew it very well. After a word with the lieutenant, he went a few paces higher, and sat there, a dominant figure, his sweat-marked horse swishing its tail, while he looked down on his men, on his orderly, a nonentity among the crowd.

The young soldier's heart was like fire in his chest, and he breathed with difficulty. The officer, looking downhill, saw three of the young soldiers, two pails of water between them, staggering across a sunny green field. A table had been set up under a tree, and there the slim lieutenant stood importantly busy. Then the captain summoned himself to an act of courage. He called his orderly.

The flame leapt into the young soldier's throat as he heard the command, and he rose blindly, stifled. He saluted, standing below the officer. He did not look up. But there was the flicker in the captain's voice.

"Go to the inn and fetch me – –" – the officer gave his commands. "Quick!" he added.

At the last word, the heart of the servant leapt with a flash, and he felt the strength come over his body. But he turned in mechanical obedience, and set off at a heavy run downhill, looking almost like a bear, his trousers bagging over his military boots. And the officer watched this blind, plunging run all the way.

But it was only the outside of the orderly's body that was obeying so humbly and mechanically. Inside had gradually accumulated a core into which all the energy of that young life was compact and concentrated. He executed his commission, and plodded quickly back uphill. There was a pain in his head, as he walked, that made him twist his features unknowingly. But hard there in the centre of his chest was himself, himself, firm, and not to be plucked to pieces.

The captain had gone up into the wood. – The orderly plodded through the hot, powerfully smelling zone of the company's atmosphere. He had a curious mass of energy inside him now. The captain was less real than himself. He approached the green entrance to the wood. There, in the half-shade, he saw the horse standing, the sunshine and the flickering shadow of leaves dancing over his brown body. There was a clearing where timber had lately been felled. Here, in the gold-green shade beside the brilliant cup of sunshine, stood two figures, blue and pink, the bits of pink showing out plainly. The captain was talking to his lieutenant.

The orderly stood on the edge of the bright clearing, where great trunks of trees, stripped and glistening, lay stretched like naked, brown-skinned bodies. Chips of wood littered the trampled floor, like splashed light, and the bases of the felled trees stood here and there, with their raw, level tops. Beyond was the brilliant, sunlit green of a beech.

"Then I will ride forward," the orderly heard his captain say. The lieutenant saluted and strode away. He himself went forward. A hot flash passed through his belly, as he tramped towards his officer.

The captain watched the rather heavy figure of the young soldier stumble forward, and his veins too ran hot. This was to be man to man between them. He yielded before the solid, stumbling figure with bent head. The orderly stooped and put the food on a level-sawn tree-base. The captain watched the glistening, sun-inflamed, naked hands. He wanted to speak to the young soldier, but could not. The servant propped a bottle against his thigh, pressed open the cork, and poured out the beer into the mug. He kept his head bent. The captain accepted the mug.

"Hot!" he said, as if amiably.

The flame sprang out of the orderly's heart, nearly suffocating him.

"Yes Sir," he replied, between shut teeth.

And he heard the sound of the captain's drinking, and he clenched his fists, such a strong torment came into his wrists. Then came the faint clang of the closing of the pot-lid. He looked up. The captain was watching him. He glanced swiftly away. Then he saw the officer stoop and take a piece of bread from the tree-base. Again the flash of flame went through the young soldier, seeing the stiff body stoop beneath him, and his hands jerked. He looked away. He could feel the officer was nervous. The bread fell as it was being broken. The officer ate the other piece. The two men stood tense and still, the master laboriously chewing his bread, the servant staring with averted face, his fists clenched.

Then the young soldier started. The officer had pressed open the lid of the mug again. The orderly watched the lid of the mug, and the white hand that clenched the handle, as if he were fascinated. It was raised. The youth followed it with his eyes. And then he saw the thin, strong throat of the elder man moving up and down as he drank, the strong jaw working. And the instinct which had been jerking at the young man's wrists suddenly jerked free. He jumped, feeling as if he were rent in two by a strong flame.

The spur of the officer caught in a tree-root, he went down backwards with a crash, the middle of his back thudding sickeningly against the sharp-edged tree-base, the pot flying away. And in a second the orderly, with serious, earnest young face, and underlip between his teeth, had got his knee in the officer's chest and was pressing the chin backward over the farther edge of the tree-stump, pressing, with all his heart behind in a passion of relief, the tension of his wrists exquisite with relief. And with the base of his palms he shoved at the chin, with all his might. And it was pleasant too to have that chin, that hard jaw already slightly rough with beard, in his hands. He did not relax one hair's-breadth but, all the force of all his blood exulting in his thrust, he shoved back the head of the other man, till there was a little 'cluck' and a crunching sensation. Then he felt as if his heart went to vapour. Heavy convulsions shook the body of the officer, frightening and horrifying the young soldier. Yet it pleased him too to repress them. It pleased him to keep his hands pressing back the chin, to feel the chest of the other man yield in expiration to the weight of his strong young knee, to feel the hard twitchings of the prostrate body jerking his own whole frame, which was pressed down on it.

But it went still. He could look into the nostrils of the other man, the eyes he could scarcely see. How curiously the mouth was pushed out, exaggerating the full lips, and the moustache bristling up from them. Then, with a start, he noticed the nostrils gradually filled with blood. The red brimmed, hesitated, ran over, and went in a thin trickle down the face to the eyes.

It shocked and distressed him. Slowly, he got up. The body twitched and sprawled there inert. He stood and looked at it in silence. It was a pity it was broken. It represented more than the thing which had kicked and bullied him. He was afraid to look at the eyes. They were hideous now, only the whites showing, and the blood running to them. The face of the orderly was drawn with horror at the sight. Well, it was so. In his heart he was satisfied. He had hated the face of the captain. _death_ It was extinguished now. There was a heavy relief in the orderly's soul. That was as it should be. But he could not bear to see the long, military body lying broken over the tree-base, the fine fingers crisped. He wanted to hide it away.

Quickly, busily, he gathered it up and pushed it under the felled tree-trunks, which rested their beautiful smooth length either end on logs. The face was horrible with blood. He covered it with the helmet. Then he pushed the limbs straight and decent, and brushed the dead leaves off the fine cloth of the uniform. So, it lay quite still in the shadow under there. A little strip of sunshine ran along the breast, from a chink between the logs. The orderly sat by it for a few moments. Here his own life also ended.

Then, through his daze, he heard the lieutenant, in a loud voice, explaining to the men outside the wood that they were to suppose the bridge on the river below was held by the enemy. Now they were to march to the attack in such and such a manner. The lieutenant had no gift of expression. The orderly, listening from habit, got muddled. And when the lieutenant began it all again, he ceased to hear.

He knew he must go. He stood up. It surprised him that the leaves were glittering in the sun, and the chips of wood reflecting white from the ground. For him a change had come over the world. But for the rest it had not – all seemed the same. Only he had left it. And he could not go back. – It was his duty to return with the beer-pot and the bottle. He could not. He had left all that. The lieutenant was still hoarsely explaining. He must go, or they would overtake him. And he could not bear contact with anyone now.

He drew his fingers over his eyes, trying to find out where he was. Then he turned away. He saw the horse standing in the path. He went up to it and mounted. It hurt him to sit in the saddle. The pain of keeping his seat occupied him as they cantered through the wood. He would not have minded anything, but he could not get away from the sense of being divided from the others. The path led out of the trees. On the edge of the wood he pulled up and stood watching. There in the spacious sunshine of the valley soldiers were moving in a little swarm. Every now and then, a man harrowing on a strip of fallow shouted to his oxen, at the turn. The village and the white-towered church was small in the sunshine. And he no longer belonged to it – he sat there, beyond, like a man outside in the dark. He had gone out from everyday life into the unknown, and he could not, he even did not want to go back.

Turning from the sun-blazing valley, he rode deep into the wood. Tree-trunks, like people standing grey and still, took no notice as he went. A doe, herself a moving bit of sunshine and shadow, went running through the flecked shade. There were bright green rents in the foliage. Then it was all pine-wood, dark and cool. And he was sick with pain, he had an intolerable great pulse in his head, and he was sick. He had never been ill in his life. He felt lost, quite dazed with all this.

Trying to get down from the horse, he fell, astonished at the pain and his lack of balance. The horse shifted uneasily. He jerked its bridle and sent it cantering jerkily away. It was his last connection with the rest of things.

But he only wanted to lie down and not be disturbed. Stumbling through the trees, he came on a quiet place where beeches and pine trees grew on a slope. Immediately he had lain down and closed his eyes, his consciousness went racing on without him. A big pulse of sickness beat in him as if it throbbed through the whole earth. He was burning with dry heat. But he was too busy, too tearingly active in the incoherent race of delirium, to observe.

3

He came to with a start. His mouth was dry and hard, his heart beat heavily, but he had not the energy to get up. His heart beat heavily. Where was he? – the barracks, – at home? There was something knocking. And, making an effort, he looked round – trees, and glitter of greenery, and reddish bright, still pieces of sunshine on the floor. He did not believe he was himself, he did not believe what he saw. Something was knocking. He made a struggle towards consciousness, but relapsed. Then he struggled again. And gradually his surroundings fell into relationship with himself. He knew, and a great pang of fear went through his heart. Somebody was knocking. He could see the heavy, black rags of a fir-tree overhead. Then everything went black. Yet he did not believe he had closed his eyes. He had not. Out of the blackness sight slowly emerged again. And someone was knocking. Quickly, he saw the blood-disfigured face of his captain, which he hated. And he held himself still with horror. Yet, deep inside him, he knew that it was so, the captain should be dead. But the physical delirium got hold of him. Someone was knocking. He lay perfectly still, as if dead, with fear. And he went unconscious.

When he opened his eyes again, he started, seeing something creeping swiftly up a tree-trunk. It was a little bird. And a bird was whistling overhead. Tap-tap-tap – it was the small, quick bird rapping the tree-trunk with its beak, as if its head were a little round hammer. He watched it curiously. It shifted sharply, in its creeping fashion. Then, like a mouse, it slid down the bare trunk. Its swift creeping sent a flash of revulsion through him. He raised his head. It felt a great weight. Then, the little bird ran out of the shadow across a still patch of sunshine, its little head bobbing swiftly, its white legs twinkling brightly for a moment. How neat it was in its build, so compact, with pieces of white on its wings. There were several of them. They were so pretty – but they crept like swift, erratic mice, running here and there among the beech-mast.

He lay down again exhausted, and his consciousness lapsed. He had a horror of the little creeping birds. All his blood seemed to be darting and creeping in his head. And yet he could not move.

He came to with a further ache of exhaustion. There was the pain in his head, and the horrible sickness, and his inability to move. He had never been ill in his life. He did not know where he was or what he was. Probably he had got sunstroke. Or what else? – he had silenced the captain for ever – some time ago – oh, a long time ago. There had been blood on his face, and his eyes had turned upwards. It was all right, somehow. It was peace. But now he had got beyond himself. He had never been here before. Was it life, or not-life? He was by himself. They were in a big, bright place, those others, and he was outside. The town, all the country, a big bright place of light: and he was outside, here, in the darkened open beyond, where each thing existed alone. But they would all have to come out there sometime, those others. Little, and left behind him, they all were. There had been father and mother and sweetheart. What did they all matter. This was the open land.

He sat up. Something scuffled. It was a little brown squirrel running in lovely, undulating bounds over the floor, its red tail completing the undulation of its body – and then, as it sat up, furling and unfurling. He watched it, pleased. It ran on again, friskily, enjoying itself. It flew wildly at another squirrel, and they were chasing each other, and making little scolding, chattering noises. The soldier wanted to speak to them. But only a hoarse sound came out of his throat. The squirrels burst away – they flew up the trees. And then he saw the one peeping round at him, half way up a tree-trunk. A start of fear went through him, though, in so far as he was conscious, he was amused. It still stayed, its little keen face staring at him half way up the tree-trunk, its little ears pricked up, its clawey little hands clinging to the bark, its white breast reared. He started from it in panic.

Struggling to his feet, he lurched away. He went on walking, walking, looking for something – for a drink. His brain felt hot and inflamed for want of water. He stumbled on. Then he did not know anything. He went unconscious as he walked. Yet he stumbled on, his mouth open.

When, to his dumb wonder, he opened his eyes on the world again, he no longer tried to remember what it was. There was thick, golden light behind golden-green glitterings, and tall, grey-purple shafts, and darknesses further off, surrounding him, growing deeper. He was conscious of a sense of arrival. He was amid the reality, on the real, dark bottom. But there was the thirst burning in his brain. He felt lighter, not so heavy. He supposed it was newness. The air was muttering with thunder. He thought he was walking wonderfully swiftly and was coming straight to relief – or was it to water?

Suddenly he stood still with fear. There was a tremendous flare of gold, immense – just a few dark trunks like bars between him and it. All the young level wheat was burnished, gold glaring on its silky green. A woman, full-skirted, a black cloth on her head for head dress, was passing like a block of shadow through the glistering green corn, into the full glare. There was a farm, too, pale blue in shadow, and the timber black. And there was a church spire nearly fused away in the gold. The woman moved on, away from him. He had no language with which to speak to her. She was the bright, solid unreality. She would make a noise of words that would confuse him, and her eyes would look at him without seeing him. She was crossing there to the other side. He stood against a tree.

When at last he turned, looking down the long, bare groove whose flat bed was already filling dark, he saw the mountains in a wonder-light, not far away, and radiant. Behind the soft, grey ridge of the nearest range the further mountains stood golden and pale grey, the snow all radiant like pure, soft gold. So still, gleaming in the sky, fashioned pure out of the ore of the sky, they shone in their silence. He stood and looked at them, his face illuminated. And like the golden, lustrous gleaming of the snow he felt his own thirst bright in him. He stood and gazed, leaning against a tree. And then everything slid away into space.

During the night the lightning fluttered perpetually, making the whole sky white. He must have walked again. The world hung livid around him for moments, fields a level sheen of grey-green light, trees in dark bulk, and a range of clouds black across a white sky. Then the darkness fell like a shutter, and the night was whole. A faint flutter of a half-revealed world, that could not quite leap out of the darkness! – Then there again stood a sweep of pallor for the land, dark shapes looming, a range of clouds hanging overhead. The world was a ghostly shadow, thrown for a moment upon the pure darkness, which returned ever whole and complete.

And the mere delirium of sickness and fever went on inside him – his brain opening and shutting like the night – then sometimes convulsions of terror from something with great eyes that stared round a tree – then the long agony of the march, and the sun decomposing his blood – then the pang of hate for the captain, followed by a pang of tenderness and ease. But everything was distorted, born of an ache and resolving into an ache.

In the morning he came definitely awake. Then his brain flamed with the sole horror of thirstiness. The sun was on his face, the dew was steaming from his wet clothes. Like one possessed, he got up. There, straight in front of him, blue and cool and tender, the mountains ranged across the pale edge of the morning sky. He wanted them – he wanted them alone – he wanted to leave himself and be identified with them. They did not move, they were still and soft, with white, gentle markings of snow. He stood still, mad with suffering, his hands crisping and clutching. Then he was twisting in a paroxysm on the grass.

He lay still, in a kind of dream of anguish. His thirst seemed to have separated itself from him, and to stand apart, a single demand. Then the pain he felt was another single self. Then there was the clog of his body, another separate thing. He was divided among all kinds of separate beings. There was some strange, agonised connection between them, but they were drawing further apart. Then they would all split. The sun, drilling down on him, was drilling through the bond. Then they would all fall, fall through the everlasting lapse of space.

Then again his consciousness reasserted itself. He roused onto his elbow and stared at the gleaming mountains. There they ranked, all still and wonderful between earth and heaven. He stared till his eyes went black, and the mountains as they

147

stood in their beauty, so clean and cool, seemed to have it, that which was lost in him.

4

When the soldiers found him, three hours later, he was lying with his face over his arm, his black hair giving off heat under the sun. But he was still alive. Seeing the open, black mouth the young soldiers dropped him in horror.

He died in the hospital at night, without having seen again.

The doctors saw the bruises on his legs, behind, and were silent.

The bodies of the two men lay together, side by side, in the mortuary, the one white and slender, but laid rigidly at rest, the other looking as if every moment it must rouse into life again, so young and unused, from a slumber.

Tickets Please

There is in the Midlands a single-line tramway system which boldly leaves the county town and plunges off into the black, industrial countryside, up hill and down dale, through the long, ugly villages of workmen's houses, over canals and railways, past churches perched high and nobly over the smoke and shadows, through stark, grimy, cold little market-places, tilting away in a rush past cinemas and shops down to the hollow where the collieries are, then up again, past a little rural church, under the ash trees, on in a rush to the terminus, the last little ugly place of industry, the cold little town that shivers on the edge of the wild, gloomy country beyond. There the green and creamy-coloured tram-car seems to pause and purr with curious satisfaction. But in a few minutes – the clock on the turret of the Co-operative Wholesale Society's Shops gives the time – away it starts once more on the adventure. Again there are the reckless swoops downhill, bouncing the loops: again the chilly wait in the hill-top market-place: again the breathless slithering round the precipitous drop under the church: again the patient halts at the loops, waiting for the outcoming car: so on and on, for two long hours, till at last the city looms beyond the fat gas works, the narrow factories draw near, we are in the sordid streets of the great town, once more we sidle to a standstill at our terminus, abashed by the great crimson and cream-coloured city cars, but still perky, jaunty, somewhat dare-devil, green as a jaunty sprig of parsley out of a black colliery garden.

To ride on these cars is always an adventure. Since we are in war-time, the drivers are men unfit for active service: cripples and hunchbacks. So they have the spirit of the devil in them. The ride becomes a steeplechase. Hurray! – we have leapt in a clean jump over the canal bridges – now for the four-lane corner. With a shriek and a trail of sparks we are clear again. To be sure, a tram often leaps the rails – but what matter! It sits in a ditch till other trams come to haul it out. It is quite common for a car packed with one solid mass of living people to come to a dead halt in the midst of unbroken blackness, the heart of nowhere on a dark night, and for the driver and the girl conductor to call – "All get off – car's on fire." Instead, however, of rushing out in a panic, the passengers stolidly reply: "Get on – get on. We're not coming out. We're stopping where we are. Push on, George." So till flames actually appear.

The reason for this reluctance to dismount is that the nights are howlingly cold, black, and wind-swept, and a car is a haven of refuge. From village to village the miners travel, for a change of cinema, of girl, of pub. The trams are desperately packed. Who is going to risk himself in the black gulf outside, to wait perhaps an hour for another tram, then to see the forlorn notice – "Depot Only" – because there is something wrong: or to greet a unit of three bright cars all so tight with people that they sail past with a howl of derision. Trams that pass in the night.

This, the most dangerous tram service in England, as the authorities themselves declare with pride, is entirely conducted by girls and driven by rash young men, a little crippled, or by delicate young men, who creep forward in terror. The girls are fearless young hussies. In their ugly blue uniforms, skirts up to their knees, shapeless old peaked caps on their heads, they have all the *sang froid* of an old non-commissioned officer. With a tram packed with howling colliers, roaring hymns downstairs and a sort of antiphony of obscenities upstairs, the lasses are perfectly at their ease. They pounce on the youths who try to evade their ticket-machine. They push off the men at the end of their distance. They are not going to be done in the eye – not they. They fear nobody – and everybody fears them.

"Halloa, Annie!"

"Halloa, Ted!"

"Oh, mind my corn, Miss Stone. It's my belief you've got a heart of stone, for you've trod on it again."

"You should keep it in your pocket," replies Miss Stone, and she goes sturdily upstairs in her high boots.

"Tickets, please."

She is peremptory, suspicious, and ready to hit first. She can hold her own against ten thousand. The step of that tram-car is her Thermopylae.°

Therefore, there is a certain wild romance aboard these cars – and in the sturdy bosom of Annie herself. The time for soft romance is in the morning, between ten o'clock and one, when things are rather slack: that is, except market day and Saturday. Then Annie has time to look about her. Then she often hops off her car and into a shop where she has spied something, while her driver chats in the main road. There is very good feeling between the girls and the drivers. Are they not companions in peril, shipmates aboard this careering vessel of a tram-car, for ever rocking on the waves of a stormy land.

Then, also, during the easy hours, the inspectors are most in evidence. For some reason, everybody employed in this tram-service is young: there are no grey heads. It would not do. Therefore the inspectors are of the right age, and one, the chief, is also good-looking. See him stand on a wet gloomy morning, in his long oil-skin, his peaked cap well down over his eyes, waiting to board a car. His face is ruddy, his small brown moustache is weathered, he has a faint impudent smile. Fairly tall and agile, even in his water-proof, he springs aboard a car and greets Annie.

"Halloa, Annie – keeping the wet out?"

"Trying to."

There are only two people in the car. Inspecting is soon over. Then for a long and impudent chat on the foot-board – a good, easy, twelve-mile chat.

The inspector's name is John Thomas Raynor: always called John Thomas,° except sometimes, in malice, Coddy.° His face sets in fury when he is addressed, from a distance, with this abbreviation. There is considerable scandal about John Thomas in half a dozen villages. He flirts with the girl conductors in the morning, and walks out with them in the dark night, when they leave their tram-car at the depôt. Of course the girls quit the service frequently. Then he flirts and walks out with the new-comer: always providing she is sufficiently attractive, and that she will consent to walk. It is remarkable, however, that most of the girls are quite comely, they are all young, and this roving life aboard the car gives them a sailor's dash and recklessness. What matter how they behave when the ship is in port. Tomorrow they will be aboard again.

Annie, however, was something of a tartar, and her sharp tongue had kept John Thomas at arm's length for many months. Perhaps, therefore, she liked him all the more: for he always came up smiling, with impudence. She watched him vanquish one girl, then another. She could tell by the movement of his mouth and eyes, when he flirted with her in the morning, that he had been walking out with this lass, or the other, the night before. A fine Cock-of-the-walk he was. She could sum him up pretty well.

In their subtle antagonism, they knew each other like old friends, they were as shrewd with one another almost as man and wife. But Annie had always kept him sufficiently at arm's length. Besides, she had a boy of her own.

The Statutes fair, however, came in November, at Bestwood. It happened that Annie had the Monday night off. It was a drizzling ugly night, yet she dressed herself up and went to the fair ground. She was alone, but she expected soon to find a pal of some sort.

The roundabouts were veering round and grinding out their music, the side shows were making as much commotion as possible. In the cocoa-nut shies there were no cocoa-nuts, but artificial war-time substitutes, which the lads declared were fastened into the irons. There was a sad decline in brilliance and luxury. None the less, the ground was muddy as ever, there was the same crush, the press of faces lighted up by the flares and the electric lights, the same smell of naphtha and of new-fried potatoes, and of electricity.

Who should be the first to greet Miss Annie, on the show ground, but John Thomas. He had a black overcoat buttoned up to his chin, and a tweed cap pulled down over his brows, his face between was ruddy and smiling and hardy as ever. She knew so well the way his mouth moved.

She was very glad to have a "boy". To be at the Statutes without a fellow was no fun. Instantly, like the gallant he was, he took her on the Dragons, grim-toothed, round-about switchbacks. It was not nearly so exciting as a tram-car, actually. But then, to be seated in a shaking green dragon, uplifted above the sea of bubble faces, careering in a rickety fashion in the lower heavens, whilst John Thomas, leaned over her, his cigarette in his mouth, was after all the right style. She was a plump, quick, alive little creature. So she was quite excited and happy.

John Thomas made her stay on for the next round. And therefore she could hardly for shame repulse him when he put his arm round her and drew her a little nearer to him, in a very warm and cuddly manner. Besides, he was fairly discreet, he kept his movement as hidden as possible. She looked down, and saw that his red, clean hand was out of sight of the crowd. And they knew each other so well. So they warmed up to the fair.

After the dragons they went on the horses. John Thomas paid each time, so she could but be complaisant. He of course sat astride on the outer horse – named "Black Bess" – and she sat sideways, towards him, on the inner horse – named "Wildfire". But of course John Thomas was not going to sit discreetly on "Black Bess", holding the brass bar. Round they spun and heaved, in the light. And round he swung on his wooden steed, flinging one leg across her mount, and perilously tipping up and down, across the space, half lying back, laughing at her. He was perfectly happy, she was afraid her hat was on one side, but she was excited.

He threw quoits on a table, and won her two large, pale blue hat-pins. And then, hearing the noise of the cinema, announcing another performance, they climbed the boards and went in.

Of course, during these performances, pitch darkness falls from time to time, when the machine goes wrong. Then there is a wild whooping, and a loud smacking of simulated kisses. In these moments John Thomas drew Annie towards him. After all, he had a wonderfully warm, cosy way of holding a girl with his arm, he seemed to make such a nice fit. And after all it was pleasant to be so held: so very comforting and cosy and nice. He leaned over her and she felt his breath on her hair, she knew he wanted to kiss her on the lips. And after all, he was so warm and she fitted in to him so softly. After all, she wanted him to touch her lips.

But the light sprang up, she also started electrically, and put her hat straight. He left his arm lying nonchalant behind her. Well, it was fun, it was exciting to be at the Statutes with John Thomas.

When the cinema was over they went for a walk across the dark, damp fields. He had all the arts of love-making. He was especially good at holding a girl, when he sat with her on a stile in the black, drizzling darkness. He seemed to be holding her in space, against his own warmth and gratification. And his kisses were soft and slow and searching.

So Annie walked out with John Thomas, though she kept her own boy dangling in the distance. Some of the tram-girls chose to be huffy. But there, you must take things as you find them, in this life.

There was no mistake about it, Annie liked John Thomas a good deal. She felt so rich and warm in herself, whenever he was near. And John Thomas really liked Annie, more than usual. The soft, melting way in which she could flow into a fellow, as if she melted into his very bones, was something rare and good. He fully appreciated this.

But with a developing acquaintance there began a developing intimacy. Annie wanted to consider him a person, a man, she wanted to take an intelligent interest in him, and to have an intelligent response. She did not want a *mere* nocturnal presence: which was what he was so far. And she prided herself that he could not leave her.

Here she made a mistake. John Thomas intended to remain a nocturnal presence, he had no idea of becoming an all-round individual to her. When she started to take an intelligent interest in him and his life and his character, he sheered off. He hated intelligent interest. And he knew that the only way to stop it was to avoid it. The possessive female was aroused in Annie. So he left her.

It was no use saying she was not surprised. She was at first startled, thrown out of her count. For she had been so *very* sure of holding him. For a while she was staggered, and everything became uncertain to her. Then she wept with fury, indignation, desolation and misery. Then she had a spasm of despair. And then, when he came, still impudently, on to her car, still familiar, but letting her see by the movement of his head that he had gone away to somebody else, for the time being, and was enjoying pastures new, then she determined to have her own back.

She had a very shrewd idea what girls John Thomas had taken out. She went to Nora Purdy. Nora was a tall, rather pale, but well-built girl, with beautiful yellow hair. She was rather secretive.

"Hey!" said Annie, accosting her: then softly: "Who's John Thomas on with now?"

"I don't know," said Nora.

"Why tha does," said Annie, ironically lapsing into dialect. "Tha knows as well as I do."

155

"Well, I do then," said Nora. "It isn't me, so don't bother."

"It's Cissy Meakin, isn't it?"

"It is for all I know."

"Hasn't he got a face on him!" said Annie. "I don't half like his cheek! I could knock him off the foot-board when he comes round at me."

"He'll get dropped on° one of these days," said Nora.

"Ay, he will when somebody makes up their mind to drop it on him. I should like to see him taken down a peg or two, shouldn't you?"

"I shouldn't mind," said Nora.

"You've got quite as much cause to as I have," said Annie. "But we'll drop on him one of these days, my girl. What? Don't you want to?"

"I don't mind," said Nora.

But as a matter of fact, Nora was much more vindictive than Annie.

One by one Annie went the round of the old flames. It so happened that Cissy Meakin left the tramway service in quite a short time. Her mother made her leave. Then John Thomas was on the *qui vive.*° He cast his eyes over his old flock. And his eyes lighted on Annie. He thought she would be safe now. Besides, he liked her.

She arranged to walk home with him on Sunday night. It so happened that her car would be in the depôt at half-past nine: the last car would come in at 10.15. So John Thomas was to wait for her there.

At the depôt the girls had a little waiting-room of their own. It was quite rough, but cosy, with a fire and an oven and a mirror, and table and wooden chairs. The half dozen girls who knew John Thomas only too well had arranged to take service this Sunday afternoon. So as the cars began to come in, early, the girls dropped in to the waiting-room. And instead of hurrying off home, they sat round the fire and had a cup of tea. Outside was the darkness and lawlessness of war-time.

John Thomas came on the car after Annie, at about a quarter to ten. He poked his head easily into the girls' waiting-room.

"Prayer meeting?" he asked.

"Ay," said Laura Sharp. "Ladies only."

"That's me!" said John Thomas. It was one of his favourite exclamations.

"Shut the door, boy," said Muriel Baggaley.

"On which side of me?" said John Thomas.

"Which tha likes," said Polly Birkin.

He had come in, and closed the door behind him. The girls moved in their circle, to make a place for him near the fire. He took off his great-coat and pushed back his hat.

"Who handles the tea-pot?" he said.

Nora Purdy silently poured him out a cup of tea.

"Want a bit o' my bread and drippin'?" said Muriel Baggaley to him.

"Ay, give us a bit."

And he began to eat his piece of bread.

"There's no place like home, girls," he said.

They all looked at him as he uttered this piece of impudence. He seemed to be sunning himself in the presence of so many damsels.

"Especially if you're not afraid to go home in the dark," said Laura Sharp.

"Me! By myself I am."

They sat till they heard the last tram come in. In a few minutes, Emma Houselay entered.

"Come on, my old duck," cried Polly Birkin.

"It *is* perishing," said Emma, holding her fingers to the fire.

"'But – I'm afraid to, go home in, the dark,'" sang Laura Sharp, the tune having got into her mind.

"Who're you going with tonight, John Thomas?" asked Muriel Baggaley, coolly.

"Tonight?" said John Thomas. "Oh, I'm going home by myself, tonight – all on my lonely-O."

"That's me!" said Nora Purdy, using his own ejaculation. The girls laughed shrilly.

"Me as well, Nora," said John Thomas.

"Don't know what you mean," said Laura.

"Yes, I'm toddling," said he, rising and reaching for his overcoat.

"Nay," said Polly. "We're all here waiting for you."

"We've got to be up in good time in the morning," he said, in the benevolent official manner.

They all laughed.

"Nay," said Muriel, "don't leave us all lonely, John Thomas. Take one!"

"I'll take the lot, if you like," he responded gallantly.

"That you won't, either," said Muriel. "Two's company, seven's too much of a good thing."

"Nay, take one," said Laura. "Fair and square, all above board, and say which one."

"Ay," cried Annie, speaking for the first time. "Pick, John Thomas, let's hear thee."

"Nay," he said. "I'm going home quiet tonight. Feeling good, for once."

"Whereabouts?" said Annie. "Take a good un, then. But tha's got to take one of us!"

"Nay, how can I take one," he said, laughing uneasily. "I don't want to make enemies."

"You'd only make *one*," said Annie.

"The chosen *one*," added Laura.

"Oh ay! Who said girls!" exclaimed John Thomas, again turning, as if to escape. "Well, good-night."

"Nay, you've got to make your pick," said Muriel. "Turn your face to the wall, and say which one touches you. Go on – we shall only just touch your back – one of us – go on – turn your face to the wall, and don't look, and say which one touches you."

He was uneasy, mistrusting them. Yet he had not the courage to break away. They pushed him to a wall and stood him there with his face to it. Behind his back they all grimaced, tittering. He looked so comical. He looked around uneasily.

"Go on!" he cried.

"You're looking – you're looking!" they shouted.

He turned his head away. And suddenly, with a movement like a swift cat, Annie went forward and fetched him a box on the side of the head that sent his cap flying, and himself staggering. He started round.

But at Annie's signal they all flew at him, slapping him, pinching him, pulling his hair, though more in fun than in spite or anger. He however saw red. His blue eyes flamed with strange fear as well as fury, and he butted through the girls to the door. It was locked. He wrenched at it. Roused, alert, the girls stood round and looked at him. He faced them, at bay. At that moment they were rather horrifying to him, as they stood in their short uniforms. He was distinctly afraid.

"Come on, John Thomas! Come on! Choose!" said Annie.

"What are you after? Open the door," he said.

"We sha'n't – not till you've chosen," said Muriel.

"Chosen what?" he said.

"Chosen the one you're going to marry," she replied.

He hesitated a moment: –

"Open the blasted door," he said, "and get back to your senses." He spoke with official authority.

"You've got to choose," cried the girls.

"Come on!" cried Annie, looking him in the eye. "Come on! Come on!"

He went forward, rather vaguely. She had taken off her belt, and swinging it, she fetched him a sharp blow over the head, with the buckle end. He sprang and seized her. But immediately the other girls rushed upon him, pulling and tearing and beating him. Their blood was now thoroughly up. He was their sport now. They were going to have their own back, out of him. Strange, wild creatures,° they hung on him and rushed at him to bear him down. His tunic was torn right up the back. Nora had hold at the back of his collar, and was actually strangling him. Luckily the button burst. He struggled in a wild frenzy of fury and terror, almost mad terror. His tunic was simply torn off his back, his shirt-sleeves were torn away, his arms were naked. The girls rushed at him, clenched their hands on him and pulled at him: or they rushed at him and pushed him, butted him with all their might: or they struck him wild blows. He ducked and cringed and struck sideways. They became more intense.

At last he was down. They rushed on him, kneeling on him. He had neither breath nor strength to move. His face was bleeding with a long scratch, his brow was bruised.

Annie knelt on him, the other girls knelt and hung on to him. Their faces were flushed, their hair wild, their eyes were all glittering strangely. He lay at last quite still, with face averted, as an animal lies when it is defeated and at the mercy of the captor. Sometimes his eye glanced back at the wild faces of the girls. His breast rose heavily, his wrists were torn.

"Now then, my fellow!" gasped Annie at length. "Now then – now –"

At the sound of her terrifying, cold triumph, he suddenly started to struggle as an animal might, but the girls threw themselves upon him with unnatural strength and power, forcing him down.

"Yes – now then – !" gasped Annie at length.

And there was a dead silence, in which the thud of heart-beating was to be heard. It was a suspense of pure silence in every soul.

"Now you know where you are," said Annie.

The sight of his white, bare arm maddened the girls. He lay in a kind of trance of fear and antagonism. They felt themselves filled with supernatural strength.

Suddenly Polly started to laugh – to giggle wildly – helplessly – and Emma and Muriel joined in. But Annie and Nora and Laura remained the same, tense, watchful, with gleaming eyes. He winced away from these eyes.

"Yes," said Annie, in a curious low tone, secret and deadly. "Yes! You've got it now! *You* know what you've done, don't you? – You know what you've done."

He made no sound nor sign, but lay with bright, averted eyes, and averted, bleeding face.

"You ought to be *killed*, that's what you ought," said Annie, tensely. "You ought to be *killed*." And there was a terrifying lust in her voice.

Polly was ceasing to laugh, and giving long-drawn Oh-h-hs and sighs as she came to herself.

"He's got to choose," she said vaguely.

"Oh, yes, he has," said Laura, with vindictive decision.

"Do you hear – do you hear?" said Annie. And with a sharp movement, that made him wince, she turned his face to her.

"Do you hear?" she repeated, shaking him.

But he was quite dumb. She fetched him a sharp slap on the face. He started, and his eyes widened. Then his face darkened with defiance, after all.

"Do you hear?" she repeated.

He only looked at her with hostile eyes.

"Speak!" she said, putting her face devilishly near his.

"What?" he said, almost overcome.

"You've got to *choose*!" she cried, as if it were some terrible menace, and as if it hurt her that she could not exact more.

"What?" he said, in fear.

"Choose your girl, Coddy. You've got to choose her now. And you'll get your neck broken if you play any more of your tricks, my boy. You're settled now."

There was a pause. Again he averted his face. He was cunning in his overthrow. He did not give in to them really – no, not if they tore him to bits.

161

"All right then," he said, "I choose Annie." His voice was strange and full of malice. Annie let go of him as if he had been a hot coal.

"He's chosen Annie!" said the girls in chorus.

"Me!" cried Annie. She was still kneeling, but away from him. He was still lying prostrate, with averted face. The girls grouped uneasily around.

"Me!" repeated Annie, with a terrible bitter accent.

Then she got up, drawing away from him with strange disgust and bitterness.

"I wouldn't touch him," she said.

But her face quivered with a kind of agony, she seemed as if she would fall. The other girls turned aside. He remained lying on the floor, with his torn clothes and bleeding, averted face.

"Oh, if he's chosen –" said Polly.

"I don't want him – he can choose again," said Annie, with the same rather bitter hopelessness.

"Get up," said Polly, lifting his shoulder. "Get up."

He rose slowly, a strange, ragged dazed creature. The girls eyed him from a distance, curiously, furtively, dangerously.

"Who wants him?" cried Laura roughly.

"Nobody," they answered, with contempt. Yet each one of them waited for him to look at her, hoped he would look at her. All except Annie, and something was broken in her.

He, however, kept his face closed and averted from them all. There was a silence of the end. He picked up the torn pieces of his tunic, without knowing what to do with them. The girls stood about uneasily, flushed, panting, tidying their hair and their dress unconsciously, and watching him. He looked at none of them. He espied his cap in a corner, and went and picked it up. He put it on his head, and one of the girls burst into a shrill, hysteric laugh at the sight he presented. He, however, took no heed, but went straight to where his overcoat hung on a peg. The girls moved away from contact with him

162

as if he had been an electric wire. He put on his coat and buttoned it down. Then he rolled his tunic-rags into a bundle, and stood before the locked door, dumbly.

"Open the door, somebody," said Laura.

"Annie's got the key," said one.

Annie silently offered the key to the girls. Nora unlocked the door.

"Tit for tat, old man," she said. "Show yourself a man, and don't bear a grudge."

But without a word or sign he had opened the door and gone, his face closed, his head dropped.

"That'll learn him," said Laura.

"Coddy!" said Nora.

"Shut up, for God's sake!" cried Annie fiercely, as if in torture.

"Well, I'm about ready to go, Polly. Look sharp!" said Muriel.

The girls were all anxious to be off. They were tidying themselves hurriedly, with mute, stupefied faces.

The Blind Man

Isabel Pervin was listening for two sounds – for the sound of wheels on the drive outside and for the noise of her husband's footsteps in the hall. Her dearest and oldest friend, a man who seemed almost indispensable to her living, would drive up in the rainy dusk of the closing November day. The trap had gone to fetch him from the station. And her husband, who had been blinded in Flanders, and who had a disfiguring mark on his brow, would be coming in from the out-houses.

He had been home for a year now. He was totally blind. Yet they had been very happy. The Grange was Maurice's own place. The back was a farmstead, and the Wernhams, who occupied the rear premises, acted as farmers. Isabel lived with her husband in the handsome rooms in front. She and he had been almost entirely alone together since he was wounded. They talked and sang and read together in a wonderful and unspeakable intimacy. Then she reviewed books for a Scottish newspaper, carrying on her old interest, and he occupied himself a good deal with the farm. Sightless, he could still discuss everything with Wernham, and he could also do a good deal of work about the place, menial work, it is true, but it gave him satisfaction. He milked the cows, carried in the pails, turned the separator, attended to the pigs and horses. Life was still very full and strangely serene for the blind man, peaceful with the almost incomprehensible peace of immediate contact in darkness. With his wife he had a whole world, rich and real and invisible.

They were newly and remotely happy. He did not even regret the loss of his sight in these times of dark, palpable joy. A certain exultance swelled his soul.

But as time wore on, sometimes the rich glamour would leave them. Sometimes, after months of this intensity, a sense of burden overcame Isabel, a weariness, a terrible *ennui*, in that silent house approached between a colonnade of tall-shafted pines. Then she felt she would go mad, for she could not bear it. And sometimes he had devastating fits of depression, which seemed to lay waste his whole being. It was worse than depression – a black misery, when his own life was a torture to him, and when his presence was unbearable to his wife. The dread went down to the roots of her soul as these black days recurred. In a kind of panic she tried to wrap herself up still further in her husband. She forced the old spontaneous cheerfulness and joy to continue. But the effort it cost her was almost too much. She knew she could not keep it up. She felt she would scream with the strain, and would give anything, anything, to escape. She longed to possess her husband utterly; it gave her inordinate joy to have him entirely to herself. And yet, when again he was gone in a black and massive misery, she could not bear him, she could not bear herself; she wished she could be snatched away off the earth altogether, anything rather than live at this cost.

Dazed, she schemed for a way out. She invited friends, she tried to give him some further connection with the outer world. But it was no good. After all their joy and suffering, after their dark, great year of blindness and solitude and unspeakable nearness, other people seemed to them both shallow, prattling, rather impertinent. Shallow prattle seemed presumptuous. He became impatient and irritated, she was wearied. And so they lapsed into their solitude again. For they preferred it.

But now, in a few weeks' time, her second baby would be born. The first had died, an infant, when her husband first went out to France. She looked with joy and relief to the coming of the second. It would be her salvation. But also she felt some anxiety. She was thirty years old, her husband was a year younger. They both wanted the child very much. Yet she could not help feeling afraid. She had her husband on her hands, a terrible joy to her, and a terrifying burden. The child would occupy her love and attention. And then, what of Maurice? What would he do? If only she could feel that he, too, would be at peace and happy when the child came! She did so want to luxuriate in a rich, physical satisfaction of maternity. But the man, what would he do? How could she provide for him, how avert those shattering black moods of his, which destroyed them both?

She sighed with fear. But at this time Bertie Reid wrote to Isabel. He was her old friend, a second or third cousin, a Scotchman, as she was a Scotchwoman. They had been brought up near to one another, and all her life he had been her friend, like a brother, but better than her own brothers. She loved him – though not in the marrying sense. There was a sort of kinship between them, an affinity. They understood one another instinctively. But Isabel would never have thought of marrying Bertie. It would have seemed like marrying in her own family.

Bertie was a barrister and a man of letters, a Scotchman of the intellectual type, quick, ironical, sentimental, and on his knees before the woman he adored but did not want to marry. Maurice Pervin was different. He came of a good old country family – the Grange was not a very great distance from Oxford. He was passionate, sensitive, perhaps over-sensitive, wincing – a big fellow with heavy limbs and a forehead that flushed painfully. For his mind was slow, as if drugged by the strong provincial blood that beat in his veins. He was very sensitive to his own mental slowness, his feelings being quick and acute. So that he was just the opposite to Bertie, whose mind was much quicker than his emotions, which were not so very fine.

From the first the two men did not like each other. Isabel felt that they *ought* to get on together. But they did not. She felt that if only each could have the clue to the other there would be such a rare understanding between them. It did not come off, however. Bertie adopted a slightly ironical attitude, very offensive to Maurice, who returned the Scotch irony with

English resentment, a resentment which deepened sometimes into stupid hatred.

This was a little puzzling to Isabel. However, she accepted it in the course of things. Men were made freakish and unreasonable. Therefore, when Maurice was going out to France for the second time, she felt that, for her husband's sake, she must discontinue her friendship with Bertie. She wrote to the barrister to this effect. Bertram Reid simply replied that in this, as in all other matters, he must obey her wishes, if these were indeed her wishes.

For nearly two years nothing had passed between the two friends. Isabel rather gloried in the fact: she had no compunction. She had one great article of faith, which was, that husband and wife should be so important to one another, that the rest of the world simply did not count. She and Maurice were husband and wife. They loved one another. They would have children. Then let everybody and everything else fade into insignificance outside this connubial felicity. She professed herself quite happy and ready to receive Maurice's friends. She was happy and ready: the happy wife, the ready woman in possession. Without knowing why, the friends retired abashed, and came no more. Maurice, of course, took as much satisfaction in this connubial absorption as Isabel did.

He shared in Isabel's literary activities, she cultivated a real interest in agriculture and cattle-raising. For she, being at heart perhaps an emotional enthusiast, always cultivated the practical side of life, and prided herself on her mastery of practical affairs. Thus the husband and wife had spent the five years of their married life. The last had been one of blindness and unspeakable intimacy. And now Isabel felt a great indifference coming over her, a sort of lethargy. She wanted to be allowed to bear her child in peace, to nod by the fire and drift vaguely, physically, from day to day. Maurice was like an ominous thunder-cloud. She had to keep waking up to remember him.

When a little note from Bertie, asking if he were to put up a tombstone to their dead friendship, and speaking of the real pain he felt on account of her husband's loss of sight, she felt a pang, a fluttering agitation of re-awakening. And she read the letter to Maurice.

"Ask him to come down," he said.

"Ask Bertie to come here!" she re-echoed.

"Yes – if he wants to."

Isabel paused for a few moments.

"I know he wants to – he'd only be too glad," she replied. "But what about you, Maurice? How would you like it?"

"I should like it."

"Well – in that case – But I thought you didn't care for him –"

"Oh, I don't know. I might think different of him now," the blind man replied. It was rather abstruse to Isabel.

"Well, dear," she said, "if you're quite sure –"

"I'm sure enough. Let him come," said Maurice.

So Bertie was coming, coming this evening, in the November rain and darkness. Isabel was agitated, racked with her old restlessness and indecision. She had always suffered from this pain of doubt, just an agonising sense of uncertainty. It had begun to pass off, in the lethargy of maternity. Now it returned, and she resented it. She struggled as usual to maintain her calm, composed, friendly bearing, a sort of mask she wore over all her body.

A woman had lighted a tall lamp beside the table, and spread the cloth. The long dining-room was dim, with its elegant but rather severe pieces of old furniture. Only the round table glowed softly under the light. It had a rich, beautiful effect. The white cloth glistened and dropped its heavy, pointed lace corners almost to the carpet, the china was old and handsome, creamy-yellow, with a blotched pattern of harsh red and deep blue, the cups large and bell-shaped, the teapot gallant. Isabel looked at it with superficial appreciation.

Her nerves were hurting her. She looked automatically again at the high, uncurtained windows. In the last dusk she could just perceive outside a huge fir-tree swaying its boughs: it was as if she thought it rather than saw it. The rain came flying on the window panes. Ah, why had she no peace? These two men, why did they tear at her? Why did they not come – why was there this suspense?

She sat in a lassitude that was really suspense and irritation. Maurice, at least, might come in – there was nothing to keep him out. She rose to her feet. Catching sight of her reflection in a mirror, she glanced at herself with a slight smile of recognition, as if she were an old friend to herself. Her face was oval and calm, her nose a little arched. Her neck made a beautiful line down to her shoulder. With hair knotted loosely behind, she had something of a warm, maternal look. Thinking this of herself, she arched her eyebrows and her rather heavy eye-lids, with a little flicker of a smile, and for a moment her grey eyes looked amused and wicked, a little sardonic, out of her transfigured Madonna face.

Then, resuming her air of womanly patience – she was really fatally self-determined – she went with a little jerk towards the door. Her eyes were slightly reddened.

She passed down the wide hall, and through a door at the end. Then she was in the farm premises. The scent of dairy, and of farm-kitchen, and of farm-yard and of leather almost overcame her: but particularly the scent of dairy. They had been scalding out the pans. The flagged passage in front of her was dark, puddled and wet. Light came out from the open kitchen door. She went forward and stood in the doorway. The farm-people were at tea, seated at a little distance from her, round a long, narrow table, in the centre of which stood a white lamp. Ruddy faces, ruddy hands holding food, red mouths working, heads bent over the tea-cups: men, land-girls, boys: it was tea-time, feeding-time. Some faces caught sight of her. Mrs. Wernham, going round behind the chairs with a large black tea-pot, halting slightly in her walk, was not aware of her for a moment. Then she turned suddenly.

"Oh, is it Madam!" she exclaimed. "Come in, then, come in! We're at tea." And she dragged forward a chair.

"No, I won't come in," said Isabel. "I'm afraid I interrupt your meal."

"No – no – not likely, Madam, not likely."

"Hasn't Mr. Pervin come in, do you know?"

"I'm sure I couldn't say! Missed him, have you, Madam?"

"No, I only wanted him to come in," laughed Isabel, as if shyly.

"Wanted him, did ye? Get up, boy – get up, now –"

Mrs. Wernham knocked one of the boys on the shoulder. He began to scrape to his feet, chewing largely.

"I believe he's in top stable," said another face from the table.

"Ah! No, don't get up. I'm going myself," said Isabel.

"Don't you go out of a dirty night like this. Let the lad go. Get along wi' ye, boy," said Mrs. Wernham.

"No, no," said Isabel, with a decision that was always obeyed. "Go on with your tea, Tom. I'd like to go across to the stable, Mrs. Wernham."

"Did ever you hear tell!" exclaimed the woman.

"Isn't the trap late?" asked Isabel.

"Why, no," said Mrs. Wernham, peering into the distance at the tall, dim clock. "No, Madam – we can give it another quarter or twenty minutes yet, good – yes, every bit of a quarter."

"Ah! It seems late when darkness falls so early," said Isabel.

"It do, that it do. Bother the days, that they draw in so," answered Mrs. Wernham. "Proper miserable!"

"They are," said Isabel, withdrawing.

She pulled on her overshoes, wrapped a large Tartan shawl around her, put on a man's felt hat, and ventured out along the causeways of the first yard. It was very dark. The wind was roaring in the great elms behind the outhouses. When she came to the second yard the darkness seemed deeper. She was unsure of her footing. She wished she had brought a lantern. Rain blew against her. Half she liked it, half she felt unwilling to battle.

She reached at last the just visible door of the stable. There was no sign of a light anywhere. Opening the upper half, she looked in: into a simple well of darkness. The smell of horses, and ammonia, and of warmth was startling to her, in that full night. She listened with all her ears, but could hear nothing save the night, and the stirring of a horse.

"Maurice!" she called, softly and musically, though she was afraid. "Maurice – are you there?"

Nothing came from the darkness. She knew the rain and wind blew in upon the horses, the hot animal life. Feeling it wrong, she entered the stable, and drew the lower half of the door shut, holding the upper part close. She did not stir, because she was aware of the presence of the dark hind-quarters of the horses, though she could not see them, and she was afraid. Something wild stirred in her heart.

She listened intensely. Then she heard a small noise in the distance – far away, it seemed – the chink of a pan, and a man's voice speaking a brief word. It would be Maurice, in the other part of the stable. She stood motionless, waiting for him to come through the partition door. The horses were so terrifyingly near to her, in the invisible.

The loud jarring of the inner door-latch made her start; the door was opened. She could hear and feel her husband entering and invisibly passing among the horses near to her, in darkness as they were, actively intermingled. The rather low sound of his voice as he spoke to the horses came velvety to her nerves. How near he was, and how invisible! The darkness seemed to be in a strange swirl of violent life, just upon her. She turned giddy.

Her presence of mind made her call, quietly and musically:
"Maurice! Maurice – dea-ar!"

"Yes," he answered. "Isabel?"

She saw nothing, and the sound of his voice seemed to touch her.

"Hello!" she answered cheerfully, straining her eyes to see him. He was still busy, attending to the horses near her, but she saw only darkness. It made her almost desperate.

"Won't you come in, dear?" she said.

"Yes, I'm coming. Just half a minute. *Stand over – now!* Trap's not come, has it?"

"Not yet," said Isabel.

His voice was pleasant and ordinary, but it had a slight suggestion of the stable to her. She wished he would come away. Whilst he was so utterly invisible, she was afraid of him.

"How's the time?" he asked.

"Not yet six," she replied. She disliked to answer into the dark. Presently he came very near to her, and she retreated out of doors.

"The weather blows in here," he said, coming steadily forward, feeling for the doors. She shrank away. At last she could dimly see him.

"Bertie won't have much of a drive," he said, as he closed the doors.

"He won't indeed!" said Isabel calmly, watching the dark shape at the door.

"Give me your arm, dear," she said.

She pressed his arm close to her, as she went. But she longed to see him, to look at him. She was nervous. He walked erect, with face rather lifted, but with a curious tentative movement of his powerful, muscular legs. She could feel the clever, careful, strong contact of his feet with the earth, as she balanced against him. For a moment he was a tower of darkness to her, as if he rose out of the earth.

In the house-passage he wavered, and went cautiously, with a curious look of silence about him as he felt for the bench. Then he sat down heavily. He was a man with rather sloping shoulders, but with heavy limbs, powerful legs that seemed to know the earth. His head was small, usually carried high and light. As he bent down to unfasten his gaiters and boots, he did not look blind. His hair was brown and crisp, his hands were large, reddish, intelligent, the veins stood out in the wrists; and his thighs and knees seemed massive. When he stood up his face and neck were surcharged with blood, the veins stood out on his temples. She did not look at his blindness.

Isabel was always glad when they had passed through the dividing door into their own regions of repose and beauty. She was a little afraid of him, out there in the animal grossness of the back. His bearing also changed, as he smelt the familiar indefinable odour that pervaded his wife's surroundings, a delicate, refined scent, very faintly spicy. Perhaps it came from the pot-pourri bowls.

He stood at the foot of the stairs, arrested, listening. She watched him, and her heart sickened. He seemed to be listening to fate.

"He's not here yet," he said. "I'll go up and change."

"Maurice," she said, "you're not wishing he wouldn't come, are you?"

"I couldn't quite say," he answered. "I feel myself rather on the *qui vive*."◇

"I can see you are," she answered. And she reached up and kissed his cheek. She saw his mouth relax into a slow smile.

"What are you laughing at?" she said, roguishly.

"You consoling me," he answered.

"Nay," she answered. "Why should I console you? You know we love each other – you know *how* married we are! What does anything else matter?"

"Nothing at all, my dear."

He felt for her face, and touched it, smiling.

"*You're* all right, aren't you?" he asked, anxiously.

"I'm wonderfully all right, love," she answered. "It's you I am a little troubled about, at times."

"Why me?" he said, touching her cheeks delicately with the tips of his fingers. The touch had an almost hypnotising effect on her.

He went away upstairs. She saw him mount into the darkness, unseeing and unchanging. He did not know that the lamps on the upper corridor were unlighted. He went on into the darkness with unchanging step. She heard him in the bath-room.

Pervin moved about almost unconsciously in his familiar surroundings, dark though everything was. He seemed to know the presence of objects before he touched them. It was a pleasure to him to rock thus through a world of things, carried on the flood in a sort of blood-prescience. He did not think much or trouble much. So long as he kept this sheer immediacy of blood-contact with the substantial world he was happy, he wanted no intervention of visual consciousness. In this state there was a certain rich positivity, bordering sometimes on rapture. Life seemed to move in him like a tide lapping, lapping, and advancing, enveloping all things darkly. It was a pleasure to stretch forth the hand and meet the unseen object, clasp it, and possess it in pure contact. He did not try to remember, to visualise. He did not want to. The new way of consciousness substituted itself in him.

The rich suffusion of this state generally kept him happy, reaching its culmination in the consuming passion for his wife. But at times the flow would seem to be checked and thrown back. Then it would beat inside him like a tangled sea, and he was tortured in the shattered chaos of his own blood. He grew to dread this arrest, this throw-back, this chaos inside himself, when he seemed merely at the mercy of his own powerful and conflicting elements. How to get some measure of control or surety, this was the question. And when the question rose maddening in him, he would clench his fists as if he would *compel* the whole universe to submit to him. But it was in vain. He could not even compel himself.

To-night, however, he was still serene, though little tremors of unreasonable exasperation ran through him. He had to handle the razor very carefully, as he shaved, for it was not at one with him, he was afraid of it. His hearing also was too much sharpened. He heard the woman lighting the lamps on the corridor, and attending to the fire in the visitors' room. And then, as he went to his room, he heard the trap arrive. Then came Isabel's voice, lifted and calling, like a bell ringing:

"Is it you, Bertie? Have you come?"

And a man's voice answered out of the wind:

"Hello, Isabel! There you are."

"Have you had a miserable drive? I'm so sorry we couldn't send a closed carriage. I can't see you at all, you know."

"I'm coming. No, I liked the drive – it was like Perthshire. Well, how are you? You're looking fit as ever, as far as I can see."

"Oh, yes," said Isabel. "I'm wonderfully well. How are you? Rather thin, I think –"

"Worked to death – everybody's old cry. But I'm all right, Ciss. How's Pervin? – isn't he here?"

"Oh, yes, he's upstairs changing. Yes, he's awfully well. Take off your wet things; I'll send them to be dried."

"And how are you both, in spirits? He doesn't fret?"

"No – no, not at all. No, on the contrary, really. We've been wonderfully happy, incredibly. It's more than I can understand – so wonderful: the nearness, and the peace –"

"Ah! Well, that's awfully good news –"

They moved away. Pervin heard no more. But a childish sense of desolation had come over him, as he heard their brisk voices. He seemed shut out – like a child that is left out. He was aimless and excluded, he did not know what to do with himself. The helpless desolation came over him. He fumbled nervously as he dressed himself, in a state almost of childishness. He disliked the Scotch accent in Bertie's speech, and the slight response it found on Isabel's tongue. He disliked

176

the slight purr of complacency in the Scottish speech. He disliked intensely the glib way in which Isabel spoke of their happiness and nearness. It made him recoil. He was fretful and beside himself like a child, he had almost a childish nostalgia to be included in the life circle. And at the same time he was a man, dark and powerful and infuriated by his own weakness. By some fatal flaw, he could not be by himself, he had to depend on the support of another. And this very dependence enraged him. He hated Bertie Reid, and at the same time he knew the hatred was nonsense, he knew it was the outcome of his own weakness.

He went downstairs. Isabel was alone in the dining-room. She watched him enter, head erect, his feet tentative. He looked so strong-blooded and healthy, and, at the same time, cancelled. Cancelled – that was the word that flew across her mind. Perhaps it was his scar suggested it.

"You heard Bertie come, Maurice?" she said.

"Yes – isn't he here?"

"He's in his room. He looks very thin and worn."

"I suppose he works himself to death."

A woman came in with a tray – and after a few minutes Bertie came down. He was a little dark man, with a very big forehead, thin, wispy hair, and sad, large eyes. His expression was inordinately sad – almost funny. He had odd, short legs.

Isabel watched him hesitate under the door, and glance nervously at her husband. Pervin heard him and turned.

"Here you are, now," said Isabel. "Come, let us eat."

Bertie went across to Maurice.

"How are you, Pervin?" he said, as he advanced.

The blind man stuck his hand out into space, and Bertie took it.

"Very fit. Glad you've come," said Maurice.

Isabel glanced at them, and glanced away, as if she could not bear to see them.

"Come," she said. "Come to table. Aren't you both awfully hungry? I am, tremendously."

"I'm afraid you waited for me," said Bertie, as they sat down.

Maurice had a curious monolithic way of sitting in a chair, erect and distant. Isabel's heart always beat when she caught sight of him thus.

"No," she replied to Bertie. "We're very little later than usual. We're having a sort of high tea, not dinner. Do you mind? It gives us such a nice long evening, uninterrupted."

"I like it," said Bertie.

Maurice was feeling, with curious little movements, almost like a cat kneading her bed, for his plate, his knife and fork, his napkin. He was getting the whole geography of his cover into his consciousness. He sat erect and inscrutable, remote-seeming. Bertie watched the static figure of the blind man, the delicate tactile discernment of the large, ruddy hands, and the curious mindless silence of the brow, above the scar. With difficulty he looked away, and without knowing what he did, picked up a little crystal bowl of violets from the table, and held them to his nose.

"They are sweet-scented," he said. "Where do they come from?"

"From the garden – under the windows," said Isabel.

"So late in the year – and so fragrant! Do you remember the violets under Aunt Bell's south wall?"

The two friends looked at each other and exchanged a smile, Isabel's eyes lighting up.

"Don't I?" she replied. "*Wasn't* she queer!"

"A curious old girl," laughed Bertie. "There's a streak of freakishness in the family, Isabel."

"Ah – but not in you and me, Bertie," said Isabel. "Give them to Maurice, will you?" she added, as Bertie was putting down the flowers. "Have you smelled the violets, dear? Do! – they are so scented."

Maurice held out his hand, and Bertie placed the tiny bowl against his large, warm-looking fingers. Maurice's hand closed over the thin white fingers of the barrister. Bertie carefully extricated himself. Then the two watched the blind man smelling the violets. He bent his head and seemed to be thinking. Isabel waited.

"Aren't they sweet, Maurice?" she said at last, anxiously.

"Very," he said. And he held out the bowl. Bertie took it. Both he and Isabel were a little afraid, and deeply disturbed.

The meal continued. Isabel and Bertie chatted spasmodically. The blind man was silent. He touched his food repeatedly, with quick, delicate touches of his knife-point, then cut irregular bits. He could not bear to be helped. Both Isabel and Bertie suffered: Isabel wondered why. She did not suffer when she was alone with Maurice. Bertie made her conscious of a strangeness.

After the meal the three drew their chairs to the fire, and sat down to talk. The decanters were put on a table near at hand. Isabel knocked the logs on the fire, and clouds of brilliant sparks went up the chimney. Bertie noticed a slight weariness in her bearing.

"You will be glad when your child comes now, Isabel?" he said.

She looked up to him with a quick, wan smile.

"Yes, I shall be glad," she answered. "It begins to seem long. Yes, I shall be very glad. So will you, Maurice, won't you?" she added.

"Yes, I shall," replied her husband.

"We are both looking forward so much to having it," she said.

"Yes, of course," said Bertie.

He was a bachelor, three or four years older than Isabel. He lived in beautiful rooms overlooking the river, guarded by a faithful Scottish man-servant. And he had his friends among the fair sex – not lovers, friends. So long as he could avoid any danger of courtship or marriage, he adored a few good women with constant and unfailing homage, and he was chivalrously fond of quite a number. But if they seemed to encroach on him, he withdrew and detested them.

Isabel knew him very well, knew his beautiful constancy, and kindness, also his incurable weakness, which made him unable ever to enter into close contact of any sort. He was ashamed of himself, because he could not marry, could not approach women physically. He wanted to do so. But he could not. At the centre of him he was afraid, helplessly and even brutally afraid. He had given up hope, had ceased to expect any more that he could escape his own weakness. Hence he was a brilliant and successful barrister, also a *littérateur*◇ of high repute, a rich man, and a great social success. At the centre he felt himself neuter, nothing.

Isabel knew him well. She despised him even while she admired him. She looked at his sad face, his little short legs, and felt contempt of him. She looked at his dark grey eyes, with their uncanny, almost childlike intuition, and she loved him. He understood amazingly – but she had no fear of his understanding. As a man she patronised him.

And she turned to the impassive, silent figure of her husband. He sat leaning back, with folded arms, and face a little uptilted. His knees were straight and massive. She sighed, picked up the poker, and again began to prod the fire, to rouse the clouds of soft brilliant sparks.

"Isabel tells me," Bertie began suddenly, "that you have not suffered unbearably from the loss of sight."

Maurice straightened himself to attend, but kept his arms folded.

"No," he said, "not unbearably. Now and again one struggles against it, you know. But there are compensations."

"They say it is much worse to be stone deaf," said Isabel.

"I believe it is," said Bertie. "Are there compensations?" he added, to Maurice.

"Yes. You cease to bother about a great many things."
Again Maurice stretched his figure, stretched the strong
muscles of his back, and leaned backwards, with uplifted face.

"And that is a relief," said Bertie. "But what is there in place
of the bothering? What replaces the activity?"

There was a pause. At length the blind man replied, as out
of a negligent, unattentive thinking:

"Oh, I don't know. There's a good deal when you're not
active."

"Is there?" said Bertie. "What, exactly? It always seems to
me that when there is no thought and no action, there is
nothing."

Again Maurice was slow in replying.

"There is something," he replied. "I couldn't tell you what
it is."

And the talk lapsed once more, Isabel and Bertie chatting
gossip and reminiscence, the blind man silent.

At length Maurice rose restlessly, a big, obtrusive figure. He
felt tight and hampered. He wanted to go away.

"Do you mind," he said, "if I go and speak to Wernham?"

"No – go along, dear," said Isabel.

And he went out. A silence came over the two friends. At
length Bertie said:

"Nevertheless, it is a great deprivation, Cissie."

"It is, Bertie. I know it is."

"Something lacking all the time," said Bertie.

"Yes, I know. And yet – and yet – Maurice is right. There
is something else, something *there*, which you never knew was
there, and which you can't express."

"What is there?" asked Bertie.

"I don't know – it's awfully hard to define it – but something
strong and immediate. There's something strange in Maurice's
presence – indefinable – but I couldn't do without it. I agree
that it seems to put one's mind to sleep. But when we're alone

I miss nothing; it seems awfully rich, almost splendid, you know."

"I'm afraid I don't follow," said Bertie.

They talked desultorily. The wind blew loudly outside, rain chattered on the window-panes, making a sharp drum-sound, because of the closed, mellow-golden shutters inside. The logs burned slowly, with hot, almost invisible small flames. Bertie seemed uneasy, there were dark circles round his eyes. Isabel, rich with her approaching maternity, leaned looking into the fire. Her hair curled in odd, loose strands, very pleasing to the man. But she had a curious feeling of old woe in her heart, old, timeless night-woe.

"I suppose we're all deficient somewhere," said Bertie.

"I suppose so," said Isabel wearily.

"Damned, sooner or later."

"I don't know," she said, rousing herself. "I feel quite all right, you know. The child coming seems to make me indifferent to everything, just placid. I can't feel that there's anything to trouble about, you know."

"A good thing, I should say," he replied slowly.

"Well, there it is. I suppose it's just Nature. If only I felt I needn't trouble about Maurice, I should be perfectly content –"

"But you feel you must trouble about him?"

"Well – I don't know –" She even resented this much effort.

The night passed slowly. Isabel looked at the clock.

"I say," she said. "It's nearly ten o'clock. Where can Maurice be? I'm sure they're all in bed at the back. Excuse me a moment."

She went out, returning almost immediately.

"It's all shut up and in darkness," she said. "I wonder where he is. He must have gone out to the farm –"

Bertie looked at her.

"I suppose he'll come in," he said.

"I suppose so," she said. "But it's unusual for him to be out now."

"Would you like me to go out and see?"

"Well – if you wouldn't mind. I'd go, but –" She did not want to make the physical effort.

Bertie put on an old overcoat and took a lantern. He went out from the side door. He shrank from the wet and roaring night. Such weather had a nervous effect on him: too much moisture everywhere made him feel almost imbecile. Unwilling, he went through it all. A dog barked violently at him. He peered in all the buildings. At last, as he opened the upper door of a sort of intermediate barn, he heard a grinding noise, and looking in, holding up his lantern, saw Maurice, in his shirt-sleeves, standing listening, holding the handle of a turnip-pulper. He had been pulping sweet roots, a pile of which lay dimly heaped in a corner behind him.

"That you, Wernham?" said Maurice, listening.

"No, it's me," said Bertie.

A large, half-wild grey cat was rubbing at Maurice's leg. The blind man stooped to rub its sides. Bertie watched the scene, then unconsciously entered and shut the door behind him. He was in a high sort of barn-place, from which, right and left, ran off the corridors in front of the stalled cattle. He watched the slow, stooping motion of the other man, as he caressed the great cat.

Maurice straightened himself.

"You came to look for me?" he said.

"Isabel was a little uneasy," said Bertie.

"I'll come in. I like messing about doing these jobs."

The cat had reared her sinister, feline length against his leg, clawing at his thigh affectionately. He lifted her claws out of his flesh.

"I hope I'm not in your way at all at the Grange here," said Bertie, rather shy and stiff.

"My way? No, not a bit. I'm glad Isabel has somebody to talk to. I'm afraid it's I who am in the way. I know I'm not very lively company. Isabel's all right, don't you think? She's not unhappy, is she?"

"I don't think so."

"What does she say?"

"She says she's very content – only a little troubled about you."

"Why me?"

"Perhaps afraid that you might brood," said Bertie, cautiously.

"She needn't be afraid of that." He continued to caress the flattened grey head of the cat with his fingers. "What I am a bit afraid of," he resumed, "is that she'll find me a dead weight, always alone with me down here."

"I don't think you need think that," said Bertie, though this was what he feared himself.

"I don't know," said Maurice. "Sometimes I feel it isn't fair that she's saddled with me." Then he dropped his voice curiously. "I say," he asked, secretly struggling, "is my face much disfigured? Do you mind telling me?"

"There is the scar," said Bertie, wondering. "Yes, it is a disfigurement. But more pitiable than shocking."

"A pretty bad scar, though," said Maurice.

"Oh, yes."

There was a pause.

"Sometimes I feel I am horrible," said Maurice, in a low voice, talking as if to himself. And Bertie actually felt a quiver of horror.

"That's nonsense," he said.

Maurice again straightened himself, leaving the cat.

"There's no telling," he said. Then again, in an odd tone, he added: "I don't really know you, do I?"

"Probably not," said Bertie.

"Do you mind if I touch you?"

The lawyer shrank away instinctively. And yet, out of very philanthropy, he said, in a small voice: "Not at all."

But he suffered as the blind man stretched out a strong, naked hand to him. Maurice accidentally knocked off Bertie's hat.

"I thought you were taller," he said, starting. Then he laid his hand on Bertie Reid's head, closing the dome of the skull in a soft, firm grasp, gathering it, as it were; then, shifting his grasp and softly closing again, with a fine, close pressure, till he had covered the skull and the face of the smaller man, tracing the brows, and touching the full, closed eyes, touching the small nose and the nostrils, the rough, short moustache, the mouth, the rather strong chin. The hand of the blind man grasped the shoulder, the arm, the hand of the other man. He seemed to take him, in the soft, travelling grasp.

"You seem young," he said quietly, at last.

The lawyer stood almost annihilated, unable to answer.

"Your head seems tender, as if you were young," Maurice repeated. "So do your hands. Touch my eyes, will you? – touch my scar."

Now Bertie quivered with revulsion. Yet he was under the power of the blind man, as if hypnotised. He lifted his hand, and laid the fingers on the scar, on the scarred eyes. Maurice suddenly covered them with his own hand, pressed the fingers of the other man upon his disfigured eye-sockets, trembling in every fibre, and rocking slightly, slowly, from side to side. He remained thus for a minute or more, whilst Bertie stood as if in a swoon, unconscious, imprisoned.

Then suddenly Maurice removed the hand of the other man from his brow, and stood holding it in his own.

"Oh, my God," he said, "we shall know each other now, shan't we? We shall know each other now."

Bertie could not answer. He gazed mute and terror-struck, overcome by his own weakness. He knew he could not answer. He had an unreasonable fear, lest the other man should suddenly destroy him. Whereas Maurice was actually filled with hot, poignant love, the passion of friendship. Perhaps it was this very passion of friendship which Bertie shrank from most.

"We're all right together now, aren't we?" said Maurice. "It's all right now, as long as we live, so far as we're concerned?"

"Yes," said Bertie, trying by any means to escape.

Maurice stood with head lifted, as if listening. The new delicate fulfilment of mortal friendship had come as a revelation and surprise to him, something exquisite and unhoped-for. He seemed to be listening to hear if it were real.

Then he turned for his coat.

"Come," he said, "we'll go to Isabel."

Bertie took the lantern and opened the door. The cat disappeared. The two men went in silence along the causeways. Isabel, as they came, thought their footsteps sounded strange. She looked up pathetically and anxiously for their entrance. There seemed a curious elation about Maurice. Bertie was haggard, with sunken eyes.

"What is it?" she asked.

"We've become friends," said Maurice, standing with his feet apart, like a strange colossus.

"Friends!" re-echoed Isabel. And she looked again at Bertie. He met her eyes with a furtive, haggard look; his eyes were as if glazed with misery.

"I'm so glad," she said, in sheer perplexity.

"Yes," said Maurice.

He was indeed so glad. Isabel took his hand with both hers, and held it fast.

"You'll be happier now, dear," she said.

But she was watching Bertie. She knew that he had one desire – to escape from this intimacy, this friendship, which had been thrust upon him. He could not bear it that he had been touched by the blind man, his insane reserve broken in. He was like a mollusc whose shell is broken.

Hadrian

The Pottery House was a square, ugly, brick house girt in by the wall that enclosed the whole grounds of the pottery itself. To be sure, a privet hedge partly masked the house and its grounds from the pottery-yard and works: but only partly. Through the hedge could be seen the desolate yard, and the many-windowed, factory-like pottery, over the hedge could be seen the chimneys and the out-houses. But inside the hedge, a pleasant garden and lawn sloped down to a willow pool, which had once supplied the works.

The pottery itself was now closed, the great doors of the yard permanently shut. No more the great crates, with yellow straw showing through, stood in stacks by the packing shed. No more the drays drawn by great horses rolled down the hill with a high load. No more the pottery-lasses in their clay-coloured overalls, their faces and hair splashed with grey fine mud, shrieked and larked with the men. All that was over.

"We like it much better – oh, much better – quieter," said Matilda Rockley.

"Oh, yes," assented Emmie Rockley, her sister.

"I'm sure you do," agreed the visitor.

But whether the two Rockley girls really liked it better, or whether they only imagined they did, is a question. Certainly their lives were much more grey and dreary now that the grey clay had ceased to spatter its mud and silt its dust over the premises. They did not quite realise how they missed the shrieking, shouting lasses, whom they had known all their lives and disliked so much.

Matilda and Emmie were already old maids. In a thorough industrial district, it is not easy for the girls who have expectations above the common to find husbands. The ugly industrial town was full of men, young men who were ready to marry. But they were all colliers or pottery-hands, mere workmen. The Rockley girls would have about ten thousand pounds each when their father died: ten thousand pounds' worth of profitable house-property. It was not to be sneezed at: they felt so themselves, and refrained from sneezing away such a fortune on any mere member of the proletariat. Consequently, bank-clerks or nonconformist clergymen or even school-teachers having failed to come forward, Matilda had begun to give up all idea of ever leaving the Pottery House.

Matilda was a tall, thin, graceful fair girl, with a rather large nose. She was the Mary to Emmie's Martha:° that is, Matilda loved painting and music, and read a good many novels, whilst Emmie looked after the housekeeping. Emmie was shorter, plumper than her sister, and she had no accomplishments. She looked up to Matilda, whose mind was naturally refined and sensible.

In their quiet, melancholy way, the two girls were happy. Their mother was dead. Their father was ill also. He was an intelligent man who had had some education, but preferred to remain as if he were one with the rest of the working people. He had a passion for music and played the violin pretty well. But now he was getting old, he was very ill, dying of a kidney disease. He had been rather a heavy whiskey-drinker.

This quiet household, with one servant-maid, lived on year after year in the Pottery House. Friends came in, the girls went out, the father drank himself more and more ill. Outside in the street there was a continual racket of the colliers and their dogs and children. But inside the pottery wall was a deserted quiet.

In all this ointment there was one little fly. Ted Rockley, the father of the girls, had had four daughters, and no son. As his girls grew, he felt angry at finding himself always in a household of women. He went off to London and adopted a boy out of a Charity Institution. Emmie was fourteen years old, and Matilda sixteen, when their father arrived home with his prodigy, the boy of six, Hadrian.

Hadrian was just an ordinary boy from a Charity Home, with ordinary brownish hair and ordinary bluish eyes and of ordinary rather cockney speech. The Rockley girls – there were three at home at the time of his arrival – had resented his being sprung on them. He, with his watchful, charity-institution instinct, knew this at once. Though he was only six years old, Hadrian had a subtle, jeering look on his face when he regarded the three young women. They insisted he should address them as Cousin: Cousin Flora, Cousin Matilda, Cousin Emmie. He complied, but there seemed a mockery in his tone.

The girls, however, were kind-hearted by nature. Flora married and left home. Hadrian did very much as he pleased with Matilda and Emmie, though they had certain strictnesses. He grew up in the Pottery House and about the Pottery premises, went to an elementary school, and was invariably called Hadrian Rockley. He regarded Cousin Matilda and Cousin Emmie with a certain laconic indifference, was quiet and reticent in his ways. The girls called him sly, but that was unjust. He was merely cautious, and without frankness. His Uncle, Ted Rockley, understood him tacitly, their natures were somewhat akin. Hadrian and the elderly man had a real but unemotional regard for one another.

When he was thirteen years old the boy was sent to a High School in the County town. He did not like it. His Cousin Matilda had longed to make a little gentleman of him, but he refused to be made. He would give a little contemptuous curve to his lip, and take on a shy, charity-boy grin, when refinement was thrust upon him. He played truant from the High School, sold his books, his cap with its badge, even his very scarf and pocket-handkerchief, to his school-fellows, and went raking off heaven knows where with the money. So he spent two very unsatisfactory years.

When he was fifteen he announced that he wanted to leave England to go to the Colonies. He had kept touch with the Home. The Rockleys knew that, when Hadrian made a declaration, in his quiet, half-jeering manner, it was worse than useless to oppose him. So at last the boy departed, going to Canada under the protection of the Institution to which he had belonged. He said good-bye to the Rockleys without a word of thanks, and parted, it seemed without a pang. Matilda and Emmie wept often to think of how he left them: even on their father's face a queer look came. But Hadrian wrote fairly regularly from Canada. He had entered some electricity works near Montreal, and was doing well.

At last, however, the war came. In his turn, Hadrian joined up and came to Europe. The Rockleys saw nothing of him. They lived on, just the same, in the Pottery House. Ted Rockley was dying of a sort of dropsy, and in his heart he wanted to see the boy. When the armistice° was signed, Hadrian had a long leave, and wrote that he was coming home to the Pottery House.

The girls were terribly fluttered. To tell the truth, they were a little afraid of Hadrian. Matilda, tall and thin, was frail in her health, both girls were worn with nursing their father. To have Hadrian, a young man of twenty-one, in the house with them, after he had left them so coldly five years before, was a trying circumstance.

They were in a flutter. Emmie persuaded her father to have his bed made finally in the morning-room downstairs, whilst his room upstairs was prepared for Hadrian. This was done, and preparations were going on for the arrival, when, at ten o'clock in the morning the young man suddenly turned up, quite unexpectedly. Cousin Emmie, with her hair bobbed up in absurd little bobs round her forehead, was busily polishing the stair-rods, while Cousin Matilda was in the kitchen washing the drawing-room ornaments in a lather, her sleeves rolled back on her thin arms, and her head tied up oddly and coquettishly in a duster.

Cousin Matilda blushed deep with mortification when the self-possessed young man walked in with his kit-bag, and put his cap on the sewing machine. He was little and self-confident, with a curious neatness about him that still suggested the Charity Institution. His face was brown, he had a small moustache, he was vigorous enough in his smallness.

"*Well*, is it Hadrian!" exclaimed Cousin Matilda, wringing the lather off her hands. "We didn't expect you till to-morrow."

"I got off Monday night," said Hadrian, glancing round the room.

"Fancy!" said Cousin Matilda. Then, having dried her hands, she went forward, held out her hand, and said:

"How are you?"

"Quite well, thank you," said Hadrian.

"You're quite a man,' said Cousin Matilda.

Hadrian glanced at her. She did not look her best: so thin, so large-nosed, with that pink-and-white checked duster tied round her head. She felt her disadvantage. But she had had a good deal of suffering and sorrow, she did not mind any more.

The servant entered – one that did not know Hadrian.

"Come and see my father," said Cousin Matilda.

In the hall they roused Cousin Emmie like a partridge from cover. She was on the stairs pushing the bright stair-rods into place. Instinctively her hand went to the little knobs, her front hair bobbed on her forehead.

"Why!" she exclaimed, crossly. "What have you come today for?"

"I got off a day earlier," said Hadrian, and his man's voice so deep and unexpected was like a blow to Cousin Emmie.

"Well, you've caught us in the midst of it," she said, with resentment. Then all three went into the middle room.

Mr. Rockley was dressed – that is, he had on his trousers and socks – but he was resting on the bed, propped up just under the window, from whence he could see his beloved and resplendent garden, where tulips and apple-trees were ablaze. He did not look as ill as he was, for the water puffed him up, and his face kept its colour. His stomach was much swollen. He glanced round swiftly, turning his eyes without turning his head. He was the wreck of a handsome, well-built man.

Seeing Hadrian, a queer, unwilling smile went over his face. The young man greeted him sheepishly.

"You wouldn't make a life-guardsman," he said. "Do you want something to eat?"

Hadrian looked round – as if for the meal.

"I don't mind," he said.

"What shall you have – egg and bacon?" asked Emmie shortly.

"Yes, I don't mind," said Hadrian.

The sisters went down to the kitchen, and sent the servant to finish the stairs.

"Isn't he *altered?*" said Matilda, *sotto voce.*$^\diamond$

"Isn't he!" said Cousin Emmie. "*What* a little man!"

They both made a grimace, and laughed nervously.

"Get the frying-pan," said Emmie to Matilda.

"But he's as cocky as ever," said Matilda, narrowing her eyes and shaking her head knowingly, as she handed the frying-pan.

"Mannie!"$^\diamond$ said Emmie sarcastically. Hadrian's new-fledged, cock-sure manliness evidently found no favour in her eyes.

"Oh, he's not bad," said Matilda. "You don't want to be prejudiced against him."

"I'm not prejudiced against him, I think he's all right for looks," said Emmie, "but there's too much of the little mannie about him."

"Fancy catching us like this," said Matilda.

"They've no thought for anything," said Emmie with contempt. "You go up and get dressed, our Matilda. I don't care about him. I can see to things, and you can talk to him. I shan't."

"He'll talk to my father," said Matilda, meaningful.

"*Sly – !*" exclaimed Emmie, with a grimace.

The sisters believed that Hadrian had come hoping to get something out of their father – hoping for a legacy. And they were not at all sure he would not get it.

Matilda went upstairs to change. She had thought it all out how she would receive Hadrian, and impress him. And he had caught her with her head tied up in a duster, and her thin arms in a basin of lather. But she did not care. She now dressed herself most scrupulously, carefully folded her long, beautiful, blonde hair, touched her pallor with a little rouge, and put her long string of exquisite crystal beads over her soft green dress. Now she looked elegant, like a heroine in a magazine illustration, and almost as unreal.

She found Hadrian and her father talking away. The young man was short of speech as a rule, but he could find his tongue with his "uncle". They were both sipping a glass of brandy, and smoking, and chatting like a pair of old cronies. Hadrian was telling about Canada. He was going back there when his leave was up.

"You wouldn't like to stop in England, then?" said Mr. Rockley.

"No, I wouldn't stop in England," said Hadrian.

"How's that? There's plenty of electricians here," said Mr. Rockley.

"Yes. But there's too much difference between the men and the employers over here – too much of that for me," said Hadrian.

The sick man looked at him narrowly, with oddly smiling eyes.

"That's it, is it?" he replied.

Matilda heard and understood. "So that's your big idea, is it, my little man," she said to herself. She had always said of Hadrian that he had no proper *respect* for anybody or anything, that he was sly and *common*. She went down to the kitchen for a *sotto voce* confab with Emmie.

"He thinks a rare lot of himself!" she whispered.

"He's somebody, he is!" said Emmie with contempt.

"He thinks there's too much difference between masters and men, over here," said Matilda.

"Is it any different in Canada?" asked Emmie.

"Oh yes – democratic," replied Matilda. "He thinks they're all on a level over there."

"Ay, well he's over here now," said Emmie drily, "so he can keep his place."

As they talked they saw the young man sauntering down the garden, looking casually at the flowers. He had his hands in his pockets, and his soldier's cap neatly on his head. He looked quite at his ease, as if in possession. The two women, fluttered, watched him through the window.

"We know what he's come for," said Emmie churlishly. Matilda looked a long time at the neat khaki figure. It had something of the charity-boy about it still; but now it was a man's figure, laconic, charged with plebeian energy. She thought of the derisive passion in his voice as he had declaimed against the propertied classes, to her father.

"You don't know, Emmie. Perhaps he's not come for that," she rebuked her sister. They were both thinking of the money.

They were still watching the young soldier. He stood away at the bottom of the garden, with his back to them, his hands in his pockets, looking into the water of the willow pond. Matilda's dark-blue eyes had a strange, full look in them, the lids, with the faint blue veins showing, dropped rather low. She carried her head light and high, but she had a look of pain. The young man at the bottom of the garden turned and looked up the path. Perhaps he saw them through the window. Matilda moved into shadow.

That afternoon their father seemed weak and ill. He was easily exhausted. The doctor came, and told Matilda that the sick man might die suddenly at any moment – but then he might not. They must be prepared.

So the day passed, and the next. Hadrian made himself at home. He went about in the morning in his brownish jersey and his khaki trousers, collarless, his bare neck showing. He explored the pottery premises, as if he had some secret purpose in so doing, he talked with Mr. Rockley, when the sick man had strength. The two girls were always angry when the two men sat talking together like cronies. Yet it was chiefly a kind of politics they talked.

On the second day after Hadrian's arrival, Matilda sat with her father in the evening. She was drawing a picture which she wanted to copy. It was very still, Hadrian was gone out somewhere, no one knew where, and Emmie was busy. Mr. Rockley reclined on his bed, looking out in silence over his evening-sunny garden.

"If anything happens to me, Matilda," he said, "you won't sell this house – you'll stop here –"

Matilda's eyes took their slightly haggard look as she stared at her father.

"Well, we couldn't do anything else," she said.

"You don't know what you might do," he said. "Everything is left to you and Emmie, equally. You do as you like with it – only don't sell this house, don't part with it."

"No," she said.

"And give Hadrian my watch and chain, and a hundred pounds out of what's in the bank – and help him if he ever wants helping. I haven't put his name in the will."

"Your watch and chain, and a hundred pounds – yes. But you'll be here when he goes back to Canada, father."

"You never know what'll happen," said her father.

Matilda sat and watched him, with her full, haggard eyes, for a long time, as if tranced. She saw that he knew he must go soon – she saw like a clairvoyant.

Later on she told Emmie what her father had said about the watch and chain and the money.

"What right has *he*" – he – meaning Hadrian – "to my father's watch and chain – what has it to do with him? Let him have the money, and get off," said Emmie. She loved her father.

That night Matilda sat late in her room. Her heart was anxious and breaking, her mind seemed entranced. She was too much entranced even to weep, and all the time she thought of her father, only her father. At last she felt she must go to him.

It was near midnight. She went along the passage and to his room. There was a faint light from the moon outside. She listened at his door. Then she softly opened and entered. The room was faintly dark. She heard a movement on the bed.

"Are you asleep?" she said softly, advancing to the side of the bed.

"Are you asleep?" she repeated gently, as she stood at the side of the bed. And she reached her hand in the darkness to touch his forehead. Delicately, her fingers met the nose and the eyebrows, she laid her fine, delicate hand on his brow. It seemed fresh and smooth – very fresh and smooth. A sort of surprise stirred her, in her entranced state. But it could not waken her. Gently, she leaned over the bed and stirred her fingers over the low-growing hair on his brow.

"Can't you sleep to-night?" she said.

There was a quick stirring in the bed. "Yes, I can," a voice answered. It was Hadrian's voice. She started away. Instantly, she was wakened from her late-at-night trance. She remembered that her father was downstairs, that Hadrian had his room. She stood in the darkness as if stung.

"Is that you, Hadrian?" she said. "I thought it was my father." She was so startled, so shocked, that she could not move. The young man gave an uncomfortable laugh, and turned in his bed.

At last she got out of the room. When she was back in her own room, in the light, and her door was closed, she stood holding up her hand that had touched him, as if it were hurt. She was almost too shocked, she could not endure.

"Well," said her calm and weary mind, "it was only a mistake, why take any notice of it."

But she could not reason her feelings so easily. She suffered, feeling herself in a false position. Her right hand, which she had laid so gently on his face, on his fresh skin, ached now, as if it were really injured. She could not forgive Hadrian for the mistake: it made her dislike him deeply.

Hadrian too slept badly. He had been awakened by the opening of the door, and had not realised what the question meant. But the soft, straying tenderness of her hand on his face startled something out of his soul. He was a charity boy, aloof and more or less at bay. The fragile exquisiteness of her caress startled him most, revealed unknown things to him.

In the morning she could feel the consciousness in his eyes, when she came downstairs. She tried to bear herself as if nothing at all had happened, and she succeeded. She had the calm self-control, self-indifference, of one who has suffered and borne her suffering. She looked at him from her darkish, almost drugged blue eyes, she met the spark of consciousness in his eyes, and quenched it. And with her long, fine hand she put the sugar in his coffee.

But she could not control him as she thought she could. He had a keen memory stinging his mind, a new set of sensations working in his consciousness. Something new was alert in him. At the back of his reticent, guarded mind he kept his secret alive and vivid. She was at his mercy, for he was unscrupulous, his standard was not her standard.

He looked at her curiously. She was not beautiful, her nose was too large, her chin was too small, her neck was too thin. But her skin was clear and fine, she had a high-bred sensitiveness. This queer, brave, high-bred quality she shared with her father. The charity boy could see it in her tapering fingers, which were white and ringed. The same glamour that he knew in the elderly man he now saw in the woman. And he wanted to possess himself of it, he wanted to make himself master of it. As he went about through the old pottery-yard, his secretive mind schemed and worked. To be master of that strange soft delicacy such as he had felt in her hand upon his face, – this was what he set himself towards. He was secretly plotting.

He watched Matilda as she went about, and she became aware of his attention, as of some shadow following her. But her pride made her ignore it. When he sauntered near her, his hands in his pockets, she received him with that same commonplace kindliness which mastered him more than any contempt. Her superior breeding seemed to control him. She made herself feel towards him exactly as she had always felt: he was a young boy who lived in the house with them, but was a stranger. Only, she dared not remember his face under her hand. When she remembered that, she was bewildered. Her hand had offended her, she wanted to cut it off. And she wanted, fiercely, to cut off the memory in him. She assumed she had done so.

One day, when he sat talking with his "uncle", he looked straight into the eyes of the sick man, and said:

"But I shouldn't like to live and die here in Rawsley."

"No – well – you needn't," said the sick man.

"Do you think Cousin Matilda likes it?"

"I should think so."

"I don't call it much of a life," said the youth. "How much older is she than me, Uncle?"

The sick man looked at the young soldier.

"A good bit," he said.

"Over thirty?" said Hadrian.

"Well, not so much. She's thirty-two."

Hadrian considered a while.

"She doesn't look it," he said.

Again the sick father looked at him.

"Do you think she'd like to leave here?" said Hadrian.

"Nay, I don't know," replied the father, restive.

Hadrian sat still, having his own thoughts. Then in a small, quiet voice, as if he were speaking from inside himself, he said:

"I'd marry her if you wanted me to."

The sick man raised his eyes suddenly, and stared. He stared for a long time. The youth looked inscrutably out of the window.

"*You!*" said the sick man, mocking, with some contempt. Hadrian turned and met his eyes. The two men had an inexplicable understanding.

"If you wasn't against it," said Hadrian.

"Nay," said the father, turning aside, "I don't think I'm against it. I've never thought of it. But – But Emmie's the youngest."

He had flushed, and looked suddenly more alive. Secretly he loved the boy.

"You might ask her," said Hadrian.

The elder man considered.

"Hadn't you better ask her yourself?" he said.

"She'd take more notice of you," said Hadrian.

They were both silent. Then Emmie came in.

For two days Mr. Rockley was excited and thoughtful. Hadrian went about quietly, secretly, unquestioning. At last the father and daughter were alone together. It was very early morning, the father had been in much pain. As the pain abated, he lay still, thinking.

"Matilda!" he said suddenly, looking at his daughter.

"Yes, I'm here," she said.

"Ay! I want you to do something –"

She rose in anticipation.

"Nay, sit still. – I want you to marry Hadrian –"

She thought he was raving. She rose, bewildered and frightened.

"Nay, sit you still, sit you still. You hear what I tell you."

"But you don't know what you're saying, father."

"Ay, I know well enough. – I want you to marry Hadrian, I tell you."

She was dumbfounded. He was a man of few words.

"You'll do what I tell you," he said.

She looked at him slowly.

"What put such an idea in your mind?" she said proudly.

"He did."

Matilda almost looked her father down, her pride was so offended.

"Why, it's disgraceful," she said.

"Why?"

She watched him slowly.

"What do you ask me for?" she said. "It's disgusting."

"The lad's sound enough," he replied, testily.

"You'd better tell him to clear out," she said coldly.

He turned and looked out of the window. She sat flushed and erect, for a long time. At length her father turned to her, looking really malevolent.

"If you won't," he said, "you're a fool, and I'll make you pay for your foolishness, do you see?"

Suddenly a cold fear gripped her. She could not believe her senses. She was terrified and bewildered. She stared at her father, believing him to be delirious, or mad, or drunk. What could she do?

"I tell you," he said. "I'll send for Whittle to-morrow if you don't. You shall neither of you have anything of mine."

Whittle was the solicitor. She understood her father well enough: he would send for his solicitor, and make a will leaving all his property to Hadrian: neither she nor Emmie should have anything. It was too much. She rose and went out of the room, up to her own room, where she locked herself in.

She did not come out for some hours. At last, late at night, she confided in Emmie.

"The sliving° demon, he wants the money," said Emmie. "My father's out of his mind."

The thought that Hadrian merely wanted the money was another blow to Matilda. She did not love the impossible youth – but she had not yet learned to think of him as a thing of evil. He now became hideous to her mind.

Emmie had a little scene with her father next day.

"You don't mean what you said to our Matilda yesterday, do you, father?" she asked aggressively.

"Yes," he replied.

"What, that you'll alter your will?"

"Yes."

"You won't," said his angry daughter.

But he looked at her with a malevolent little smile.

"Annie!" he shouted. "Annie!"

He had still power to make his voice carry. The servant maid came in from the kitchen.

"Put your things on, and go down to Whittle's office, and say I want to see Mr. Whittle as soon as he can, and will he bring a will-form."

The sick man lay back a little – he could not lie down. His daughter sat as if she had been struck. Then she left the room.

Hadrian was pottering about in the garden. She went straight down to him.

"Here," she said. "You'd better get off. You'd better take your things and go from here, quick."

Hadrian looked slowly at the infuriated girl.

"Who says so?" he asked.

"*We* say so – get off, you've done enough mischief and damage."

"Does Uncle say so?"

"Yes, he does."

"I'll go and ask him."

But like a fury Emmie barred his way.

"No, you needn't. You needn't ask him nothing at all. We don't want you, so you can go."

"Uncle's boss here."

"A man that's dying, and you crawling round and working on him for his money! – you're not fit to live."

"Oh!" he said. "Who says I'm working for his money?"

"I say. But my father told our Matilda, and *she* knows what you are. *She* knows what you're after. So you might as well clear out, for all you'll get – gutter-snipe!"

He turned his back on her, to think. It had not occurred to him that they would think he was after the money. He *did* want the money – badly. He badly wanted to be an employer himself, not one of the employed. But he knew, in his subtle, calculating way, that it was not for money he wanted Matilda. He wanted both the money and Matilda. But he told himself the two desires were separate, not one. He could not do with Matilda, *without* the money. But he did not want her *for* the money.

When he got this clear in his mind, he sought for an opportunity to tell it her, lurking and watching. But she avoided him. In the evening the lawyer came. Mr. Rockley seemed to have a new access of strength – a will was drawn up, making the previous arrangements wholly conditional. The old will held good, if Matilda would consent to marry Hadrian. If she refused then at the end of six months the whole property passed to Hadrian.

Mr. Rockley told this to the young man, with malevolent satisfaction. He seemed to have a strange desire, quite unreasonable, for revenge upon the women who had surrounded him for so long, and served him so carefully.

"Tell her in front of me," said Hadrian.

So Mr. Rockley sent for his daughters.

At last they came, pale, mute, stubborn. Matilda seemed to have retired far off, Emmie seemed like a fighter ready to fight to the death. The sick man reclined on the bed, his eyes bright, his puffed hand trembling. But his face had again some of its old, bright handsomeness. Hadrian sat quiet, a little aside: the indomitable, dangerous charity boy.

"There's the will," said their father, pointing them to the paper.

The two women sat mute and immovable, they took no notice.

"Either you marry Hadrian, or he has everything," said the father with satisfaction.

"Then let him have everything," said Matilda coldly.

"He's not! He's not!" cried Emmie fiercely. "He's not going to have it. The gutter-snipe!"

An amused look came on her father's face.

"You hear that, Hadrian," he said.

"I didn't offer to marry Cousin Matilda for the money," said Hadrian, flushing and moving in his seat.

Matilda looked at him slowly, with her dark-blue, drugged eyes. He seemed a strange little monster to her.

"Why, you liar, you know you did," cried Emmie.

The sick man laughed. Matilda continued to gaze strangely at the young man.

"She knows I didn't," said Hadrian.

He too had his courage, as a rat has indomitable courage in the end. Hadrian had some of the neatness, the reserve, the underground quality of the rat. But he had perhaps the ultimate courage, the most unquenchable courage of all.

Emmie looked at her sister.

"Oh, well," she said. "Matilda – don't you bother. Let him have everything, we can look after ourselves."

"I know he'll take everything," said Matilda abstractedly.

Hadrian did not answer. He knew in fact that if Matilda refused him he would take everything, and go off with it.

"A clever little mannie – !" said Emmie, with a jeering grimace.

The father laughed noiselessly to himself. But he was tired. ...

205

"Go on then," he said. "Go on, let me be quiet."

Emmie turned and looked at him.

"You deserve what you've got," she said to her father bluntly.

"Go on," he answered mildly. "Go on."

Another night passed – a night nurse sat up with Mr. Rockley. Another day came. Hadrian was there as ever, in his woollen jersey and coarse khaki trousers and bare neck. Matilda went about, frail and distant, Emmie black-browed in spite of her blondness. They were all quiet, for they did not intend the mystified servant to learn everything.

Mr. Rockley had very bad attacks of pain, he could not breathe. The end seemed near. They all went about quiet and stoical, all unyielding. Hadrian pondered within himself. If he did not marry Matilda he would go to Canada with twenty thousand pounds. This was itself a very satisfactory prospect. If Matilda consented he would have nothing – she would have her own money.

Emmie was the one to act. She went off in search of the solicitor and brought him home with her. There was an interview, and Whittle tried to frighten the youth into withdrawal – but without avail. Then clergyman and relatives were summoned – but Hadrian stared at them and took no notice. It made him angry, however.

He wanted to catch Matilda alone. Many days went by, and he was not successful: she avoided him. At last, lurking, he surprised her one day as she came to pick gooseberries, and he cut off her retreat. He came to the point at once.

"You don't want me then?" he said, in his subtle, insinuating voice.

"I don't want to speak to you," she said, averting her face.

"You put your hand on me, though," he said. "You shouldn't have done that, and then I should never have thought of it. You shouldn't have touched me."

"If you were anything decent, you'd know that was a mistake, and forget it," she said.

"I know it was a mistake – but I shan't forget it. If you wake a man up, he can't go to sleep again because he's told to."

"If you had any decent feeling in you, you'd have gone away," she replied.

"I didn't want to," he replied.

She looked away into the distance. At last she asked:

"What do you persecute me for, if it isn't for the money? I'm old enough to be your mother. In a way I've been your mother."

"Doesn't matter," he said. "You've been no mother to me. Let us marry and go out to Canada – you might as well – you've touched me."

She was white and trembling. Suddenly she flushed with anger.

"It's so *indecent*," she said.

"How?" he retorted. "You touched me."

But she walked away from him. She felt as if he had trapped her. He was angry and depressed, he felt again despised.

That same evening, she went into her father's room.

"Yes," she said suddenly. "I'll marry him."

Her father looked up at her. He was in pain, and very ill.

"You like him now, do you?" he said, with a faint smile.

She looked down into his face, and saw death not far off. She turned and went coldly out of the room.

The solicitor was sent for, preparations were hastily made. In all the interval Matilda did not speak to Hadrian, never answered him if he addressed her. He approached her in the morning.

"You've come round to it, then?" he said, giving her a pleasant look from his twinkling, almost kindly eyes. She looked down at him and turned aside. She looked down on him both literally and figuratively. Still he persisted, and triumphed.

Emmie raved and wept, the secret flew abroad. But Matilda was silent and unmoved, Hadrian was quiet and satisfied, and nipped with fear also. But he held out against his fear. Mr. Rockley was very ill, but unchanged.

On the third day the marriage took place. Matilda and Hadrian drove straight home from the registrar, and went straight into the room of the dying man. His face lit up with a clear twinkling smile.

"Hadrian, – you've got her?" he said, a little hoarsely.

"Yes," said Hadrian, who was pale round the gills.

"Ay, my lad, I'm glad you're mine," replied the dying man. Then he turned his eyes closely on Matilda.

"Let's look at you, Matilda," he said. Then his voice went strange and unrecognisable. "Kiss me," he said.

She stooped and kissed him. She had never kissed him before, not since she was a tiny child. But she was quiet, very still.

"Kiss him," the dying man said.

Obediently, Matilda put forward her mouth and kissed the young husband.

"That's right! That's right!" murmured the dying man.

The Rocking-Horse Winner

There was a woman who was beautiful, who started with all the advantages, yet she had no luck. She married for love, and the love turned to dust. She had bonny children, yet she felt they had been thrust upon her, and she could not love them. They looked at her coldly, as if they were finding fault with her. And hurriedly, she felt she must cover up some fault in herself. Yet what it was that she must cover up, she never knew. Nevertheless, when her children were present, she always felt the centre of her heart go hard. This troubled her, and in her manner she was all the more gentle and anxious for her children, as if she loved them very much. Only she herself knew that at the centre of her heart was a hard little place that could not feel love, no, not for anybody. Everybody else said of her: "She is such a good mother. She adores her children." Only she herself, and her children themselves, knew it was not so. They read it in each other's eyes.

There was a boy and two little girls. They lived in a pleasant house, with a garden, and they had discreet servants, and felt themselves superior to anyone in the neighbourhood.

Although they lived in style, they felt always an anxiety in the house. There was never enough money. The mother had a small income, and the father had a small income, but not nearly enough for the social position which they had to keep up. The father went in to town to some office. But though he had good prospects, these prospects never materialised. There was always the grinding sense of the shortage of money, though the style was always kept up.

At last the mother said: "I will see if *I* can't make something." But she did not know where to begin. She racked her brains, and tried this thing and the other, but could not find anything successful. The failure made deep lines come into her face. Her children were growing up, they would have to go to school. There must be more money, there must be more money. The father, who was always very handsome and expensive in his tastes, seemed as if he never *would* be able to do anything worth doing. And the mother, who had a great belief in herself, did not succeed any better, and her tastes were just as expensive.

And so the house came to be haunted by the unspoken phrase: *There must be more money*! *There must be more money*! The children could hear it all the time, though nobody ever said it aloud. They heard it at Christmas, when the expensive and splendid toys filled the nursery. Behind the shining modern rocking-horse, behind the smart doll's house, a voice would start whispering: There *must* be more money! There *must* be more money! And the children would stop playing, to listen for a moment. They would look into each other's eyes, to see if they had all heard. And each one saw in the eyes of the other two, that they too had heard. "There *must* be more money! There *must* be more money."

It came whispering from the springs of the still-swaying rocking-horse, and even the horse, bending his wooden, champing head, heard it. The big doll, sitting so pink and smirking in her new pram, could hear it quite plainly, and seemed to be smirking all the more self-consciously because of it. The foolish puppy, too, that took the place of the teddy bear, he was looking so extraordinarily foolish for no other reason but that he heard the secret whisper all over the house: "There must be more money."

Yet nobody ever said it aloud. The whisper was everywhere, and therefore no-one spoke it. Just as no-one ever says: "We are breathing!", in spite of the fact that breath is coming and going all the time.

"Mother!" said the boy Paul one day. "Why don't we keep a car of our own? Why do we always use uncle's, or else a taxi?"

"Because we're the poor members of the family," said the mother.

"But why *are* we, Mother?"

"Well – I suppose – " she said slowly and bitterly – "it's because your father has no luck."

The boy was silent for some time.

"Is luck money, Mother?" he asked, rather timidly.

"No, Paul! Not quite. It's what causes you to have money."

"Oh!" said Paul vaguely. "I thought when Uncle Oscar said *filthy lucker* it meant money."

"*Filthy lucre* does mean money," said the mother. "But it's lucre, not luck."

"Oh!" said the boy. "Then what *is* luck, Mother?"

"It's what causes you to have money. If you're lucky you have money. That's why it's better to be born lucky than rich. If you're rich, you may lose your money. But if you're lucky, you will always get more money."

"Oh! Will you! And is father not lucky?"

"Very unlucky, I should say," she said bitterly.

The boy watched her with unsure eyes.

"Why?" he asked.

"I don't know. Nobody ever knows why one person is lucky and another unlucky."

"Don't they? Nobody at all? Does *nobody* know?"

"Perhaps God! But he never tells."

"He ought to then. – And aren't you lucky either, Mother?"

"I can't be, if I married an unlucky husband."

"But by yourself, aren't you?"

"I used to think I was, before I married. Now I think I am very unlucky indeed."

"Why?"

"Well – never mind! Perhaps I'm not really," she said.

The child looked at her, to see if she meant it. But he saw, by the lines at her mouth, that she was only trying to hide something from him.

"Well anyhow," he said stoutly, "I'm a lucky person."

"Why?" said his mother, with a sudden laugh.

He stared at her. He didn't even know why he had said it.

"God told me," he asserted, brazening it out.

"I hope he did, Dear!" she said, again with a laugh, but rather bitter.

"He did, Mother!"

"Excellent!" said the mother, using one of her husband's exclamations.

The boy saw she did not believe him: or rather, that she paid no attention to his assertion. This angered him somewhere, and made him want to compel her attention.

He went off by himself, vaguely, in a childish way, seeking for the clue to "luck". Absorbed, taking no heed of other people, he went about with a sort of stealth, seeking inwardly for luck. He wanted luck, he wanted it, he wanted it. When the two girls were playing dolls, in the nursery, he would sit on his big rocking-horse, charging madly into space, with a frenzy that made the little girls peer at him uneasily. Wildly the horse careered, the waving dark hair of the boy tossed, his eyes had a strange glare in them. The little girls dared not speak to him.

When he had ridden to the end of his mad little journey, he climbed down and stood in front of his rocking-horse, staring fixedly into its lowered face. Its red mouth was slightly open, its big eye was wide and glassy bright.

"Now!" he would silently command the snorting steed. "Now take me to where there is luck! Now take me!"

And he would slash the horse on the neck with the little whip he had asked Uncle Oscar for. He *knew* the horse could take him to where there was luck, if only he forced it. So he would mount again, and start on his furious ride, hoping at last to get there. He knew he could get there.

"You'll break your horse, Paul!" said the nurse.

"He's always riding like that! I wish he'd leave off!" said his elder sister Joan.

But he only glared down on them in silence. Nurse gave him up. She could make nothing of him. Anyhow he was growing beyond her.

One day his mother and his Uncle Oscar came in when he was on one of his furious rides. He did not speak to them.

"Hello! you young jockey! Riding a winner?" said his Uncle.

"Aren't you growing too big for a rocking-horse? You're not a very little boy any longer, you know," said his mother.

But Paul only gave a blue glare from his big, rather close-set eyes. He would speak to nobody when he was in full tilt. His mother watched him with a curious expression on her face.

At last he suddenly stopped forcing his horse into the mechanical gallop, and slid down.

"Well I got there!" he announced fiercely, his blue eyes still flaring, and his sturdy long legs straddling apart.

"Where did you get to?" asked his mother.

"Where I wanted to go to," he flared back at her.

"That's right, Son!" said Uncle Oscar. "Don't you stop till you get there. – What's the horse's name?"

"He doesn't have a name," said the boy.

"Gets on without all right?" asked the uncle.

"Well, he has different names. He was called Sansovino last week."

"Sansovino, eh? Won the Ascot.* How did you know his name?"

"He always talks about horse-races with Bassett," said Joan.

The uncle was delighted to find that his small nephew was posted with all the racing news. Bassett, the young gardener who had been wounded in the left foot in the war, and had got his present job through Oscar Cresswell, whose batman* he had been, was a perfect blade of the "turf".* He lived in the racing events. And the small boy lived with him.

Oscar Cresswell got it all from Bassett.

"Master Paul comes and asks me, so I can't do more than tell him, Sir," said Bassett, his face terribly serious, as if he were speaking of religious matters.

"And does he ever put anything on a horse he fancies?"

"Well – I don't want to give him away – he's a young sport, a fine sport, Sir. Would you mind asking him himself? He sort of takes a pleasure in it, and perhaps he'd feel I was giving him away, Sir, if you don't mind."

Bassett was serious as a church.

The uncle went back to his nephew, and took him off for a ride in the car.

"Say, Paul, old man, do you ever put anything on a horse?" the uncle asked.

The boy watched the handsome man closely.

"Why, do you think I oughtn't to?" he parried.

"Not a bit of it! I thought perhaps you might give me a tip for the Lincoln."◇

The car sped on into the country, going down to Uncle Oscar's place in Hampshire.

"Honour bright?" said the nephew.

"Honour bright, Son!" said the Uncle.

"Well then, Daffodil."

"Daffodil! I doubt it, Sonny. What about Mirza?"

"I only know the winner," said the boy. "That's Daffodil!"

"Daffodil, eh?"

There was a pause. Daffodil was an obscure horse, comparatively.

"Uncle!"

"Yes Son!"

"You won't let it go any further, will you? I promised Bassett."

"Bassett be damned, old man! What's he got to do with it?"

"We're partners! We've been partners from the first! Uncle, he lent me my first five shillings which I lost. I promised him, honour bright, it was only between me and him: only you gave

214

me that ten shilling note I started winning with, so I thought you were lucky. You won't let it go any further, will you?"

The boy gazed at his uncle from those big, hot blue eyes, set rather close together. The uncle stirred and laughed uneasily.

"Right you are, Son! I'll keep your tip private. Daffodil, eh? – How much are you putting on him?"

"All except twenty pounds," said the boy. "I keep that in reserve."

The uncle thought it a good joke.

"You keep twenty pounds in reserve, do you, you young romancer? What are you betting, then?"

"I'm betting three hundred," said the boy gravely. "But it's between you and me, Uncle Oscar! Honour bright?"

The uncle burst into a roar of laughter.

"It's between you and me all right, you young Nat Gould,"° he said, laughing. "But where's your three hundred?"

"Bassett keeps it for me. We're partners."

"You are, are you! And what is Bassett putting on Daffodil?"

"He won't go quite as high as I do, I expect. Perhaps he'll go a hundred and fifty."

"What, pennies?" laughed the uncle.

"Pounds," said the child, with a surprised look at his uncle. "Bassett keeps a bigger reserve than I do."

Between wonder and amusement, Uncle Oscar was silent. He pursued the matter no further, but he determined to take his nephew with him to the Lincoln races.

"Now Son," he said, "I'm putting twenty on Mirza, and I'll put five for you on any horse you fancy. What's your pick?"

"Daffodil, Uncle!"

"No, not the fiver on Daffodil!"

"I should if it was my own fiver," said the child.

"Good! Good! Right you are! A fiver for me and a fiver for you, on Daffodil."

The child had never been to a race-meeting before, and his eyes were blue fire. He pursed his mouth tight, and watched. A Frenchman just in front had put his money on Lancelot. Wild with excitement, he flayed his arms up and down, yelling *Lancelot*! *Lancelot*! – in his French accent.

Daffodil came in first, Lancelot second, Mirza third. The child, flushed and with eyes blazing, was curiously serene. His uncle brought him five five-pound notes: four to one.

"What am I to do with these?" he cried, waving them before the boy's eyes.

"I suppose we'll talk to Bassett," said the boy. "I expect I have fifteen hundred now: and twenty in reserve: and this twenty."

His uncle studied him for some moments.

"Look here, Son!" he said. "You're not serious about Bassett and that fifteen hundred, are you?"

"Yes, I am. But it's between you and me, Uncle! Honour bright!"

"Honour bright all right, Son! But I must talk to Bassett."

"If you'd like to be a partner, Uncle, with Bassett and me, we could all be partners. Only you'd have to promise, Honour bright, Uncle, not to let it go beyond us three. Bassett and I are lucky, and you must be lucky, because it was your ten shillings I started winning with –"

Uncle Oscar took both Bassett and Paul into Richmond Park for an afternoon, and there they talked.

"It's like this, you see, Sir," Bassett said. "Master Paul would get me talking about racing events, spinning yarns you know, Sir. And he was always keen on knowing if I'd made or if I'd lost. It's about a year since, now, that I put five shillings on Blush of Dawn for him: and we lost. Then the luck turned, with that ten shillings he had from you, that we put on Singhalese. And since that time, it's been pretty steady, all things considering. What do you say, Master Paul?"

"We're all right when we're *sure*," said Paul. "It's when we're not quite sure that we go down."

"Oh, but we're careful then," said Bassett.

"But when are you *sure*?" smiled Uncle Oscar.

"It's Master Paul, Sir!" said Bassett, in a secret, religious voice. "It's as if he had it from heaven. Like Daffodil, now, for the Lincoln. That was as sure as eggs."

"Did you put anything on Daffodil?" asked Oscar Cresswell.

"Yes Sir! I made my bit."

"And my nephew?"

Bassett was obstinately silent, looking at Paul.

"I made twelve hundred, didn't I, Bassett? I told Uncle I was putting three hundred on Daffodil."

"That's right!" said Bassett, nodding.

"But where's the money?" asked the uncle.

"I keep it safe locked up, Sir. Master Paul, he can have it any minute he likes to ask for it."

"What, fifteen hundred pounds?"

"And twenty! And *forty*, that is, with the twenty he made on the course."

"It's amazing!" said the uncle.

"If Master Paul offers you to be partners, Sir, I would if I were you: if you'll excuse me," said Bassett.

Oscar Cresswell thought about it.

"I'll see the money," he said.

They drove home again, and sure enough, Bassett came round to the garden house with fifteen hundred pounds in notes. The twenty pounds reserve was left with Joe Glee, in the Turf Commission deposit.

"You see it's all right, Uncle, when I'm *sure*! Then we go strong, for all we're worth. Don't we, Bassett?"

"We do that, Master Paul."

"And when are you sure?" said the uncle, laughing.

"Oh well, sometimes I'm *absolutely* sure, like about Daffodil," said the boy. "And sometimes I have an idea; and sometimes I haven't even an idea, do I Bassett? Then we're careful, because we mostly go down."

"You do, do you! And when you're sure, like about Daffodil, what makes you sure, Sonny?"

"Oh well, I don't know," said the boy uneasily. "I'm sure, you know, Uncle, that's all."

"It's as if he had it from heaven, Sir!" Bassett reiterated.

"I should say so!" said the uncle.

But he became a partner. And when the Leger◇ was coming on, Paul was "sure" about Lively Spark, which was a quite inconsiderable horse. The boy insisted on putting a thousand on the horse, Bassett went for five hundred, and Oscar Cresswell two hundred. Lively Spark came in first, and the betting had been ten to one against him. Paul had made ten thousand.

"You see," he said, "I was absolutely sure of him."

Even Oscar Cresswell had cleared two thousand.

"Look here, Son," he said. "This sort of thing makes me nervous."

"It needn't, Uncle! Perhaps I shan't be sure again for a long time."

"But what are you going to do with your money?" asked the uncle.

"Of course," said the boy, "I started it for mother. She said she had no luck, because father is unlucky, so I thought if I was lucky, it might stop whispering."

"What might stop whispering?"

"Our house! I *hate* our house for whispering."

"What does it whisper?"

"Why? Why?" – the boy fidgetted – "Why, I don't know! But it's always short of money, you know, Uncle."

"I know it, Son, I know it."

"You know people send mother Writs, don't you, Uncle?"

"I'm afraid I do," said the uncle.

218

"And then the house whispers like people laughing at you behind your back. It's awful, that is! I thought if I was lucky –"

"You might stop it – " added the uncle.

The boy watched him with big blue eyes, that had an uncanny cold fire in them, and he said never a word.

"Well then!" said the uncle. "What are we doing?"

"I shouldn't like mother to know I was lucky," said the boy.

"Why not, Son?"

"She'd stop me."

"I don't think she would."

"Oh!" – and the boy writhed in an odd way. "I *don't* want her to know, Uncle."

"All right, Son! We'll manage it without her knowing."

They managed it very easily. Paul, at the other's suggestion, handed over five thousand pounds to his uncle, who deposited it with the family lawyer, who was then to inform Paul's mother that a relative had put five thousand pounds into his hands, which sum was to be paid out a thousand pounds at a time, on the mother's birthday, for the next five years.

"So she'll have a birthday present of a thousand pounds for five successive years," said Uncle Oscar. "I hope it won't make it all the harder for her later."

Paul's mother had her birthday in November. The house had been "whispering" worse than ever, lately, and even in spite of his luck, Paul could not bear up against it. He was very anxious to see the effect of the birthday letter, telling his mother about the thousand pounds.

When there were no visitors, Paul now took his meals with his parents, as he was beyond the nursery control. His mother went in to town nearly every day. She had discovered that she had an odd knack of sketching furs and dress materials, so she worked secretly in the studio of a friend who was the chief "artist" for the leading drapers. She drew the figures of ladies in furs and ladies in silk and sequins, for the newspaper advertisements. This young woman artist earned several thousand pounds a year, but Paul's mother only made several hundreds, and she was again dissatisfied. She so wanted to be first in something, and she did not succeed, even in making sketches for drapery advertisements.

She was down to breakfast on the morning of her birthday. Paul watched her face as she read her letters. He knew the lawyer's letter. As his mother read it, her face hardened and became more expressionless. Then a cold, determined look came on her mouth. She hid the letter under the pile of others, and said not a word about it.

"Didn't you have anything nice in the post, for your birthday, Mother?" said Paul.

"Quite moderately nice," she said, her voice cold and absent.

She went away to town without saying more.

But in the afternoon Uncle Oscar appeared. He said Paul's mother had had a long interview with the lawyer, asking if the whole five thousand could not be advanced at once, as she was in debt.

"What do you think, Uncle?" said the boy.

"I leave it to you, Son."

"Oh, let her have it, then! We can get some more with the other," said the boy.

"A bird in the hand is worth two in the bush, Laddie!" said Uncle Oscar.

"But I'm sure to *know* for the Grand National: or the Lincoln: or else the Derby.° I'm sure to know for *one* of them," said Paul.

So Uncle Oscar signed the agreement, and Paul's mother touched the whole five thousand. Then something very curious happened. The voices in the house suddenly went mad, like a chorus of frogs on a spring evening. There were certain new furnishings, and Paul had a tutor. He was *really* going to Eton, his father's school, in the following autumn. There were flowers in the winter, and a blossoming of the luxury Paul's mother had been used to. And yet the voices in the house, behind the sprays of mimosa and almond blossom, and from under the piles of iridescent cushions, simply trilled and screamed in a sort of ecstasy: "There *must* be more money! Oh-h-h! There must be more money! Oh now, now-w! now-w-w! – there *must* be more money!" – More than ever! More than ever!

It frightened Paul terribly. He studied away at his Latin and Greek, with his tutor. But his intense hours were spent with Bassett. The Grand National had gone by: he had not "known", and had lost a hundred pounds. Summer was at hand. He was in agony, for the Lincoln. But even for the Lincoln, he didn't "know", and he lost fifty pounds. He became wild-eyed and strange, as if something were going to explode in him.

"Let it alone, Son! Don't you bother about it!" urged Uncle Oscar. But it was as if the boy couldn't really hear what his uncle was saying.

"I've got to know for the Derby! I've *got* to know for the Derby!" the child re-iterated, his big blue eyes blazing with a sort of madness.

His mother noticed how overwrought he was.

"You'd better go to the seaside! Wouldn't you like to go now to the seaside, instead of waiting? I think you'd better!" she said, looking down at him anxiously, her heart curiously heavy because of him.

But the child lifted his uncanny blue eyes.

"I couldn't possibly go before the Derby, Mother!" he said. "I couldn't possibly!"

"Why not?" she said, her voice becoming heavy when she was opposed. "Why not? You can still go from the seaside to see the Derby, with your Uncle Oscar, if that's what you wish. No need for you to wait here. – Besides, I think you care too much about these races. It's a bad sign. My family has been a gambling family, and you won't know till you grow up how much damage it has done. But it has done damage. I shall have to send Bassett away, and ask Uncle Oscar not to talk racing to you, unless you promise to be reasonable about it: go away to the seaside and forget it. You're all nerves!"

"I'll do what you like, Mother, so long as you don't send me away till after the Derby," the boy said.

"Send you away from where? just from this house?"

"Yes!" he said, gazing at her.

"Why, you curious child, what makes you care about this house so much, suddenly? I never knew you loved it!"

He gazed at her without speaking. He had a secret within a secret, something he had not divulged, even to Bassett or to his Uncle Oscar.

But his mother, after standing undecided and a little bit sullen for some moments, said:

"Very well, then! Don't go to the seaside till after the Derby, if you don't wish it. But promise me you won't let your nerves go to pieces! Promise you won't think so much about horse-racing and *events*, as you call them!"

"Oh no!" said the boy, casually. "I won't think much about them, Mother. You needn't worry. I wouldn't worry, Mother, if I were you."

"If you were me and I were you," said his mother, "I wonder what we *should* do!"

"But you know you needn't worry, Mother, don't you?" the boy repeated.

"I should be awfully glad to know it," she said wearily.

"Oh well, you *can*, you know. I mean you *ought* to know you needn't worry!" he insisted.

"Ought I? Then I'll see about it," she said.

Paul's secret of secrets was his wooden horse, that which had no name. Since he was emancipated from a nurse and a nursery governess, he had had his rocking-horse removed to his own bedroom at the top of the house.

"Surely you're too big for a rocking-horse!" his mother had remonstrated.

"Well, you see, Mother, till I can have a *real* horse, I like to have *some* sort of animal about," had been his quaint answer.

"Do you feel he keeps you company?" she laughed.

"Oh yes! He's very good, he always keeps me company, when I'm there," said Paul.

So the horse, rather shabby, stood in an arrested prance in the boy's bedroom.

The Derby was drawing near, and the boy grew more and more tense. He hardly heard what was spoken to him, he was very frail, and his eyes were really uncanny. His mother had sudden strange seizures of uneasiness about him. Sometimes, for half an hour, she would feel a sudden anxiety about him, that was almost anguish. She wanted to rush to him at once, and know he was safe.

Two nights before the Derby, she was at a big party in town, when one of her rushes of anxiety about her boy, her first-born, gripped her heart till she could hardly speak. She fought with the feeling, might and main, for she believed in common-sense. But it was too strong. She had to leave the dance and go downstairs to telephone to the country. The children's nursery governess was terribly surprised and startled at being rung up in the night.

"Are the children all right, Miss Wilmot?"

"Oh yes, they are quite all right."

"Master Paul? Is he all right?"

"He went to bed as right as a trivet.◇ Shall I run up and look at him?"

"No!" said Paul's mother reluctantly. "No! Don't trouble. It's all right. Don't sit up. We shall be home fairly soon." She did not want her son's privacy intruded upon.

"Very good!" said the governess.

It was about one o'clock when Paul's mother and father drove up to their house. All was still. Paul's mother went to her room and slipped off her white fur cloak. She had told her maid not to wait up for her. She heard her husband downstairs, mixing a whiskey and soda.

And then, because of the strange anxiety at her heart, she stole upstairs to her son's room. Noiselessly she went along the upper corridor. Was there a faint noise? What was it?

She stood with arrested muscles outside his door, listening. There was a strange, heavy and yet not loud noise. Her heart stood still. It was a soundless noise, yet rushing and powerful. Something huge, in violent, hushed motion. What was it? What in God's name was it? She ought to know. She felt that she *knew* the noise. She knew what it was.

Yet she could not place it. She couldn't say what it was. And on and on it went, like a madness.

Softly, frozen with anxiety and fear, she turned the door-handle.

The room was dark. Yet in the space near the window, she heard and saw something plunging to and fro. She gazed in fear and amazement.

Then suddenly she switched on the light, and saw her son, in his green pyjamas, madly surging on his rocking-horse. The blaze of light suddenly lit him up, as he urged the wooden horse, and lit her up, as she stood, blonde, in her dress of pale green and crystal, in the doorway.

"Paul!" she cried. "Whatever are you doing?"

"It's Malabar!"◊ he screamed, in a powerful strange voice. "It's Malabar!"

His eyes blazed at her for one strange and senseless second, as he ceased urging his wooden horse. Then he fell with a crash to the ground, and she, all her tormented motherhood flooding upon her, rushed to gather him up.

But he was unconscious, and unconscious he remained, with some brain fever. He talked and tossed, and his mother sat stonily by his side.

"Malabar! It's Malabar! Bassett, Bassett, I *know*: it's Malabar!"

So the child cried, trying to get up and urge the rocking-horse that gave him his inspiration.

"What does he mean by Malabar?" asked the heart-frozen mother.

"I don't know," said the father, stonily.

"What does he mean by Malabar?" she asked her brother Oscar.

"It's one of the horses running for the Derby," was the answer.

And in spite of himself, Oscar Cresswell spoke to Bassett, and himself put a thousand on Malabar: at fourteen to one.

The third day of the illness was critical: they were watching for a change. The boy, with his rather long, curly hair, was tossing ceaselessly on the pillow. He neither slept nor regained consciousness, and his eyes were like blue stones. His mother sat, feeling her heart had gone, turned actually into a stone.

In the evening, Oscar Cresswell did not come, but Bassett sent a message, saying could he come up for one moment, just one moment. Paul's mother was angry at the intrusion, but on second thoughts she agreed. The boy was the same. Perhaps Bassett might bring him to consciousness.

The gardener, a shortish fellow with a little brown moustache and sharp little brown eyes, tiptoed into the room, touched his imaginary cap to Paul's mother, and stole to the bedside, staring with glittering, smallish eyes at the tossing, dying child.

"Master Paul!" he whispered. "Master Paul! Malabar came in first all right, a clean win. I did as you told me. You've made over seventy thousand pounds, you have, you've got over eighty thousand. Malabar came in all right, Master Paul."

"Malabar! Malabar! Did I say Malabar, Mother? Did I say Malabar? Do you think I'm lucky, Mother? I knew Malabar, didn't I? Over eighty thousand pounds! I call that lucky, don't you, Mother? Over eighty thousand pounds! I knew, didn't I know I knew? Malabar came in all right! If I ride my horse till

I'm sure, then I tell you, Bassett, you can go as high as you like. Did you go for all you were worth, Bassett?"

"I went a thousand on it, Master Paul."

"I never told you, Mother, that if I can ride my horse, and *get there*, then I'm absolutely sure – Oh absolutely! Mother, did I ever tell you? I *am* lucky!"

"No, you never did," said the mother.

But the boy died in the night.

And even as he lay dead, his mother heard her brother's voice saying to her: "My God, Hester, you're eighty-odd thousand to the good, and a poor devil of a son to the bad. But poor devil, poor devil, he's best gone out of a life where he rides his rocking-horse to find a winner."

The Man Who Loved Islands

First Island

There was a man who loved islands. He was born on one, but it didn't suit him, as there were too many other people on it, besides himself. He wanted an island all of his own: not necessarily to be alone on it, but to make it a world of his own.

An island, if it is big enough, is no better than a continent. It has to be really quite small, before it *feels like* an island; and this story will show how tiny it has to be, before you can presume to fill it with your own personality.

Now circumstances so worked out, that this lover of islands, by the time he was thirty-five, actually acquired an island of his own. He didn't own it as freehold property, but he had a ninety-nine years lease of it, which, as far as a man and an island are concerned, is as good as everlasting. Since, if you are like Abraham, and want your offspring to be numberless as the sands of the sea-shore,° you don't choose an island to start breeding on. Too soon there would be overpopulation, overcrowding, and slum conditions. Which is a horrid thought, for one who loves an island for its insulation. No, an island is a nest which holds one egg, and one only. This egg is the islander himself.

The island acquired by our potential islander was not in the remote oceans. It was quite near at home, no palm trees nor boom of surf on the reef, nor any of that kind of thing; but a good solid dwelling-house, rather gloomy, above the landing-place, and beyond, a small farm-house with sheds, and a few outlying fields. Down on the little landing bay were three cottages in a row, like coastguards' cottages, all neat and whitewashed.

What could be more cosy and home-like? It was four miles if you walked all round your island, through the gorse and the blackthorn bushes, above the steep rocks of the sea and down in the little glades where the primroses grew. If you walked straight over the two humps of hills, the length of it, through the rocky fields where the cows lay chewing, and through the rather sparse oats, on into the gorse again, and so to the low cliffs' edge, it took you only twenty minutes. And when you came to the edge, you could see another, bigger island lying beyond. But the sea was between you and it. And as you returned over the turf where the short, downland cowslips nodded, you saw to the east still another island, a tiny one this time, like the calf of the cow. This tiny island also belonged to the islander.

Thus it seems that even islands like to keep each other company.

Our islander loved his island very much. In early spring, the little ways and glades were a snow of blackthorn, a vivid white among the celtic stillness of close green and grey rock, blackbirds calling out in the whiteness their first long, triumphing calls. After the blackthorn and the nestling primroses came the blue apparition of hyacinths, like elfin lakes and slipping sheets of blue, among the bushes and under the glade of trees. And many birds with nests you could peep into, on the island all your own. Wonderful what a great world it was!

Followed summer, and the cowslips gone, the wild roses faintly fragrant through the haze. There was a field of hay, the foxgloves stood looking down. In a little cove, the sun was on the pale granite where you bathed, and the shadow was in the rocks. Before the mist came stealing, and you went home through the ripening oats, the glare of the sea fading from the high air as the fog-horn started to moo from the other island. And then the sea-fog went, it was autumn, the oat-sheaves lying prone; the great moon, another island, rose golden out of the sea, and, rising higher, the world of the sea was white.

So autumn ended with rain, and winter came, dark skies and dampness and rain, but rarely frost. The island, your island, cowered dark, holding away from you. You could feel, down in the wet, sombre hollows, the resentful spirit coiled upon itself, like a wet dog coiled in gloom, or a snake that is neither asleep nor awake. Then in the night, when the wind left off blowing in great gusts and volleys, as at sea, you felt that your island was a universe, infinite and old as the darkness; not an island at all, but an infinite dark world where all the souls from all the other bygone nights lived on, and the infinite distance was near.

Strangely, from your little island in space, you were gone forth into the dark, great realms of time, where all the souls that never die veer and swoop on their vast, strange errands. The little earthly island has dwindled, like a jumping-off place, into nothingness, for you have jumped off, you know not how, into the dark wide mystery of time, where the past is vastly alive, and the future is not separated off.

This is the danger of becoming an islander. When, in the city, you wear your white spats and dodge the traffic with the fear of death down your spine, then you are quite safe from the terrors of infinite time. The moment is your little islet in time, it is the spatial universe that careers round you.

But once isolate yourself on a little island in the sea of space, and the moment begins to heave and expand in great circles, the solid earth is gone, and your slippery, naked dark soul finds herself out in the timeless world, where the chariots of the so-called dead dash down the old streets of centuries, and souls crowd on the footways that we, in the moment, call bygone years. The souls of all the dead are alive again, and pulsating actively around you. You are out in the other infinity.

Something of this happened to our islander. Mysterious "feelings" came upon him, that he wasn't used to; strange awarenesses of old, far-gone men, and other influences; men of Gaul, with big moustaches, who had been on his island, and had vanished from the face of it, but not out of the air of night. They were there still, hurtling their big, violent, unseen bodies through the night. And there were priests, with golden knives and mistletoe; then other priests with a crucifix; then pirates with murder on the sea.

Our islander was uneasy. He didn't believe, in the daytime, in any of this nonsense. But at night it just was so. He had reduced himself to a single point in space, and a point being that which has neither length nor breadth, he had to step off it into somewhere else. Just as you must step into the sea, if the waters wash your foothold away, so he had, at night, to step off into the otherworld of undying time.

He was uncannily aware, as he lay in the dark, that the blackthorn grove that seemed a bit uncanny even in the realm of space and day, at night was crying with old men of an invisible race, around the altar stone. What was a ruin under the hornbeam trees by day, was a moaning of bloodstained priests with crucifixes, on the ineffable night. What was a cave and a hidden beach between coarse rocks, became in the invisible dark the purple-lipped imprecation of pirates.

To escape any more of this sort of awareness, our islander daily concentrated upon his material island. Why should it not be the Happy Isle at last? Why not the last small isle of the Hesperides,° the perfect place, all filled with his own gracious, blossom-like spirit? A minute world of pure perfection, made by man, himself.

He began, as we begin all our attempts to regain Paradise, by spending money. The old, semi-feudal dwelling-house he restored, let in more light, put clear lovely carpets on the floor, clear, flower-petal curtains at the sullen windows, and wines in the cellars of rock. He brought over a buxom housekeeper from the world, and a soft-spoken, much-experienced butler. These too were to be islanders.

In the farm-house he put a bailiff, with two farm-hands. There were Jersey cows, tinkling a slow bell, among the gorse. There was a call to meals at midday, and the peaceful smoking of chimneys at evening, when rest descended.

A jaunty sailing-boat with a motor accessory rode in the shelter in the bay, just below the row of three white cottages. There was also a little yawl, and two row-boats drawn up on the sand. A fishing net was drying on its supports, a boat-load of new white planks stood criss-cross, a woman was going to the well with a bucket.

In the end cottage lived the skipper of the yacht, and his wife and son. He was a man from the other, large island, at home on this sea. Every fine day he went out fishing, with his son, every fine day there was fresh fish on the island.

In the middle cottage lived an old man and wife, a very faithful couple. The old man was a carpenter, and man of many jobs. He was always working, always the sound of his plane or his saw: lost in his work, he was another kind of islander.

In the third cottage was the mason, a widower with a son and two daughters. With the help of his boys, this man dug ditches and built fences, raised buttresses and erected a new outbuilding, and hewed stone from the little quarry. His daughter worked at the big house.

It was a quiet, busy little world. When the islander brought you over as his guest, you met first the dark-bearded, thin, smiling skipper, Arnold, then his boy Charles. At the house, the smooth-lipped butler who had lived all over the world valeted you, and created that curious creamy-smooth, disarming sense of luxury around you which only a perfect and rather untrustworthy servant can create. He disarmed you and had you at his mercy. The buxom housekeeper smiled and treated you with the subtly respectful familiarity, that is only dealt out to the true gentry. And the rosy maid threw a glance at you, as if you were very wonderful, coming from the great outer world. Then you met the smiling but watchful bailiff, who came from Cornwall, and the shy farm-hand from Berkshire, with his clean wife and two little children, then the rather sulky farm-hand from Suffolk. The mason, a Kent man, would talk to you by the yard, if you let him. Only the old carpenter was gruff and elsewhere absorbed.

Well then, it was a little world to itself, and everybody feeling very safe, and being very nice to you, as if you were really something special. But it was the islander's world, not yours. He was the master. The special smile, the special attention was to the Master. They all knew how well off they were. So the islander was no longer Mr. So-and-so. To everyone on the island, even to you yourself, he was "the Master".

Well, it was ideal. The Master was no tyrant. Ah no! He was a delicate, sensitive, handsome Master, who wanted everything perfect and everybody happy. Himself, of course, to be the fount of this happiness and perfection.

But in his way, he was a poet. He treated his guests royally, his servants liberally. Yet he was shrewd, and very wise. He never came the boss over his people. Yet he kept his eye on everything, like a shrewd, blue-eyed young Hermes.° And it was amazing what a lot of knowledge he had at hand. Amazing what he knew about Jersey cows, and cheese-making, ditching and fencing, flowers and gardening, ships and the sailing of ships. He was a fount of knowledge about everything, and this knowledge he imparted to his people in an odd, half-ironical, half-portentous fashion, as if he really belonged to the quaint, half-real world of the gods.

They listened to him with their hats in their hands. He loved white clothes; or creamy white; and cloaks, and broad hats. So, in fine weather, the bailiff would see the elegant tall figure in creamy-white serge coming like some bird over the fallow, to look at the weeding of the turnips. Then there would be a doffing of hats, and a few minutes of whimsical, shrewd, wise talk, to which the bailiff answered admiringly, and the farm-hands listened in silent wonder, leaning on their hoes. The bailiff was almost tender, to the Master.

Or, on a windy morning, he would stand with his cloak blowing in the sticky sea-wind, on the edge of the ditch that was being dug to drain a little swamp, talking in the teeth of the wind to the man below, who looked up at him with steady and inscrutable eyes.

Or at evening in the rain he would be seen hurrying across the yard, the broad hat turned against the rain. And the farm-wife would hurriedly exclaim: "The Master! Get up John, and clear him a place on the sofa." And then the door opened, and it was a cry of: "Why of all things, if it isn't the Master! Why, have ye turned out then of a night like this, to come across to the like of we?" And the bailiff took his cloak, and the farm-wife his hat, the two farm-hands drew their chairs to the back, he sat on the sofa and took a child up near him. He was wonderful with children, talked to them simply wonderful, made you think of Our Saviour Himself, said the woman.

Always he was greeted with smiles, and the same peculiar deference, as if he were a higher, but also frailer being. They handled him almost tenderly, and almost with adulation. But when he left, or when they spoke of him, they had often a subtle, mocking smile on their faces. There was no need to be afraid of "the Master". Just let him have his own way. Only the old carpenter was sometimes sincerely rude to him; so he didn't care for the old man.

It is doubtful whether any of them really liked him, man to man, or even woman to man. But then it is doubtful if he really liked any of them, as man to man, or man to woman. He wanted them to be happy, and the little world to be perfect. But any one who wants the world to be perfect, must be careful not to have real likes and dislikes. A general good-will is all you can afford.

The sad fact is, alas, that general good-will is always felt as something of an insult, by the mere object of it; and so it breeds

quite a special brand of malice. Surely general good-will is a
form of egoism, that it should have such a result!

Our islander, however, had his own resources. He spent
long hours in his library, for he was compiling a book of
reference to all the flowers mentioned in the Greek and Latin
authors. He was not a great classical scholar: the usual
public-school equipment. But there are such excellent
translations nowadays. And it was so lovely, tracing flower
after flower as it blossomed in the ancient world.

So the first year on the island passed by. A great deal had
been done. Now the bills flooded in, and the Master,
conscientious in all things, began to study them. The study left
him pale and breathless. He was not a rich man. He knew he
had been making a hole in his capital, to get the island into
running order. When he came to look, however, there was
hardly anything left but hole. Thousands and thousands of
pounds had the island swallowed into nothingness.

But surely the bulk of the spending was over! Surely the
island would now begin to be self-supporting, even if it made
no profit! Surely he was safe. He paid a good many of the bills,
and took a little heart. But he had had a shock, and the next
year, the coming year, there must be economy, frugality. He
told his people so, in simple and touching language. And they
said: "Why surely! Surely!"

So, while the wind blew and the rain lashed outside, he
would sit in his library with the bailiff over a pipe and a pot of
beer, discussing farm projects. He lifted his narrow handsome
face, and his blue eye became dreamy. "*What* a wind!" It blew
like cannon shots. He thought of his island, lashed with foam,
and inaccessible, and he exulted ... No, he must not lose it. He
turned back to the farm projects with the zest of genius, and
his hands flicked white emphasis, while the bailiff intoned:
"Yes, Sir! Yes, Sir! You're right, Master!"

But the man was hardly listening. He was looking at the
Master's blue lawn shirt and curious pink tie with the fiery red

stone, at the enamel sleevelinks, and at the ring with the peculiar scarab. The brown searching eyes of the man of the soil glanced repeatedly over the fine, immaculate figure of the Master, with a sort of slow, calculating wonder. But if he happened to catch the Master's bright, exalted glance, his own eye lit up with a careful cordiality and deference, as he bowed his head slightly.

Thus between them they decided what crops should be sown, what fertilisers should be used in different places, which breed of pigs should be imported, and which line of turkeys. That is to say, the bailiff, by continually cautiously agreeing with the Master, kept out of it, and let the young man have his own way.

The Master knew what he was talking about. He was brilliant at grasping the gist of a book, and knowing how to apply his knowledge. On the whole, his ideas were sound. The bailiff even knew it. But in the man of the soil there was no answering enthusiasm. The brown eyes smiled their cordial deference, but the thin lips never changed. The Master pursed his own flexible mouth in a boyish versatility, as he cleverly sketched in his ideas to the other man, and the bailiff made eyes of admiration, but in his heart he was not attending, he was only watching the Master as he would have watched a queer, alien animal, quite without sympathy, not implicated.

So, it was settled, and the Master rang for Elvery, the butler, to bring a sandwich. He, the Master, was pleased. The butler saw it, and came back with anchovy and ham sandwiches, and a newly opened bottle of vermouth. There was always a newly opened bottle of something.

It was the same with the mason. The Master and he discussed the drainage of a bit of land, and more pipes were ordered, more special bricks, more this, more that.

Fine weather came at last, there was a little lull in the hard work on the island. The Master went for a short cruise in his yacht. It was not really a yacht, just a neat little bit of a yawl.

They sailed along the coast of the mainland, and put in at the ports. At every port some friend turned up, the butler made elegant little meals in the cabin. Then the Master was invited to villas and hotels, his people disembarked him as if he were a prince.

And oh! how expensive it turned out! He had to telegraph to the bank for money. And he went home again, to economise.

The marsh-marigolds were blazing in the little swamp where the ditches were being dug for drainage. He almost regretted, now, the work in hand. The yellow beauties would not blaze again.

Harvest came, and a bumper crop. There must be a harvest-home supper. The long barn was now completely restored and added to. The carpenter had made long tables. Lanterns hung from the beams of the high-pitched roof. All the people of the island were assembled. The bailiff presided. It was a gay scene.

Towards the end of the supper the Master, in a velvet jacket, appeared with his guests. Then the bailiff rose and proposed: "The Master! Long life and health to the Master!" – All the people drank the health with great enthusiasm and cheering. The Master replied with a little speech: They were on an island in a little world of their own. It depended on them all to make this world a world of true happiness and content. Each must do his part. He hoped he himself did what he could, for his heart was in his island, and with the people of his island.

The butler responded: As long as the island had such a Master, it could not help but be a little heaven for all the people on it. – This was seconded with virile warmth by the bailiff and the mason, the skipper was beside himself. Then there was dancing, the old carpenter was fiddler.

But under all this, things were not well. The very next morning came the farm-boy to say that a cow had fallen over the cliff. The master went to look. He peered over the not very high declivity, and saw her lying dead, on a green ledge under a bit of late-flowering broom. A beautiful, expensive creature, already looking swollen. But what a fool, to fall so unnecessarily!

It was a question of getting several men to haul her up the bank: and then of skinning and burying her. No-one would eat the meat. How repulsive it all was!

This was symbolic of the island. As sure as the spirits rose in the human breast, with a movement of joy, an invisible hand struck malevolently out of the silence. There must not be any joy, nor even any quiet peace. A man broke a leg, another was crippled with rheumatic fever. The pigs had some strange disease. A storm drove the yacht on a rock. The mason hated the butler, and refused to let his daughter serve at the house.

Out of the very air came a stony, heavy malevolence. The island itself seemed malicious. It would go on being hurtful and evil for weeks at a time. Then suddenly again one morning it would be fair, lovely as a morning in Paradise, everything beautiful and flowing. And everybody would begin to feel a great relief, and a hope for happiness.

Then as soon as the Master was opened out in spirit like an open flower, some ugly blow would fall. Somebody would send him an anonymous note, accusing some other person on the island. Somebody else would come hinting things against one of his servants.

"Some folks thinks they've got an easy job out here, with all the pickings they make!" the mason's daughter screamed at the suave butler, in the Master's hearing. He pretended not to hear.

"My man says this island is surely one of the lean kine of Egypt,° it would swallow a sight of money, and you'd never get anything back out of it," confided the farm-hand's wife to one of the Master's visitors.

The people were not contented. They were not islanders. "We feel we're not doing right by the children," said those who had children. "We feel we're not doing right by ourselves," said those who had no children. And the various families fairly came to hate one another.

Yet the island was so lovely. When there was a scent of honeysuckle, and the moon brightly flickering down on the sea, then even the grumblers felt a strange nostalgia for it. It set you yearning, with a wild yearning; perhaps for the past, to be far back in the mysterious past of the island, when the blood had a different throb. Strange floods of passion came over you, strange violent lusts and imaginations of cruelty. The blood and the passion and the lust which the island had known. Uncanny dreams, half-dreams, half-evocated yearnings.

The Master himself began to be a little afraid of his island. He felt here strange violent feelings he had never felt before, and lustful desires that he had been quite free from. He knew quite well now that his people didn't love him at all. He knew that their spirits were secretly against him, malicious, jeering, envious, and lurking to down him. He became just as wary and secretive with regard to them.

But it was too much. At the end of the second year, several departures took place. The housekeeper went. The Master always blamed self-important women most. The mason said he wasn't going to be monkeyed about any more, so he took his departure, with his family. The rheumatic farm-hand left.

And then the year's bills came in, the Master made up his accounts. In spite of good crops, the assets were ridiculous, against the spending. The island had again lost, not hundreds but thousands of pounds. It was incredible. But you simply couldn't believe it! Where had it all gone?

The Master spent gloomy nights and days, going through accounts in the library. He was thorough. It became evident, now the housekeeper had gone, that she had swindled him. Probably everybody was swindling him. But he hated to think it, so he put the thought away.

He emerged, however, pale and hollow-eyed from his balancing of unbalanceable accounts, looking as if something had kicked him in the stomach. It was pitiable. But the money had gone, and there was an end of it. Another great hole in his capital. How could people be so heartless?

It couldn't go on, that was evident. He would soon be bankrupt. He had to give regretful notice to his butler. He was afraid to find out how much his butler had swindled him. Because the man was such a wonderful butler, after all. And the farm-bailiff had to go. The Master had no regrets in that quarter. The losses on the farm had almost embittered him.

The third year was spent in rigid cutting down of expenses. The island was still mysterious and fascinating. But it was also treacherous and cruel, secretly, fathomlessly malevolent. In spite of all its fair show of white blossom and bluebells, and the lovely dignity of foxgloves bending their rose-red bells, it was your implacable enemy.

With reduced staff, reduced wages, reduced splendour, the third year went by. But it was fighting against hope. The farm still lost a good deal. And once more, there was a hole in that remnant of capital. Another hole, in that which was already a mere remnant round the old holes. The island was mysterious in this also: it seemed to pick the very money out of your pocket, as if it were an octopus with invisible arms stealing from you in every direction.

Yet the Master still loved it. But with a touch of rancour now.

He spent, however, the second half of the fourth year intensely working on the mainland, to be rid of it. And it was amazing how difficult he found it, to dispose of an island. He had thought that everybody was pining for such an island as his; but not at all. Nobody would pay any price for it. And he wanted now to get rid of it, as a man who wants a divorce at any cost.

It was not till the middle of the fifth year that he transferred it, at a considerable loss to himself, to an hotel company who were willing to speculate in it. They were to turn it into a handy honeymoon-and-golf island.

There, take that, island which didn't know when it was well off! Now be a honeymoon-and-golf island!

Second Island

The islander had to move. But he was not going to the mainland. Oh no! He moved to the smaller island, which still belonged to him. And he took with him the faithful old carpenter and wife, the couple he never really cared for; also a widow and daughter, who had kept house for him the last year; also an orphan lad, to help the old man.

The small island was very small; but being a hump of rock in the sea, it was bigger than it looked. There was a little track among rocks and bushes, winding and scrambling up and down around the islet, so that it took you twenty minutes to do the circuit. It was more than you would have expected.

Still, it was an island. The islander moved himself, with all his books, into the common-place six-roomed house up to which you had to scramble from the rocky landing-place. There were also two joined-together cottages. The old carpenter lived in one, with his wife and the lad, the widow and daughter lived in the other.

At last all was in order. The Master's books filled two rooms. It was already autumn, Orion° lifting out of the sea. And in the dark nights, the Master could see the lights on his late island, where the hotel company were entertaining guests who would advertise the new resort for honeymoon-golfers.

On his hump of rock, however, the Master was still master. He explored the crannies, the odd handbreadths of grassy level, the steep little cliffs where the last harebells hung, and the seeds of summer were brown above the sea, lonely and untouched.

He peered down the old well. He examined the stone pen where the pig had been kept. Himself, he had a goat.

Yes, it was an island. Always, always, underneath among the rocks the celtic sea sucked and washed and smote its feathery greyness. How many different noises of the sea! deep explosions, rumblings, strange long sighs and whistling noises; then voices, real voices of people clamouring as if they were in a market, under the waters: and again, the far-off ringing of a bell, surely an actual bell! then a tremulous trilling noise, very long and alarming, and an undertone of hoarse gasping.

On this island there were no human ghosts, no ghosts of any ancient race. The sea, and the spume and the wind and the weather, had washed them all out, washed them out, so there was only the sound of the sea itself, its own ghost, myriad-voiced, communing and plotting and shouting all winter long. And only the smell of the sea, with a few bristly bushes of gorse and coarse tufts of heather, among the grey, pellucid rocks, in the grey, more-pellucid air. The coldness, the greyness, even the soft, creeping fog of the sea! and the islet of rock humped up in it all, like the last point in space.

Green star Sirius stood over the sea's rim. The island was a shadow. Out at sea a ship showed small lights. Below, in the rocky cove, the row-boat and the motor-boat were safe. A light shone in the carpenter's kitchen. That was all.

Save, of course, that the lamp was lit in the house, where the widow was preparing supper, her daughter helping. The islander went in to his meal. Here he was no longer the Master, he was an islander again and he had peace. The old carpenter, the widow and daughter were all faithfulness itself. The old man worked while ever there was light to see, because he had a passion for work. The widow and her quiet, rather delicate daughter of thirty-three worked for the Master, because they loved looking after him, and they were infinitely grateful for the haven he provided them. But they didn't call him "the Master". They gave him his name: "Mr. Cathcart, Sir!" softly, and reverently. And he spoke back to them also softly, gently, like people far from the world, afraid to make a noise.

The island was no longer a "world". It was a sort of refuge. The islander no longer struggled for anything. He had no need. It was as if he and his few dependants were a small flock of sea-birds alighted on this rock, as they travelled through space, and keeping together without a word. The silent mystery of travelling birds.

He spent most of his day in his study. His book was coming along. The widow's daughter could type out his manuscript for him, she was not uneducated. It was the one strange sound on the island, the typewriter. But soon even its spattering fitted in with the sea's noises, and the wind's.

The months went by. The islander worked away in his study, the people of the island went quietly about their concerns. The goat had a little black kid with yellow eyes. There were mackerel in the sea. The old man went fishing in the row-boat, with the lad. When the weather was calm enough, they went off in the motor-boat to the biggest island, for the post. And they brought supplies, never a penny wasted. And the days went by, and the nights, without desire, without ennui.

The strange stillness from all desire was a kind of wonder to the islander. He didn't want anything. His soul at last was still in him, his spirit was like a dim-lit cave under water, where strange sea-foliage expands upon the watery atmosphere, and scarcely sways, and a mute fish shadowily slips in and slips away again. All still and soft and uncrying, yet alive as rooted sea-weed is alive.

The islander said to himself: "Is this happiness?" He said to himself: "I am turned into a dream. I feel nothing, or I don't know what I feel. Yet it seems to me I am happy."

Only he had to have something upon which his mental activity could work. So he spent long, silent hours in his study, working not very fast, nor very importantly, letting the writing spin softly from him as if it were drowsy gossamer. He no longer fretted whether it were good or not, what he produced. He slowly, softly spun it like gossamer, and if it were to melt away as gossamer in autumn melts, he would not mind. It was only the soft evanescence of gossamy things which now seemed to him permanent. The very mist of eternity was in them. Whereas stone buildings, cathedrals for example, seemed to him to howl with temporary resistance, knowing they must fall at last; the tension of their long endurance seemed to howl forth from them all the time.

Sometimes he went to the mainland and to the city. Then he went elegantly, dressed in the latest style, to his club. He sat in a stall at the theatre, he shopped in Bond Street. He discussed terms for publishing his book. But over his face was that gossamy look of having dropped out of the race of progress, which made the vulgar city people feel they had won it over him, and made him glad to go back to his island.

He didn't mind if he never published his book. The years were blending into a soft mist, from which nothing obtruded. Spring came. There was never a primrose on his island, but he found a winter-aconite. There were two little sprayed bushes of blackthorn, and some wind-flowers. He began to make a list of the flowers of his islet, and that was absorbing. He noted a wild currant bush, and watched for the elder flowers on a stunted little tree, then for the first yellow rags of the broom, and wild roses. Bladder campion, orchids, stitchwort, celandine, he was prouder of them than if they had been people on his island. When he came across the golden saxifrage, so inconspicuous in a damp corner, he crouched over it in a trance, he knew not for how long, looking at it. Yet it was nothing to look at. As the widow's daughter found, when he showed it her.

He had said to her, in real triumph:

"I found the golden saxifrage this morning."

The name sounded splendid. She looked at him with fascinated brown eyes, in which was a hollow ache that frightened him a little.

"Did you, Sir? Is it a nice flower?"

He pursed his lips and tilted his brows.

"Well – not showy exactly. I'll show it you if you like."

"I should like to see it."

She was so quiet, so wistful. But he sensed in her a persistency which made him uneasy. She said she was so happy: really happy. She followed him quietly, like a shadow, on the rocky track where there was never room for two people to walk side by side. He went first, and could feel her there, immediately behind him, following so submissively, gloating on him from behind.

It was a kind of pity for her which made him become her lover: though he never realised the extent of the power she had gained over him, and how *she* willed it. But the moment he had fallen, a jangling feeling came upon him, that it was all wrong. He felt a nervous dislike of her. He had not wanted it. And it seemed to him, as far as her physical self went, she had not wanted it either. It was just her will. He went away, and climbed at the risk of his neck down to a ledge near the sea. There he sat for hours, gazing all jangled at the sea, and saying miserably to himself: "We didn't want it. We didn't really want it."

It was the automatism of sex that had caught him again. Not that he hated sex. He deemed it, as the Chinese do, one of the great life-mysteries. But it had become mechanical, automatic, and he wanted to escape that. Automatic sex shattered him, and filled him with a sort of death. He thought he had come through, to a new stillness of desirelessness. Perhaps beyond that, there was a new fresh delicacy of desire, an unentered frail communion of two people meeting on untrodden ground.

But be that as it might, this was not it. This was nothing new or fresh. It was automatic, and driven from the will. Even she, in her true self, hadn't wanted it. It was automatic in her.

When he came home, very late, and saw her face white with fear and apprehension of his feeling against her, he pitied her, and spoke to her delicately, reassuringly. But he kept himself remote from her.

She gave no sign. She served him with the same silence, the same hidden hunger to serve him, to be near where he was. He felt her love following him with strange, awful persistency. She claimed nothing. Yet now, when he met her bright, brown, curiously vacant eyes, he saw in them the mute question. The question came direct at him, with a force and a power of will he never realised.

So he succumbed, and asked her again.

"Not," she said, "if it will make you hate me."

"Why should it?" he replied, nettled. "Of course not."

"You know I would do anything on earth for you."

It was only afterwards, in his exasperation, he remembered what she had said, and was more exasperated. Why should she pretend to do this *for him*? Why not for herself? But in his exasperation, he drove himself deeper in. In order to achieve some sort of satisfaction, which he never did achieve, he abandoned himself to her. Everybody on the island knew. But he did not care.

Then even what desire he had, left him, and he felt only shattered. He felt that only with her will had she wanted him. Now he was shattered and full of self-contempt. His island was smirched and spoiled. He had lost his place in the rare, desireless levels of Time to which he had at last arrived, and he had fallen right back. If only it had been true, delicate desire between them, and a delicate meeting on the third rare place where a man might meet a woman, when they were both true to the frail, sensitive, crocus flame of desire in them. But it had been no such thing: automatic, an act of will, not of true desire, it left him feeling humiliated.

He went away from the islet, in spite of her mute reproach. And he wandered about the continent, vainly seeking a place where he could stay. He was out of key; he did not fit in the world any more.

There came a letter from Flora – her name was Flora – to say she was afraid she was going to have a child. He sat down as if he were shot, and he remained sitting. But he replied to her: "Why be afraid? If it is so, it is so, and we should rather be pleased than afraid."

At this very moment, it happened there was an auction of islands. He got the maps, and studied them. And at the auction he bought, for very little money, another island. It was just a few acres of rock away in the north, on the outer fringe of the isles. It was low, it rose low out of the great ocean. There was not a building, not even a tree on it. Only northern sea-turf, a pool of rain-water, a bit of sedge, rock, and sea-birds. Nothing else. Under the weeping wet western sky.

He made a trip to visit his new possession. For several days, owing to the seas, he could not approach it. Then, in a light sea-mist, he landed, and saw it hazy, low, stretching apparently a long way. But it was illusion. He walked over the wet, springy turf, and dark-grey sheep tossed away from him, spectral, bleating hoarsely. And he came to the dark pool, with the sedge. Then on in the dampness, to the grey sea sucking angrily among the rocks.

This was indeed an island.

So he went home to Flora. She looked at him with guilty fear, but also with a triumphant brightness in her uncanny eyes. And again he was gentle, he reassured her, even he wanted her again, with that curious desire that was almost like toothache. So he took her to the mainland, and they were married, since she was going to have his child.

They returned to the island. She still brought in his meals, her own along with them. She sat and ate with him. He would have it so. The widowed mother preferred to stay in the kitchen. And Flora slept in the guest-room of his house, mistress of his house.

His desire, whatever it was, died in him with nauseous finality. The child would still be months coming. His island was hateful to him, vulgar, a suburb. He himself had lost all his finer distinction. The weeks passed in a sort of prison, in humiliation. Yet he stuck it out, till the child was born. But he was meditating escape. Flora did not even know.

A nurse appeared, and ate at table with them. The doctor came sometimes, and if the sea were rough, he too had to stay. He was cheery over his whiskey.

They might have been a young couple in Golders Green.º

The daughter was born at last. The father looked at the baby, and felt depressed, almost more than he could bear. The millstone was tied round his neck. But he tried not to show what he felt. And Flora did not know. She still smiled with a kind of half-witted triumph in her joy, as she got well again. Then she began again to look at him with those aching, suggestive, somehow impudent eyes. She adored him so.

This he could not stand. He told her that he had to go away for a time. She wept, but she thought she had got him. He told her he had settled the best part of his property on her, and wrote down for her what income it would produce. She hardly listened, only looked at him with those heavy, adoring, impudent eyes. He gave her a cheque-book, with the amount of her credit duly entered. This did arouse her interest. And he told her, if she got tired of the island, she could choose her home wherever she wished.

She followed him with those aching, persistent brown eyes, when he left, and he never even saw her weep.

He went straight north, to prepare his third island.

The Third Island

The third island was soon made habitable. With cement and the big pebbles from the shingle beach, two men built him a hut, and roofed it with corrugated iron. A boat brought over a bed and table, and three chairs, with a good cupboard, and a few books. He laid in a supply of coal and paraffin and food – he wanted so little.

The house stood near the flat shingle bay where he landed, and where he pulled up his light boat. On a sunny day in August the men sailed away and left him. The sea was still and pale blue. On the horizon he saw the small mail-steamer slowly passing northwards, as if she were walking. She served the outer isles twice a week. He could row out to her if need be, in calm weather, and he could signal her from a flagstaff behind his cottage.

Half-a-dozen sheep still remained on the island, as company; and he had a cat to rub against his legs. While the sweet, sunny days of the northern autumn lasted, he would walk among the rocks, and over the springy turf of his small domain, always coming to the ceaseless, restless sea. He looked at every leaf, that might be different from another, and he watched the endless expansion and contraction of the water-tossed sea-weed. He had never a tree, not even a bit of heather to guard. Only the turf, and tiny turf-plants, and the sedge by the pool, the sea-weed in the ocean. He was glad. He didn't want trees or bushes. They stood up like people, too assertive. His bare, low-pitched island in the pale blue sea was all he wanted.

He no longer worked at his book. The interest had gone. He liked to sit on the low elevation of his island, and see the sea; nothing but the pale, quiet sea. And to feel his mind turn soft and hazy, like the hazy ocean. Sometimes, like a mirage, he would see the shadow of land rise hovering to northwards. It was a big island beyond. But quite without substance.

He was soon almost startled when he perceived the steamer on the near horizon, and his heart contracted with fear, lest it were going to pause and molest him. Anxiously he watched it go, and not till it was out of sight did he feel truly relieved, himself again. The tension of waiting for human approach was cruel. He did not want to be approached. He did not want to hear voices. He was shocked by the sound of his own voice, if he inadvertently spoke to his cat. He rebuked himself for having broken the great silence. And he was irritated when his cat would look up at him and mew faintly, plaintively. He frowned at her. And she knew. She was becoming wild, lurking in the rocks, perhaps fishing.

But what he disliked most was when one of the lumps of sheep opened its mouth and baa-ed its hoarse, raucous baa. He watched it, and it looked to him hideous and gross. He came to dislike the sheep very much.

He wanted only to hear the whispering sound of the sea, and the sharp cries of the gulls, cries that came out of another world to him. And best of all, the great silence.

He decided to get rid of the sheep, when the boat came. They were accustomed to him now, and stood and stared at him with yellow or colourless eyes, in an insolence that was almost cold ridicule. There was a suggestion of cold indecency about them. He disliked them very much. And when they jumped with staccato jumps off the rocks, and their hoofs made the dry, sharp hit, and the fleece flopped on their square backs, – he found them repulsive, degrading.

The fine weather passed, and it rained all day. He lay a great deal on his bed, listening to the water trickling from his roof into the zinc water-butt, looking through the open door at the rain, the dark rocks, the hidden sea. Many gulls were on the island now: many sea-birds of all sorts. It was another world of life. Many of the birds he had never seen before. His old impulse came over him, to send for a book, to know their names. In a flicker of the old passion, to know the name of everything he saw, he even decided to row out to the steamer. The names of these birds! he must know their names, otherwise he had not got them, they were not quite alive to him.

But the desire left him, and he merely watched the birds as they wheeled or walked around him, watched them vaguely, without discrimination. All interest had left him. Only there was one gull, a big handsome fellow, who would walk back and forth, back and forth in front of the open door of the cabin, as if he had some mission there. He was big, and pearl-grey, and his roundnesses were as smooth and lovely as a pearl. Only the folded wings had shut black pinions, and on the closed black feathers were three very distinct white dots, making a pattern. The islander wondered very much, why this bit of trimming on the bird out of the far, cold seas. And as the gull walked back and forth, back and forth in front of the cabin, strutting on pale-dusky gold feet, holding up his pale yellow beak, that was curved at the tip, with curious alien importance, the man wondered over him. He was portentous, he had a meaning.

Then the bird came no more. The island, which had been full of sea-birds, the flash of wings, the sound and cut of wings and sharp eerie cries in the air, began to be deserted again. No longer they sat like living eggs on the rocks and turf, moving their heads, but scarcely rising into flight round his feet. No longer they ran across the turf among the sheep, and lifted themselves upon low wings. The host had gone. But some remained, always.

The days shortened, and the world grew eerie. One day the boat came: as if suddenly, swooping down. The islander found it a violation. It was torture to talk to those two men, in their homely clumsy clothes. The air of familiarity around them was very repugnant to him. Himself, he was neatly dressed, his cabin was neat and tidy. He resented any intrusion, the clumsy homeliness, the heavy-footedness of the two fishermen was really repulsive to him.

The letters they had brought, he left lying unopened in a little box. In one of them was his money. But he could not bear to open even that one. Any kind of contact was repulsive to him. Even to read his name on an envelope. He hid the letters away.

And the hustle and horror of getting the sheep caught and tied and put in the ship made him loathe with profound repulsion the whole of the animal creation. What repulsive god invented animals, and evil-smelling men? To his nostrils, the fishermen and the sheep alike smelled foul; an uncleanness on the fresh earth.

He was still nerve-racked and tortured when the ship at last lifted sail and was drawing away, over the still sea. And sometimes days after, he would start with repulsion, thinking he heard the munching of sheep.

The dark days of winter drew on. Sometimes there was no real day at all. He felt ill, as if he were dissolving, as if dissolution had already set in inside him. Everything was twilight, outside, and in his mind and soul. Once, when he went to the door, he saw black heads of men swimming in his bay. For some moments he swooned unconscious. It was the shock, the horror of unexpected human approach. The horror in the twilight! And not till the shock had undermined him and left him disembodied, did he realise that the black heads were the heads of seals swimming in. A sick relief came over him. But he was barely conscious, after the shock. Later on, he sat and wept with gratitude, because they were not men. But he never realised that he wept. He was too dim. Like some strange, ethereal animal, he no longer realised what he was doing.

Only he still derived his single satisfaction from being alone, absolutely alone, with the space soaking into him. The grey sea alone, and the footing of his sea-washed island. No other contact. Nothing human to bring its horror into contact with him. Only space, damp, twilit, sea-washed space! This was the bread of his soul.

For this reason, he was most glad when there was a storm, or when the sea was high. Then nothing could get at him. Nothing could come through to him from the outer world. True, the terrific violence of the wind made him suffer badly. At the same time, it swept the world utterly out of existence for him. He always liked the sea to be heavily rolling and tearing. Then no boat could get at him. It was like eternal ramparts round his island.

He kept no track of time, and no longer thought of opening a book. The print, the printed letters, so like the depravity of speech, looked obscene. He tore the brass label from his paraffin stove. He obliterated any bit of lettering in his cabin.

His cat had disappeared. He was rather glad. He shivered at her thin, obtrusive call. She had lived in the coal shed. And each morning he had put her a dish of porridge, the same as he ate. He washed her saucer with repulsion. He did not like her writhing about. But he fed her scrupulously. Then one day she did not come for her porridge: she always mewed for it. She did not come again.

He prowled about his island in the rain, in a big oil-skin coat, not knowing what he was looking at, nor what he went out to see. Time had ceased to pass. He stood for long spaces, gazing from a white, sharp face, with those keen, far-off blue eyes of his, gazing fiercely and almost cruelly at the dark sea under the dark sky. And if he saw the labouring sail of a fishing boat away on the cold waters, a strange malevolent anger passed over his features.

Sometimes he was ill. He knew he was ill, because he staggered as he walked, and easily fell down. Then he paused to think what it was. And he went to his stores and took out dried milk and malt, and ate that. Then he forgot again. He ceased to register his own feelings.

The days were beginning to lengthen. All winter the weather had been comparatively mild, but with much rain, much rain. He had forgotten the sun. Suddenly, however, the air was very cold, and he began to shiver. A fear came over him. The sky was level and grey, and never a star appeared at night. It was very cold. More birds began to arrive. The island was freezing. With trembling hands he made a fire in his grate. The cold frightened him.

And now it continued, day after day, a dull, deathly cold. Occasional crumblings of snow were in the air. The days were greyly longer, but no change in the cold. Frozen grey daylight. The birds passed away, flying away. Some he saw lying frozen. It was as if all life were drawing away, contracting away from the north, contracting southwards. "Soon," he said to himself, "it will all be gone, and in all these regions nothing will be alive." He felt a cruel satisfaction in the thought.

Then one night there seemed to be a relief: he slept better, did not tremble half awake, and writhe so much, half-conscious. He had become so used to the quaking and writhing of his body, he hardly noticed it. But when for once it slept deep, he noticed that.

He woke in the morning to a curious whiteness. His window was muffled. It had snowed. He got up and opened his door, and shuddered. Ugh! how cold! All white, with a dark leaden sea, and black rocks curiously speckled with white. The foam was no longer pure. It seemed dirty. And the sea ate at the whiteness of the corpse-like land. Crumbles of snow were silting down the dead air.

On the ground the snow was a foot deep, white and smooth and soft, windless. He took a shovel to clear round his house and shed. The pallor of morning darkened. There was a strange rumbling of far-off thunder, in the frozen air, and through the newly-falling snow, a dim flash of lightning. Snow now fell steadily down, in the motionless obscurity.

He went out for a few minutes. But it was difficult. He stumbled and fell in the snow, which burned his face. Weak, faint, he toiled home. And when he recovered, he took the trouble to make hot milk.

It snowed all the time. In the afternoon again there was a muffled rumbling of thunder, and flashes of lightning blinking reddish through the falling snow. Uneasy, he went to bed and lay staring fixedly at nothingness.

Morning seemed never to come. An eternity long he lay and waited for one alleviating pallor on the night. And at last it seemed the air was paler. His house was a cell faintly illuminated with white light. He realised the snow was walled outside his window. He got up, in the dead cold. When he opened his door, the motionless snow stopped him in a wall as high as his breast. Looking over the top of it, he felt the dead wind slowly driving, saw the snow-powder lift and travel like a funeral train. The blackish sea churned and champed, seeming to bite at the snow, impotent. The sky was grey, but luminous.

He began to work in a frenzy, to get at his boat. If he was to be shut in, it must be by his own choice, not by the mechanical power of the elements. He must get to the sea. He must be able to get at his boat.

But he was weak, and at times the snow overcame him. It fell on him, and he lay buried and lifeless. Yet every time, he struggled alive before it was too late, and fell upon the snow with the energy of fever. Exhausted, he would not give in. He crept indoors and made coffee and bacon. Long since he had cooked so much. Then he went at the snow once more. He must conquer the snow, this new, white brute force which had accumulated against him.

He worked in the awful, dead wind, pushing the snow aside, pressing it with his shovel. It was cold, freezing hard in the wind, even when the sun came out for a while, and showed him his white, lifeless surroundings, the black sea rolling sullen, flecked with dull spume, away to the horizons. Yet the sun had power on his face. It was March.

He reached the boat. He pushed the snow away, then sat down under the lee of the boat, looking at the sea, which nearly swirled to his feet, in the high tide. Curiously natural the pebbles looked, in a world gone all uncanny. The sun shone no more. Snow was falling in hard crumbs, that vanished as if by miracle as they touched the hard blackness of the sea. Hoarse waves rang in the shingle, rushing up at the snow. The wet rocks were brutally black. And all the time the myriad swooping crumbs of snow, demonish, touched the dark sea and disappeared.

During the night there was a great storm. It seemed to him he could hear the vast mass of the snow striking all the world with a ceaseless thud; and over it all, the wind roared in strange hollow volleys, in between which came a jump of blindfold lightning, then the low roll of thunder heavier than the wind. When at last the dawn faintly discoloured the dark, the storm had more or less subsided, but a steady wind drove on. The snow was up to the top of his door.

Sullenly, he worked to dig himself out. And he managed, through sheer persistency, to get out. He was in the tail of a great drift, many feet high. When he got through, the frozen snow was not more than two feet deep. But his island was gone. Its shape was all changed, great heaping white hills rose where no hills had been, inaccessible, and they fumed like volcanoes, but with snow powder. He was sickened and overcome.

His boat was in another, smaller drift. But he had not the strength to clear it. He looked at it helplessly. The shovel slipped from his hands, and he sank in the snow, to forget. In the snow itself, the sea resounded.

Something brought him to. He crept to his house. He was almost without feeling. Yet he managed to warm himself, just that part of him which leaned in snow-sleep over the coal fire.

Then again, he made hot milk. After which, carefully, he built up the fire.

The wind dropped. Was it night again? In the silence, it seemed he could hear the panther-like dropping of infinite snow. Thunder rumbled nearer, crackled quick after the bleared reddened lightning. He lay in bed in a kind of stupor. The elements! The elements! His mind repeated the word dumbly. You can't win against the elements.

How long it went on, he never knew. Once, like a wraith, he got out, and climbed to the top of a white hill on his unrecognisable island. The sun was hot. "It is summer," he said to himself, "and the time of leaves." He looked stupidly over the whiteness of his foreign island, over the waste of the lifeless sea. He pretended to imagine he saw the wink of a sail. Because he knew too well there would never again be a sail on that stark sea.

As he looked, the sky mysteriously darkened and chilled. From far off came the mutter of the unsatisfied thunder, and he knew it was the signal of the snow rolling over the sea. He turned, and felt its breath on him.

The Lovely Lady

At seventy-two, Pauline Attenborough could still be mistaken, in the half-light, for thirty. She really was a wonderfully unaged woman, of perfect *chic*. Of course it helps a great deal to have the right frame. She would be an exquisite skeleton, and her skull would be exquisite when she was long dead; like that of some Etruscan° woman with feminine charm still in the swerve of the bone and the pretty, naïve little teeth.

But agelessness is a question rather of strength and subtlety of will than anything else. And herein lay Pauline Attenborough's secret. She had a very fine and very perfectly-wrought will of her own. It was hidden in her soft and laughing manner as her skull was hidden under the delicate, teasing smile of her face. And just as, physically, she was neither too plump nor too dry, so psychically she was neither too hard nor too emotional. She was lucky: a really well-balanced woman.

Her face was a lovely oval, and of that slightly flat type which wears best; because there is no flesh to sag. Nothing sagged about Pauline Attenborough. Her nose rode serenely, and her witty spirit travelled continually over its finely-curved bridge. Her big grey eyes were a tiny bit prominent, on the surface of her face, but they were very bright and arch, even at seventy.

Nevertheless, it was round the eyes that sometimes she was betrayed, in spite of all her skill. The bluish lids were heavy, as if they ached sometimes with the strain of keeping the eyes beneath them arch and bright; and at the corners of the eyes, the smile had worn tiny wrinkles like the wrinkles in rock, and when the smile sank in weariness, these wrinkles would go haggard with the suggestion of geological centuries. But Pauline was able to summon the smile back, and by candle-light, the wrinkles were only the gay little cracklings of half-hidden laughter. And then Pauline looked like a Leonardo woman° of a freer age, who would not be afraid to laugh outright, with a full, rich, mocking laugh.

So she seemed to the world. Her niece Cecilia was perhaps the only person who knew the working of the invisible little wire which connected Aunt Pauline's eye-wrinkles with Aunt Pauline's competent will. Only Cecilia coldly watched the eyes go old and haggard and tired as if they were centuries old, monkey-old; when Aunt Pauline was alone. And then when somebody came, or when Robert was heard outside the door, then ping! – the mysterious little wire that worked between Pauline's will and her face did its work, and the weary, haggard eyes lying dead on the surface of the dead face started alive, and Pauline was a lovely woman again, whom age could not wither.° The bluish, deadened eyelids glimmered pearly, the thin, curved eyebrows which floated in such frail arches on Pauline's forehead suddenly took on a mocking lightness, and you had the *real* Pauline. Real, that is, to everyone except Pauline's niece Cecilia.

Aunt Pauline really had the secret of everlasting youth. Or if not that, then really she could renew her youth like the eagle.° She donned it, and she doffed it. And she was sparing of it. She was wise enough not to try being young too long at a stretch, or for too many people at a time. Her son Robert, in the evenings, and sometimes Sir Wilfrid Knipe in the afternoon; and then an occasional few people to tea some day when Robert was home; these knew the lovely lady undiminished. For these she was still an aspless Cleopatra,° and a Mona Lisa who could break into a bronzy little laugh of pure humour. For Pauline was never malicious; or if she was just the spiciest bit malicious, she was never spiteful nor carping. She tolerated virtue as well as vice, and almost as wittily.

Like Mona Lisa of the sly smile, she knew a thing or two. But her niece Cecilia, who was in Aunt Pauline's opinion a negligible quantity, knew just one thing more. Cecilia, called by her aunt and by her cousin Robert just Ciss, like a cat spitting, was useful as a dilutant, as nitrogen is useful in the atmosphere. She was not very observant, not much of a live wire; moreover she was plain; more than that, she was in love, or thought she was, with her cousin Robert, who hardly noticed her existence. Finally, she was thirty, penniless, dependent on her Aunt Pauline. Oh Cecilia! why make music for her!°

Ciss was a big, dark-complexioned, pug-faced young woman who seemed to be glooming about something. She rarely said anything, and when she did, it seemed to get self-consciously stuck in her throat. She was the daughter of a congregational minister, younger brother of Aunt Pauline's long-since-faded-out husband, Ronald Attenborough. The congregational minister had been five years dead, and Cecilia had been domiciled those five years with Aunt Pauline.

In a rather small but quite perfect Queen Ann house° some thirty miles out of London. It stood in a little vale, with a little river winding through its quaint and quite perfect though not extensive grounds. Everything Aunt Pauline had was just about perfect. And Old Brinsley, as the house was called, was absolutely ideal; for Aunt Pauline, of course, at the age of seventy-two. When the kingfishers flashed up the little stream and under the balustraded bridge in the garden, something still flashed in Pauline's heart. Ah, that exquisite stab of blue! in *my* garden! – She was that kind of person.

Robert, Aunt Pauline's son, went to town every day, driving his own little car, to his chambers in one of the Inns.° He was only thirty-two years old, born when Aunt Pauline was forty. He was a barrister, and he went to town every day, and actually he made, one way or another, about a hundred pounds a year. One never knew whether he were mortified or merely indifferent, for he never told. And Pauline only laughed, and said she preferred failures. They made better lovers. She herself was such a success. So she gave her son money in little spasms.

For a long time she would be quite mean. Then suddenly she would buy him lots of things, and hand him a cheque for a hundred pounds. He never knew exactly where he was, and he hid from his mother absolutely the fact that he had an unknown account amounting almost to a thousand pounds. He was that kind of man, secret and taciturn.

To Ciss, Pauline gave fifty pounds a year, for being useful. This was not exactly munificent. But Pauline liked to feel that what was her own was her own; what was Pauline's was Pauline's. Then she could give a lovely and undeserved present now and then. It was so lovely for Ciss to get something she had not earned, and therefore did not deserve. A real present. Cecilia, however, with human perversity, found it harder and harder to take these presents in the right spirit.

Robert was a plain young man; no longer so very young. He was rather short, and broad, and looked fat, though he wasn't. He was thick-set. Only his pale, rather creamy-sallow face was fat and expressionless. He looked very clean-shaven, rather like an Italian priest, secretive and taciturn. There was something clouded and unlifting on his brow, and a slight waddle in his thick-legged walk. Yet his hands were very beautiful, and his eyes, dark-grey like his mother's, were seen, when at last he looked at you, to have a lonely warmth under their gloom, very different from his mother's arch bright glance. He wore his dark hair cut very short, and somehow this showed up the fineness of his rather low, finely-bred brow.

Cecilia, who perhaps knew him best, found in him a quality of beauty and pure breeding which she absolutely failed to find in Aunt Pauline's loveliness. But it was as if he were cut off in some mysterious way from life. He never really lived. He suffered, in a silent, perhaps unconscious way. He did not quite give in. But he went about always silent and always under a weight. Only sometimes he would lift his eyes very beautifully to his cousin, full of gloom and knowing and stoicism, yet with an undergleam of passionate warmth. Yet of this, he himself knew nothing.

He had one interest, and that was the collecting of legal *Mexicana.*° It had started when he had come across some old papers relating to the trial of English sailors before the inquisition at Vera Cruz early in the seventeenth century. This weird and tortuous affair he had followed out as far as ever he could, and while doing so had come across strange horrifying processes against nuns and priests, foreign merchants and travellers in Vice-regal Mexico.° There were so many things the modern mind just refuses openly to contemplate.

He never spoke of his interest to anyone but his mother. Pauline was genuinely thrilled over these weird and often terrible stories. She always wanted to know, to know everything, especially the worst. She had a smattering of Spanish. So when there was a new document, she and her son would sit together in the drawing-room at night, having a wonderful time deciphering it. Cecilia was never let in to this. She knew vaguely what they were working at. And she knew that Robert had a genuine scholar's passion for his old researches. But he never even mentioned them to her. And Pauline only vaguely hinted at the wonder and the thrill of these ancient scripts which were so far beyond Ciss' mental grasp. Cecilia stayed out in the cold, with the stupid and the unimportant.

Pauline rather affected a Spanish appearance. Her head was poised high on her neck in the proud Spanish-blonde style. So in her soft brown hair that was streaked only with grey she wore a high comb, and over her still proud shoulders a marvellous old brown shawl with silvery silk embroidery, very rich and heavy, with long fringe. Then she would sit at the darkly-glowing round dining-table, in her tall chair backed with old green brocade, and pearly-looking and somehow suave and loftily perky like a goose, she would sway her long ear-rings and turn to her son, saying in her roguish voice:

"Oh Robert, I am so looking forward to our work tonight! The thought of it buoys me up all day."

"But we are coming to a dull part," he would say, sensible of poor Ciss sitting out of it.

"Oh never mind *that*! It won't be dull to me," replied Pauline.

And she would take up her old silver fork again, and eat delicately, her white arms showing still beautiful and young, from her dress of dark-green silk, the brown shawl hanging negligently. She had such poise! that was her chief charm. And she made poor Ciss feel such a clumsy horse. The candles were set just right for Aunt Pauline's face, the few strings of pearls round Aunt Pauline's neck were just the right becoming sort of pearls, neither poor nor pretentious. The old green brocade of the chair-back just suited Aunt Pauline's Christmas rose sort of complexion. The pace of the dinner was just Aunt Pauline's laughing, leisurely pace. And Cecilia was just the perfect, rather stupid foil for Aunt Pauline's light poise, sitting there as she did admiring and a little overcome, even now, after five years.

They were always three at table; and they always drank champagne, Pauline two glasses, Ciss two glasses, and Robert the rest of the bottle. He preferred burgundy, but he never said so. Dinner always went with a pleasant easy rhythm. Pauline always sparkled a little at her second glass of champagne. That was her highest moment of the day. Ciss, with her black hair bobbed and her shoulders square and her hazel eyes looking rather dumbly round in wonder, always wore some becoming dress that clever Aunt Pauline had helped her to make, and some attractive old inexpensive jewel Aunt Pauline had given her. She was still rendered speechless by it all, and she could still get up from table entirely unconscious of the fact that she had not spoken a word all the meal, feeling as if she had taken part in the animation.

Nevertheless, she was collecting as curious a mass of data concerning Aunt Pauline and Cousin Robert, as ever Robert collected from his Mexican documents.

Robert said almost as little as she, and was almost as unaware of the fact. Not that Pauline rattled. She often had pauses of perfectly easy silence. But it was always her voice broke the stillness. And Robert was always on the *qui vive*° to attend to her. It was as if his mother absorbed all his faculties.

This was not the case, however. Priestlike, he was aware all the time of the young woman's presence, though he gave no sign. He was always naturally well-bred, too, and suffered when he thought Ciss was made to feel out of it. But apart from that, there was always a delicate feeler of awareness from him always touching the young woman, always, and Pauline was much too self-preoccupied to know it. But it had its effect on Cecilia.

The young woman knew that when dinner was over and he held the door for her to pass, the closeness of her physical presence moved him. And she had her arms quite bare, on purpose, and she showed a tiny glimpse of her firm small breasts, and she sailed past him in a queer way, like a ship skirting a rock. It moved him inwardly. But outwardly it had no effect. It never would have any effect. He was overcome, and would remain so.

Ciss poured coffee in the softly-shaded drawing-room, where everything again was nearly perfect, delicate old pieces of furniture and some very valuable pictures by Renoir and Gauguin and Cézanne.° This was part of the cream of all the aesthetic or antique stuff which Pauline had drawn from all over the world. She had made all her money, dealing privately in works of art, whether old furniture or modern pictures or rare things from barbaric countries. Now she was rich, and the things she had kept for herself she could afford.

The drawing-room, however, was no museum. It was pleasant, even homely. You never noticed how choice things were in it, unless you had some idea of furniture and of art. Many visitors thought Pauline's drawing-room a little faded and old-fashioned, with hopeless modern pictures. But she herself liked a sensitive, silvery-dusty sort of effect. She sat in the shade by the fire, making a note of dull colour and feminine gleam, in the dim frail room. And she mused, with her coffee cup in her hand.

This muse was a signal to Ciss not to linger. Pauline's soul was already drifting ahead to the "work" with Robert. So as soon as the coffee was finished, Ciss collected the cups on to the little tray, and said Good-night. She never kissed her aunt. Pauline was not a kisser.

"Good-night, Aunt Pauline!"

"Good-night, Ciss!" So calm and laconic! Not even: "Will you go so soon?" – No, let her go.

"Good-night Robert!"

"Good-night Ciss!" – But he rose to hold the door for her as she went out with the tray. And she passed mutely near him, her heart was always bitterly disappointed, she did not quite know why. And he, though he gave absolutely no sign, always felt a little forlorn when she went, and he was left alone, so to speak, with the lioness in her den.

But it was Pauline's hour, which, before she was seventy-two, had been her hour for her lover. In some mysterious way she had saved up her power of being thrilled, especially in connection with a man. She had saved up her power of being a little in love, and this was her secret of secrets. She was eager as a girl to be at the old manuscripts under the lamp, with Robert, whose voice was so quiet and lonely and attractive, and whose hands were so beautiful, beautiful enough to delight even a connoisseur. She looked up at him so eagerly, like a child. And then he spoke his words so slowly, and on his forehead was a patience and a gentleness that had a touch of nobility. It was as if he were the elder of the two, like a priest with a young and beautiful charge he was secretly in love with, but whom he treated only with delicate gentleness and reverence.

And his mother truly was this to him. But she was also the lioness who played with him as if he were a puppy put there for her sport. And he was to her truly a wonderful, pure man with a touch of patient nobility. But he was also the ineffectual Robert who waddled a little when he walked.

Ciss had a flat for herself just across the court-yard at the back of the house, over the old coach-house and stables. There were no horses, only Robert's car. So Ciss had three very nice rooms upstairs, opening off one another, and charmingly fitted up by Aunt Pauline. For company, she had the ticking of the stable clock, her own charge. She herself wound it up every week.

But sometimes she did not go to her rooms at once. In the turmoil of her spirits, she would wander in the garden, or sit on the lawn, where, from the open window of the drawing-room upstairs she would hear the murmur of voices, and Pauline's wonderful low laugh. But if it were winter time, she would put on a thick coat and walk slowly to the little balustraded bridge over the stream, and look at the pointed stars of Orion° rearing out of the east, or, on a dark night, see the glow from the windows of the drawing-room mistily touching the bare trees. And always she wondered, with a kind of desperation: "Where is my life? When is it my turn to live?"

She believed that Pauline intended Robert to marry her, Ciss, when Pauline was dead. She intended it out of very indifference to either of them, once her own back was turned for ever. But when would that be? Aunt Pauline would live for years and years, by the looks of things. And Robert was already incapable of acting. His will was prostrate, prostrated since he was born, almost prostituted to his mother's will. What would he be in another ten years time? A mere shell of a man who had never even been a man. It was awful! And yet, Ciss knew, he *could* love her with a manly love. Only he could never shake off his mother. He could never even think of it.

She felt for him the intense, impassioned sympathy of the young for one another, when they are overshadowed by the old. It was a secret, but very potent and dangerous feeling. Sometimes a wild passion of anarchy filled her. She did not care what she did. The thing was, however, to begin. To act! And this point was not quite reached.

But she felt it coming. Even Robert had begun to betray a twisting sort of irritability. He had had influenza several times, and it seemed as if the composition of his nature were breaking up, changing. There was now a permanent little tension of irritation between his brows. He would watch his mother with a very strange, astonished sort of irritable scrutiny, when Pauline was not aware. And then, almost guiltily, he would catch Ciss' eye. For half a second, the two young ones exchanged glances sullen and desperate as murder. Then he would look away, his face like a mask. Pauline would sniff something in the air, wake up from her abstraction, and she, Ciss, would watch the stiff, murderous mask of his face slowly and bewilderingly change again to the half vacant look of fascination, as he gazed at his young mother. He was lost once more.

But once or twice Ciss lunched with him in town, and there she saw the little pleat of agonised irritation fixed in his brow, and the sulky mask of shame and humiliation wedged into his face. He was sullen with humiliation, murderous almost. But the one he would murder would be himself. He gave strange little looks at his cousin Ciss, looks almost of hate. And he was a little brusque and impatient, as if Ciss was no good to him. He wanted to make a break, do something final and disgraceful to himself, in order to accomplish his last bodily humiliation. Poor Ciss, her little outing did not do her much good. She was merely roused to the fact that Robert was soon going to make a break; that he was going deliberately to throw himself to the dogs before long; or to the bitches.

They all took coffee in their rooms, in the morning. At nine o'clock, Ciss walked over to Sir Wilfrid Knipe's place, to give two hour's lessons to his little grand-daughter. It was her sole serious occupation; except that she played the piano. Robert set off to town about nine. Ciss rarely saw him in the morning. As a rule, Aunt Pauline appeared to lunch, then retired again. She was almost always in her room, though she liked to walk in the garden when the weather was fine. But she was inclined to fade rather rapidly, in the daylight. Her hour was candle hour.

It was her practice, when the sun shone, to take a sun-bath. This was one of her beauty secrets. The sun gave one resistance, the resistance of youth. Sometimes she took her sun-bath before noon, but usually after. Her lunch was very light. And on days of real sun, the queer little bowling-green just behind the stables was a cup of sunshine all afternoon. It was cosy in the angle of the stable buildings, and had a very fortress of thick yew walls round it. Here, within the yew enclosure, Ciss stretched out the low canvas bed and spread the silky rugs, beneath the red glow of old brick walls. Then Aunt Pauline came with her sunshade, and Ciss retired to her rooms upstairs, to keep guard.

One afternoon, in the gnawing restlessness of her spirit, Ciss suddenly climbed up the ladder at the end of the loft, out on to the roof of the stable buildings. It was a marvellous July day, clear, the great rounded tops of the beech-trees calmly abutting into the upper, cleaner world. Beautiful to go up one layer, above the harassment of the trodden world. Ciss found herself a perfect corner, under the parapet of the leaded roof, and took off her things. If sunbaths were good for Aunt Pauline, then they would be good for Ciss.

She found it very lovely, to bask her whole length in the hot sky. It even seemed to melt some of the hard bitterness out of her heart. In a dim kind of way, she realised that Aunt Pauline was really a very fine sport, playing her own game with such perfect athletic skill and isolation. It was like some dancer dancing all alone the dance of her own all-important life. Well why not? People must look out for themselves. People must look out for themselves! Here was a new creed, for Ciss, born of the sun in her. She rolled over voluptuously. Even the new idea was voluptuous, leaving her more naked and free under the grand sun.

Suddenly, as she sprawled her limbs, her blood froze, and her heart stood still. She could feel her hair creeping up on her head, as a voice said very softly, musingly in her ear:

"No, it was not my fault. For that I can't be blamed. No, Robert my child, you must not try to blame *me* that Henry died instead of marrying his Claudia. I was quite, quite willing for him to marry her, unsuitable as she was. But when he had been to see me, he realised his own false position, and I suppose that was it."

The voice ceased. Ciss sank down on her rug, powerless and perspiring with dread. The awful voice, so soft and musing and trailing, and so unnatural! It was not a human voice, really. It had a strange, void whisper, as if it spoke out of nowhere. Yet there must, there must be somebody on the roof. How unspeakably ghastly!

She lifted her weak head and peeped across the ridged leads. Nobody! The chimneys were too narrow to shelter a person. There was nothing on the roof. She felt it. – In the trees? In the beeches? – She peeped in a prostration of terror. But the leaves were massy and still, there was no-one there. Besides, the trees were too far off. No, there was no-one to utter the voice. She raised her head a little higher, to gaze around. And as she did so the voice came again, whisperingly:

"No darling! I only told you you would tire of her in six months, and you knew it was true. I wanted to spare you that. It was your own mistake, dear. You knew you were mistaken, and yet you could not throw off your mistake. That was what hurt you, my boy. Mother only made you see clearly. That silly Claudia was a pure mistake of yours. Yet you would not give up the *idea* that you wanted her and must have her. And it was that that confused you and weakened you, not me at all. If you had stuck to what your mother knew was right for you, you would not have died. No darling, it was you who let *me* down, dying like that; not I who let you down. Bitter! Bitter!"

The voice faded away. Cecilia, the tension of listening over, subsided on to her rug, too weak to move. Ah, it was awful! The sun was shining, the sky was blue, the trees stood noble and still. All seemed so lovely and afternoony and summery. Yet pervading it was this horror, this voice, this something outside of nature. Oh, and Cecilia had always hated the pretence of the supernatural, ghosts and voices and rappings, and all that. She hated it. And now it had come upon her!

That awful, unholy, bodiless voice! It had something so strangely familiar in it too, under the rusty, creeping sort of whisper of an overtone. Yet it was so utterly uncanny and inexplicable. Poor Ciss could only lie there nude in an agony of helpless resistance and terror, collapsed.

Then she heard the thing sigh: a long sigh that was not human, yet seemed weirdly familiar. "Ah well! Ah well! The heart must bleed. Perhaps it keeps it fresh. And one must have one's grief among the rest of the bouquet of life. But I cannot have you blaming *me*, Robert. Henry was a much more brilliant boy than you, and he killed himself trying to marry himself to that silly Claudia. And do you think you would be any better with our dull Ciss? When I am gone, marry her or not, as you wish. If you wanted her sex, you could no doubt have it now. She would give it you. But I can't have you kill yourself trying to marry a woman who doesn't profoundly interest you. I can't lose another son, having lost the best."

It was certainly Aunt Pauline's spirit whispering on the air. Ciss was about to give vent to loud and piercing screams, when the mention of her own name checked her, and she became cautious and hostile. It was Aunt Pauline, Aunt Pauline revealing all her enmity. Ciss lay paralysed with terror, and yet alert and cunning. It was Aunt Pauline. How was she doing it? Was it some horrible trick of ventriloquism?

The sounds were very uneven, sometimes quite inaudible, sometimes only a brushing sort of noise. Ciss listened intently. No, it could not be ventriloquism. It was not that. It was a sighing out of the inner air: worse than any ventriloquism. It was some sort of thought transference, that registered as sound. Some horror of that sort. Thought broadcasting itself, and no escaping it, once you were in key. Ciss lay weak and inert, too overcome to move. But the effort of using her reason was calming her, and as she grew calmer she grew suspicious and wary. It was some trick of that unnatural woman, Aunt Pauline. Or perhaps it was some nemesis that had overtaken her.

Aunt Pauline with a guilty conscience! Ciss had always suspected it. A woman like that ought to feel guilty. But it was about Henry that her conscience smote her. Henry was Aunt Pauline's first-born, twelve years older than Robert. He had been dead these twenty years; died quite suddenly at the age of twenty-two, just before the day fixed for his wedding with a good-looking actress. Aunt Pauline had hated the thought of the actress, and had jeered at poor Henry, who had always been so devoted to his mother. It had been too much for the poor boy. He was taken ill, and died before ever his mother could reach him, to speak to him. It had been a bitter blow to her. But Ciss' father, who hated Pauline, had declared that poor Henry would never have died if his mother had not jeered and tormented him and mixed him all up. She just broke the boy's courage, said the uncle. Ciss had often thought of her father's words, and wondered if Robert would have to be broken as well. A mother fascinating her sons, and then forcing them into death, rather than let them go. The bad woman!

"I suppose I may as well get up!" whispered the dim, unbreathing voice. "Not too much sun, any more than too much shadow. Enough sun, enough sex-thrill, enough active interest, and a woman might live forever. Why not? But not too much of any of them. Not too much. Enough to absorb vitality; then stop, before the sun begins to absorb one's vitality back from one. Absorb vitality from the sun, but don't let him get hold of you, and absorb *your* vitality."

How amazing it was! It was certainly Aunt Pauline. Those were her thoughts, broadcasting themselves. But how horrible to *have* to listen! How horrible, to have got on to the same wave-length, and to have to hear! Not able to switch off! – Must I all my life henceforward hear Aunt Pauline's thoughts? – thought Ciss, in misery. It really was too much to bear.

She lay twisted and inert, staring vacantly in front of her. Vacantly vacantly! Her eyes were staring into a hole in the lead gutter. She stared at it, and it meant nothing to her. Only it seemed to hypnotise her still more, this hole going down in the leaden gutter.

Suddenly, out of the hole came a whispered sigh, and at last voiceless breathing of words: "Ah well, Pauline! Get up, get up then! It is enough for today. Don't be slack!"

Straight out of the hole of the rain-pipe! As if it was the horn of a telephone! Exactly! Good God! It was the pipe! It was the rain-pipe acting as a speaking-tube! Surely! But was it possible? Oh, *was* it possible?

Ciss reared on her elbow and looked down the pipe. She could see nothing. But a huge relief, and a wicked sort of triumph filled her heart. Of course! of course! Aunt Pauline was lying down there and whispering straight into the rain-pipe. It was possible! Ciss knew it was possible, she believed she had even read of something similar in a book. And the sound came up – Oh, it was too awful and ridiculous! Aunt Pauline talked aloud to herself when she was alone, like a real old lady. *That* was why she locked herself so mysteriously in her bed-room. That was why she was so mysterious, always retiring and letting no-one near her! That was why she never dozed in a chair, or lay on a couch, or sat absent-minded anywhere, but always, as soon as her attention relaxed, retired to her room! Because, as soon as she slackened off, she talked in a soft crazy little voice, aloud to herself! – A sullen exultance sprang in Ciss' heart. So! This was where the invulnerable Aunt Pauline gave herself away! The young woman lay prone, in a luxury of strange, desperate exultance.

She was roused by the ringing, musical call from outside: *All right*! It was Aunt Pauline calling to say the coast was clear, as she returned to the house. And such a young, strong, resonant voice! so assured! Who could believe it was the same as the whisper that came up the rain-pipe? Ciss felt very sardonic. She could not refrain, nude as she was, from creeping across the roof and peeping over the parapet at the elegant and leisurely figure in a silk wrap and sunshade that was mounting the steps to the back door. Madame Sans Gêne!◇

Ciss rapidly cast on her few clothes and went down the loft ladder and round to the bowling-court. The silky rugs tumbled on the bright green grass, in the full sunshine, the long light couch seemed to nestle against the creeper of the old red wall. And among the leaves of the creeper, exactly opposite Aunt Pauline's mouth, if she turned over, was the dainty mouth of the rain-pipe. Oh Nemesis! Ciss grimly folded the rugs and carried them in.

She was in a seethe of thoughts and emotions. So Aunt Pauline was not superhuman? She was not even perfect to herself. She even had a great chagrin, a chagrin she would never get over: the death of her handsome and dashing Henry, whom she had admired so much more than poor Robert. Yes, Henry had been Aunt Pauline's *beau ideal*,◇ till he went and fell in love with that smirking actress. And hadn't she scathed him for it! And he had gone back on her, by dying.

But what an indomitable woman! She showed her scars to nobody. She seemed so perfect. She had to be perfect, even to herself. She could not bear to be in the wrong; she could not bear even to find herself in the wrong. No, in public or in private, she must be perfect.

Yet she was a wonderful woman. She used to say, conceitedly: My life is my work of art. – The daughter of a consul, she had been brought up in the East, then in Port Said, then in Naples. Her father was a devoted collector of exotic or precious things, and he paid little attention to his daughter. When he died, soon after his grandson Henry was born, Pauline gathered up his collection of treasures, and started to make a life for herself. She separated herself quite amicably from her husband, and took her child along. She had a certain genius for appreciating beauty, whether of texture, form, or colour. On the basis of her father's collection, she built her own fortune. She sold what it was advantageous to sell, and she went on collecting. She acquired old African wooden figures, and Papuan masks and ivories, when nobody cared about them. She bought Renoir very early. She sold to collectors and to museums, but kept herself out of sight. She had made a fortune by the time Robert was born. She allowed her husband an income till he died, some five years after Robert's birth. But she had not lived with him for years. Robert's coming had made everybody catch their breath. But then, after all, Pauline's husband sometimes came to tea.

And it was almost impossible to fasten a lover on to Pauline. She had many devoted men friends and sincere admirers. But she married none of them, and gave herself away to none of them. They were devoted just the same; perhaps more. A pure woman! Such is the baseness of humanity, that a man respects a woman much more highly if she doesn't become his lover. So that no man seemed to imagine he was the father of Robert.

Pauline did brilliant war work, and became a Dame. She kept Robert safely employed through it all, in the Intelligence

Department. She had a really choice set of friends. And she enjoyed that rare comfort of feeling herself a success. Her only concern now was for her life; she wanted to live for ever.

And now at last, this was what Ciss was determined she should not do. Ciss was attached to her cousin Robert, and she was desperate. For while Pauline lived, he would never caress her, Ciss, with those fascinating hands of his. She knew it, she knew it. Therefore, between her and her Aunt Pauline, it was a question of: Thy life, or mine.

But still Ciss did not know what to do. Only she felt, somehow, she had gained power. She had stolen some of Aunt Pauline's mysterious strength, and she had it inside herself.

Even Pauline seemed to feel a trifle diminished. She was very quiet at dinner, and after coffee, she said:

"The sun has made me sleepy. I think I shall retire. You two might have a game of chess."

When Robert had closed the door after his mother, and returned to his seat, Ciss asked him:

"Do you want to play chess?"

"If you do," he replied, looking at her with those patient and courteous grey eyes.

"No," she said. "Would you rather I went away? Would you rather be alone?"

"No-no!" he said hastily. "Why do you ask?"

The windows were open, the scent of honeysuckle wafted in, with the sound of an owl. Robert smoked in silence. There was a sort of despair in his motionless, rather squat body, and it filled Ciss with despair also. He had nothing to say. Even this tortured him.

"Do you remember cousin Henry?" Ciss asked suddenly.

"Yes! Very well," he replied, in a sort of surprise.

"What did he look like?" Ciss met her cousin's big, slow, secret-troubled eyes, in which was a wincing look almost like fear.

"Handsome," he said. "Tall, good at games; rather freckled, with mother's soft brown hair with a gleam of red in it."

Ciss wanted to say: Aunt Pauline is as grey as a badger. – But she held her tongue.

"And what kind of a character?" she asked.

"Open, rather boisterous. Women all loved him."

"And did you?" she asked. "Did you love him?"

"Yes!" he said, surprised.

"Weren't you jealous of him?"

"Why?" – He looked at her in wonder.

"Your mother loved him better than she loved you, didn't she?"

The question was insidious. He seemed never to have thought of it. His face was puzzled like a child's. Then he said, in a queer voice:

"Yes! I suppose she did – if – if one thinks of such things."

"She must have felt it a terrible slap in the eye, when he died."

He looked at her in a very strange way.

"Why that exactly?" he said, and his shapely hand trembled a little.

"I suppose he was just torn in two between the girl he wanted to marry, and your mother; and he died to get out of it."

Ciss was so desperate, she didn't care what she said, so long as she only got some of this business off her chest.

"That may very well be," he said.

And there was a pause.

"I wonder what his ghost thinks," she said, "if it ever comes back and looks at you and Aunt Pauline!"

But this he would not answer. He was profoundly upset.

"Don't you ever want to *live*, Robert?" she asked rather feebly. "I want to, so much."

"In what way, live?" he said.

"To love, and to *feel* things," she said. "To feel something before we die," she added tremulously.

After a long pause, he said caustically:

"I think we're as well out of it."

"No!" she said. "Why don't you love somebody, Robert? I mean a man's love, not a child's."

He slowly flushed a swarthy, dull crimson, and seemed to shrink in his chair.

"Can one do those things to order?" he asked, his flush belying the dryness of his question.

"Perhaps," she said. "Perhaps a man like you has to." – Then her voice went small and faltering. "Don't you love me even a little?" she said.

"I'm very fond of you," he said, in a deep voice of conviction.

"Yes – but – don't you ever love anybody?" she asked.

"I never feel a genuine physical desire for any particular person, if that's what you mean," he said, in an easy tone of voice, but his face now green with agitation.

"But you never try," she said.

"Does one have to try?" he asked dryly.

"Yes, why not? One never does anything if one doesn't try."

He kept his face averted, and was silent. Then he asked:

"And do you mean I am to try to feel a – a physical love for you?"

"I believe you would, if you'd let yourself," she said desperately.

He said nothing, but slowly shook his head.

"Don't you want to?" she said sharply. "Are you content to go on being a child and a – a dumb-bell all your life?"

A quick, nervous smile went over his face.

"Dumb-bell is rather good," he said. Then he pulled himself together, and said with sudden surprising bitterness: "It's no good, you know. My mother would know all about it before it had even started. I shouldn't wonder if she didn't know you

276

wanted to say something like this to me, so she went to bed on purpose. I'm almost sure she did."

"But what if she did?" Ciss cried. "I don't care what Aunt Pauline thinks of me!"

"Don't you?" he said dryly.

And Ciss knew it wasn't true. The thought that Aunt Pauline might know what she, Ciss, had said was somehow paralysing. When Aunt Pauline knew things, she seemed to be able to kill them with a smile. Her mysterious power of mockery, jeering at one, made one go all tangled up and perverse inside, till one absolutely cared about nothing.

No, there was nothing to do but to fight her. Ciss said Goodnight, and went away to her rooms.

The weather continued hot. Pauline continued her sun-baths, and Ciss lay on the roof eaves-dropping in the literal sense of the word. But no sound came up the pipe, not even a sigh. Pauline must be lying with her face away from the wall. Ciss could hear the faintest, faintest stirring of sound. Her aunt must be murmuring into the void. Oh bitter waste! The afternoon passed, with not an audible syllable.

At night, under the stars, Ciss sat in the garden and waited, amid the perfume of honey-suckle and hay, and the crying of the owl. She saw the lights go up in her aunt's room. She saw the lights at last go out in the drawing-room. And she waited. But he did not come. Half the night she stayed out there, motionless, silent. But she stayed alone.

And for two days she heard nothing, though the sun shone and Pauline basked. But the pipe spoke not. And for two evenings she stayed deep into the night, alone in the garden. Then when she had ceased to listen or to hope, as she sat with heavy, helpless persistence in the garden, suddenly she started. Someone had come out. She rose, and went hesitatingly over the grass. It was he.

"Don't speak!" he murmured.

And in silence they crossed the lawns and walked down to the little bridge, then over into the paddock where the hay, cut late, was standing in cock. They stood irresolute, looking up at the faint summer stars, and smelling the rich scent of hay.

"Come to the lime tree," she said.

They sat on the bench under the tree that still smelled sweet.

"You see," he said awkwardly, as if continuing a conversation, "how can I ask for love, if I don't feel any love in myself? You know my real regard for you – "

She listened, and said nothing. Then she asked, irrelevant:

"Don't you ever want to get away from here?"

"From this little paradise?" he said. "But where should I go? I don't even succeed in earning my own living."

"Oh, you would if you had to," she replied roughly. "If ever you got out of this paradise – fool's paradise – you would do something."

"A fool's paradise," he said mockingly, "where the serpent won't let one get within a mile of an apple tree.° A paradise where there is never a chance of a fall! A paradise with no temptation. And where the Lord is a lovely lady! A paradise where one lives and rots! – "

She was amazed at his sudden mocking bitterness. He had never before uttered a single word to show he was not contented.

"Then why don't you clear out?" she said.

"Yes, why don't I?" he said.

"You are a man," she asserted.

"Thanks! But what's in a word? What *kind* of man am I?" He spoke with great self-contempt.

"How should anybody know, till you get out of this paradise? But at least, you might love me a little."

"I might! Only unfortunately, I haven't any sentimental feeling for anybody."

"But why should you want to have a sentimental feeling? Have an unsentimental feeling for me. I wish you would."

"The lovely lady will know, as sure as eggs."

"If you mean Aunt Pauline, why should you mind?"

"She will feel it a most mortal offence."

"Then that's her fault. Why don't you just tell her you are going to marry me?"

"Am I going to marry you?"

"I hope so. Else I shall go away and earn my living as a governess."

"You might do worse," he said.

"I might," she replied grimly. "I might stay on here till I'm grey, a grey old hungry cat. That's what I've realised."

He sat silent for a long time. Then he took her hand and held it in his.

"I think I can do something about it. It's a question of turning oneself out of paradise, this time, and telling the lovely lady one has had enough of it. I think Adam ought to have said to the Lord, under the circumstances: 'Thank you, Sir; but we prefer to go.' "

Ciss was rather puzzled by his new tone of acrid humour. He rose. And as they went to the bridge, he said:

"I think I can do something about it. I'll let you know."

That was all she got out of him. She went angrily beside him. Now that the ice was breaking, waves of anger surged up.

"I'll see you to your door," he said as they crossed the lawn.

"Do you think you'd better risk it?" she replied.

"Miau! Miau!"

He suddenly had given two sharp cat-calls, in sheer, tom-cat mockery. Ciss was startled out of her skin. She fled indoors. If Aunt Pauline didn't hear that, she'd hear nothing.

Aunt Pauline had heard. She had been lying awake, musing and preparing herself for a struggle. The last few days she had felt her power slipping. She had such absolute authority over her immediate surroundings. She felt she must have. And these last few days, she had felt it in some way jeopardised, or questioned. She believed herself to be so absolutely the best influence, she simply *had* to shed her authority unquestioned over her own immediate world. And she had not been able to understand why the grip should have been slipping from her grasp, for a day or two.

She heard the cat-calls, and she was furious. She knew at once what it was. It was Ciss, that common she-cat, luring Robert out into the dark and inciting him to vulgar rebellion. And he was answering in real *gamin*◇ spirit. True street-arab! Pauline was furious. But now she knew what it was, she could cope with it.

Ciss was using the vulgar sex-power against her, Pauline. Pauline hated the vulgar sex-power. She liked a sublimated sex, what she called sex-imagination. A woman should use all her feminine powers to enhance the life of the imagination. The life of the imagination! In this Pauline felt at home, and immeasurably superior to all vulgar cat-calling and physical coarseness. A wave of hatred went over her, against that lumbering gutter-cat Ciss. She was perverting Robert. But Pauline would show her. She would show her who was stronger at that kind of game.

Saving herself till evening, Pauline did not appear next day until after lunch, when she came down to take her sun-bath. She took no notice of Ciss. Pauline believed that if she cut a person out of her consciousness, she cut them out altogether. And there was something in it. Ciss felt uneasy and weak, as she followed her Aunt Pauline to the bowling-green, and spread the rugs.

She was determined to go as usual to the roof, and listen. But she was feeling a little depressed. She picked up her big cat Jim, and carried him with her. He would sleep all the time, being a night-bird. But still he would be a support.

The sun was hot and biting. It seemed to bite into the flesh, and make one angry. Jim curled down in the shade near her, his blackness glistening silkily. And Ciss almost slept. She hardly listened any more for the voice.

"Chi lo sa, caro, se vale la pena!"◇ came the murmur, in a foreign language Ciss did not understand. She lay and writhed her limbs in anger, listening intently to words that conveyed nothing to her. Softly, whisperingly, with infinite caressiveness and yet with that subtle arrogance that made Ciss' blood boil, the voice went on in a velvet murmur: "Bravo, si, molto bravo, poverino! Ma uomo come te non sarà mai, mai. Non è eroe, lui, ne dell' amore ne dell' intelligenza."◇ – Oh, especially in Italian Ciss heard the poisonous charm of the voice, so ironical and so egoistic. She hated it with intensity as it sighed its insolence out of nowhere. It was so skilful and sure, it made her feel so clumsy and helpless, herself.

"No Robert dear, you will never be the man your father was. If you had it in you to be a lover such as he was, *nemmeno male!*◇ But you are a clown and fish in comparison. Mauro! Mauro! He gave himself to a woman as he gave himself to God. How he loved me! How he loved me! Soft as a flower, and as piercing as a humming-bird." The voice paused in a reverie of vanity. Then it resumed: "But you, Robert dear, are after all only an English half-breed. The rain has turned you fishy, and made you about as tempting, for a lover, as a fish-monger. You should leave love alone, dear, it will never be your *forte*. Never try to be physical; that is where your imagination quite gives out."

There was a pause in the complacency of the voice. Then it resumed:

"I am disappointed in you, Robert. You have no poignancy. Your father was a Jesuit, and poignant as a stiletto. To him, love was an art, and a secret religion. But you are like a thick old carp in a pond, and that Ciss is a common house-cat fishing for you. Of course, all she wants is a domestic establishment, and little house-cats of babies. Poor Henry did better than that: much better."

Cecilia suddenly put her mouth to the opening of the tube, and said in a quiet, angry voice:

"Leave Robert alone!"

This effort was like electric fluid rushing out of her body down the tube. It left her weak and collapsed upon the leads. The cat, rubbing against her in great uneasiness, uttered two sharp little *miaus*! Ciss lay weak and prostrate, her heart beating in great thumps. The July sun poured a thick heat, prickly with thunder. There was dead silence, for what seemed a long time. Then there came a small whisper:

"Did someone speak?"

The cat heard it, fluffed his tail and arched his back in terror, uttering a sharp, tiny *miau*! and looking anxiously at Ciss. She was oblivious, lying down and reaching her mouth to the tube to say:

"Take your will off Robert! Don't kill him as you killed me."

The cat fled. Ciss lay utterly spent on the roof, feeling as if all her life had gone down that pipe. Yet she listened avidly.

"That can't be Henry's spirit speaking?" mused the terrified voice in the tube, questioning.

Ciss bent over the pipe.

"Yes, it is!" she said, in a small but stern, voice-of-God tone.

There was a long silence. Ciss lay in utter terror, not knowing what had happened. Perhaps she had killed Aunt Pauline! She felt a shadow over her limbs, like a cool cover. Glancing up, she saw the sun had gone among yellowish, sinister cloud.

"Are you happy, Henry?" came the frightened whisper.

Ciss bent sternly over the tube.

"No! I wanted to live, and I didn't get a chance!"

She could just get these words out, then her lungs were empty.

"But you don't blame me, dear?" came the cajoling whisper.

Ciss was ready. She felt she could pour charge after charge of poison down that tube. Nothing could stop her.

"I do! I wanted to live, and you cut me off."

She spoke it, with the ultimate passion of her soul.

"But how? how?" came the remonstrance. Aunt Pauline would not give in easily, not even to a spirit.

"With your selfish will. You had power over me, and you never let me live my life."

Ciss spoke with fierce vengefulness. She did not know her own voice. She felt as if she really were possessed by Henry's vengeful spirit.

"I think you must be an evil spirit," came the troubled voice.

"I am not!" Ciss almost shouted into the tube. "You are an evil woman, and a cruel mother. I blame you for my death."

This was a truly terrible charge. She lay in terror of her own ferocity. She too felt an awful power surging up in her body. And she would use it remorselessly. She lay and panted, as the sky blackened.

"I think you must be an evil spirit, sent to try me," came the broken murmur up the tube.

"I am not. I am good! You are evil! I am watching over Robert."

Ciss lay inert, but her heart was hard and fierce. She felt as if a terrible battle were being fought down that rain-pipe. She could feel Aunt Pauline trying to save her face, trying to escape the accusation of evil. Aunt Pauline was wriggling and wriggling and wriggling to get away from the sense of her own guiltiness. And Ciss was determined she should not. She was determined to fix it on her. She should *not* escape. Evil she was, and she should be made, at last, to feel it. She should *not* escape! She should not emerge once more, for the millionth time, feeling good and blameless. This time the sense of her own guilt, her lifelong guilt of forcing her will over the lives of others, should be fixed on her. It should be fixed on her. She had escaped too often, and come out with a sense of innocence and superior righteousness. Now no more. She *must* feel her own guilt. It must be driven home into her like a stiletto, since she mentioned stilettos.

"Have you gone away?" came the faint murmur; still waiting to evade the sentence.

"No! I shall *never* go away. I shall accuse you till eternity. You are an evil woman, and you must stop working your evil."

A broken little cry of expostulation came up the tube. Then there was silence. Ciss lay and listened and listened. No sound! As if time had ceased, she lay in the deepening darkness of the sky, she knew not for how long. She felt everything darkening and darkening. And her heart was gradually loosening its tension. She seemed to be waking up. It was over. The weird game with her aunt was finished, and Ciss felt new and awkward, yet released. For the first time in her life, it seemed, she could breathe freely. Her anxiety was external.

The sky made her anxious. It was black, with fleecy yellow fringes. She felt something was going to happen. There would be a storm. Already came a breath of cold air. No sound came up the pipe. She dressed in a moment, and listened again. No sound! There was a far-off rumble of thunder, but no sound from her aunt.

Resuming her normal, housewife self, Ciss ran down and round to the corner of the bowling-green, calling:

"Are you ready, Aunt Pauline? I'm afraid there's going to be a storm."

There was no answer. She drew nearer, anxiously, and called again:

"Did you hear the thunder, Aunt Pauline?"

Still she hesitated to go round the corner of the hedge, for she was very averse from finding her aunt in a state of nudity. But thank heaven, Aunt Pauline's weak voice replied:

"Did someone call? I must have been asleep."

"Won't you go in? There's a storm coming," Ciss repeated.

And at the sound of that weak, false little voice of her aunt's, Ciss half wanted to burst into hysterical laughter.

"It's all right! I'm going!" snapped the voice.

Ciss retreated to her own regions, and waited. There was no sound. She went to the loft to watch. The thunder was coming nearer. And she saw Aunt Pauline, in her lovely blue silk wrap, creeping to the house, looking small and diminished. She had even forgotten to call.

A clap of thunder broke. Ciss rushed to carry in the rugs and the couch. She felt strong, and in spite of herself, rejoicing in the momentary overthrow of her enemy. She hardly felt it could be permanent. But she felt as if, with the thunder that now crashed, an ancient tightness was being broken in the atmosphere. There was a new freedom, an opening of the heart and of the whole soul. She no longer felt any rancour. She wanted to laugh, to laugh heartily as the thunder broke in great smashes, and the relieving rain at last fell in a stream. She wanted to laugh with relief.

The rain lasted all afternoon, and was still pouring when Ciss ran over to the house at tea-time. Aunt Pauline had telephoned down from her room, to ask her maid to take up a cup of tea. The thunder had upset her. She would not come down before dinner. So Ciss had tea alone, waiting for Robert.

It was still steadily raining when she heard the sound of the car. She went downstairs and along the covered passage to the garage. The car was splashed pale with mud, but Robert seemed bright-eyed, as if the weather had freshened him up.

"I wondered how you had got on, in the storm," she said, going near to him as if drawn by some force of attraction.

"I liked it – stir things up a bit," he said, glancing over her with a new light in his eyes. "How are you?"

"I'm all right!" she said softly.

He had pulled off his gloves, and suddenly he softly touched her cheek with his finger-tips. She flushed crimson, remembering that his father had been a Jesuit and a man to whom love was a secret religion. She looked at him searchingly, to see these new things in his face. And the hidden flame in his eyes, the pure fineness of his brow under the short dark hair, the mask-like creaminess of his cheeks seemed to show her that he too had the power for secret passion and intense secret voluptuousness.

"I think Tinia threw his third thunder,"* he said, though it meant nothing to her. Then, caressing her face again with his soft, cool fingertips, he asked, with a secret sort of casualness: "Where's mother?"

"She didn't come down to tea. But she's coming to dinner. Shall I make more tea for you?"

"No thanks!" He looked at her again, with a queer, glowing, and yet impersonal glance. And smiling faintly, he ran his finger-tips softly over her face, as a blind man might. He seemed in no hurry to go indoors.

"I suppose Annie will have telephoned up to mother that I am home," he said.

"Perhaps you had better do it," Ciss replied.

The rain left off before dinner. Ciss put on her nicest dress, of black velvet flowers on an orange chiffon background, and she took some white columbines, that stood nodding very dazed after the rain, to wear at her breast. It was almost a gala rig-out. Robert was alone in the drawing-room, as she came in with the white flowers nodding. He eyed her curiously.

"You are very handsome tonight," he said. "Is there anything special?"

"It's for you," she said, looking at him with a little smile. She saw him square his shoulders. His face had a queer, glimmering dangerous little look. Ciss could see he was holding himself together to meet his mother, and to have a silent battle of wills with her. There was a tension in the air, even though the storm had gone.

Ciss went uneasily over to the bookshelves near the door, to find a book. But she was in that frame of mind when there seemed no book she wanted, never anything she wanted. Robert stood silent on the rug by the softly-shaded lamp, waiting. The tension of waiting was almost unnerving. She felt almost paralysed, there at the book-shelves.

She heard a rustle outside, and a hand on the door, and in a sudden nervous access switched on the strong light over the books, just as her aunt, in a rather fluffy, young black dress, entered. Pauline stood for a moment in the full light in the door-way, as if bewildered. She looked a queer poppinjay, curiously withered under her careful make-up, and a little fantastic, with her artificial flowers and her pearls. She blinked irritably, as if long years of suppressed exasperation and dislike of her fellow-men had suddenly floated to the surface of her, and crumpled her like an old witch.

"Oh Aunt!" cried Cecilia, not having presence of mind to put down the book she had in her hands.

"Why Mother, you're a little old lady!" came the astounded voice of Robert: like an astonished boy, and with all the malice of youth.

"Have you only just found it out?" snapped the old woman venomously, as she hurried forward out of the light.

"Why yes!" stammered Robert. "I thought – "

"We won't trouble you for what you thought," interrupted his mother, gritty and dry and a jangle of nerves. "We'll go down."

She laid her hand viciously on his arm, and walked beside him with a wrinkled old face tilted in unspeakable irritation of nervous collapse. She had not even noticed the excess of light in the drawing-room, nor rebuked the guilty Ciss, who followed down the stairs wondering over the queer, tripping-tottering walk of her aunt tonight.

At table, Pauline sat with her face exaggeratedly calm, a crumpled mask of unspeakable irritation. She looked old, very old, and full of hate because she was old. She was something to be frightened of. But now, tonight, she was aloof, sitting somehow in the distance of her agedness and her exasperation, unable really to touch the young ones. Robert and Cecilia fetched furtive glances at her. Aunt Pauline was shattered like a piece of lovely Venetian glass that has been knocked over and broken to fragments. One ought to feel sorry for her, but one could not. She was nothing but sharp and ugly edges, like broken glass that hurts whoever touches it. Ciss saw that Robert was immeasurably repelled. He had thought her a lovely and charming woman. Now she was an ugly, repellant witch, utterly hard, and cutting as broken glass. She was not even pathetic, one could not feel sorry for her, she was so hard and rancorous.

"What kind of drive home did you have?" she snapped, suddenly becoming aware of the silence that hummed with surprise.

"It rained, of course," he said coolly.

"How clever of you to have noticed it!" she snapped, with an almost gibbering malice, a grisly grin of irritability on her face.

"In what way?" he said quietly.

But she only glanced at him sideways, with a rapid leer of hatred.

Rapidly and rather sloppily she ate her food, rushing through the meal like a crazy dog, to the utter consternation of the servant. It would all have been too horrible, if Ciss and Robert had not felt fortified by the strength of their silent sympathy. Ciss, who ought to have felt guilty, only thought to herself: Now! Now she shows up in her true colours! Now we can see what she really is, full to the brim with hate, now her will is thwarted!

The moment she had swallowed her strawberries, which she bit off their stalks showing all her teeth like a vicious dog, Pauline laid down her napkin and darted in a queer, crab-like way upstairs. It was as if she could not bear the presence of the young people, not for another second. Robert and Ciss followed in dumb amazement. On the landing Pauline looked

down with a grisly, girning° look at the face of Robert. It was
as if she were grinding her teeth.

"I'm not taking coffee," she said, and scuttled off to her
room. He was stunned with the thought: My God, how she
hates me! – He did not feel guilty. He only felt blank. Ciss, who
was the guilty one, kept her face utterly still. Pauline had not
spoken one word to her: could not trust herself. Very well! If
it was a battle to the death, it was a battle to the death. She,
Ciss, was not going to relent. With a face quite calm and
composed, she poured the coffee. Robert and she sat in silence
by the fire. It was chilly after the rain. Ciss pretended to read,
but she only stared at the print. And Robert merely smoked.
Nevertheless Ciss felt essentially at ease, at ease with him as if
he were her husband. She felt, somehow, as if their marriage
were already made.

"Mother isn't herself tonight," said Robert, out of the
silence.

"No," said Ciss, looking up at him. "I suppose it is the storm
that has upset her nerves."

The eyes of the two young people met. He understood,
really, what was happening. He and Ciss were two rebels
destroying silently and relentlessly the old authority. But he did
not know the secret of the rain-pipe. That she would never tell
him. That was part of her own private battle, in which the man
should not be mixed up. It was too ridiculous also.

"I think she had better see a doctor," he said.

"Or a priest," said Ciss.

His eyes met hers again for a second.

"You think a priest?" he said.

She did not answer, and they relapsed into silence. Why
should they talk? They both had a capacity for silence. It was
much more real to them than a lot of words, to sit there in the
stillness, in the same flow. Ciss felt at peace with him, inwardly.
Only outwardly, on the surface of her body, as it were, she was

fighting a battle with Aunt Pauline. So she sat and pretended to read, and he sat motionless, peacefully brooding.

The time passed wonderfully quickly. Ciss heard the clock softly strike ten. She ought to go. But it was so lovely, sitting there in the stillness with him, she did not want to break away.

Suddenly she heard a slight noise, and looking sharply round saw Aunt Pauline stealthily entering, wrapped in her blue wrap. Robert rose sharply from his chair. Pauline stealthily closed the door, and then looked from one to the other of the young people with that faint, gibbering smile of malice.

"You two had better get married quickly. It would look more decent," she said, in her broken, malevolent voice.

Ciss saw Robert square his shoulders.

"Really, Mother?" he said in that cool voice he used when he was outraged. "Is that your serious opinion?"

She looked at him in contempt.

"It wouldn't be, if only you were in question," she said. "But since your cousin Ciss is determined to have a husband at any price, you'd better make an open thing of it, and keep my house as clean as possible."

"You advise me to marry her, then?" he asked, with pointed coldness.

"As quickly as possible," said Aunt Pauline, girning.

"You no longer mind that we are cousins?" he asked.

"You never were," replied his mother. "Your father was an Italian priest." Pauline had advanced to the fire, and was holding her daintily slippered foot to the glow. Her body tried to repeat all the old, coquettish gestures, but her face and her voice were ugly.

"Is that true?" he asked.

"True?" she glanced round at him with that grisly smile of contempt. "You are right, it is hard to believe it. He was an *extraordinarily* distinguished man. He had to be, to be my lover. He was far too distinguished a man to have had you for a son. That small comfort was left to me."

She coolly warmed the other foot, with the old, serene gesture. She had taken her pitch on the field of battle. But her face was a horrid wrinkled mask.

Robert was silent, having nothing to say. Pauline still utterly disregarded the presence of Ciss in the room. But Ciss sat on. She was not going to be ousted either. The moments ticked off with hideous slowness, and nobody said anything.

Robert at last broke the silence, and he spoke like a lawyer.

"Whoever was my father, no doubt you are my mother," he said.

"Unfortunately," put in Aunt Pauline. "I would hardly have adopted you."

"And as my only parent, you approve of my marriage with Ciss?"

"You daren't do it without my approval, dare you?" said Pauline, looking at him with hideous jeering. It was the money she meant.

He went greeny white, but did not answer her question.

"I am to understand that you approve?" he repeated.

"You poor monkey," was all she said.

"Surely it is bad taste to talk like this!" Ciss put in softly.

Pauline turned on her.

"Who are you, living on my charity!" she said contemptuously.

"That is *very* charitable of you, Aunt Pauline," sang Ciss softly.

Again there was a sudden pause, as if a scotch◊ had been put in Pauline's wheels. Her face grinned again with aged malice.

"You are not yourself, Mother," said Robert. "You should see a doctor."

"I shall see a lawyer," she sneered. She meant her will.

"Listen Robert," said Ciss, suddenly rising. "Do you want to marry me, whatever happens? Just say the truth."

Both women fixed their eyes on him. He kept his face averted.

"I very much want to marry you, Ciss," he said rigidly.

There was a moment's pause, while Pauline curled her lip in contempt.

"You poor fool! Clinging to her petticoats already!" she sneered.

And unable to stand any more, she scuttled from the room.

Ciss and Robert looked at one another, and she saw that distress had a paralysing effect on him. But he sat down again in his chair by the dying fire, and she knew he would not *do* anything. He would remain on her side, but passive, in the strange contest.

"The only comfort left is to know I am a bastard," he said, looking up at Ciss with a wry glimmer of a smile.

"Do you mind?" she asked rather coldly.

"I am glad. Now I needn't try to be inside the pale.◦ But do *you* mind?"

"It means nothing to me," said Ciss. She shook off her inertia, and turned to go. "It is late. I'd better go. Good-night!"

"I'll come with you," he said.

They went in silence. The night was very dark. She felt she could not speak.

"It is difficult to feel the feeling of love, with this other thing hanging over one," he said, as if in apology.

"What other thing?" she asked.

"Mother! The strangle-hold," he said. "There's a feeling almost of murder in the air."

Ciss did not answer, but held his hand tight for a moment. Then she went in to her own place, leaving him. She locked her door fast, for she was frightened with an uncanny fear. It was as he said, there was a tension almost like murder in the night. Ciss was tired, and she wondered whether it would not be better to submit, to yield again to Aunt Pauline, and let the old rule sway again. It would be so much easier, and in a way, so much kinder. – But no! The fight had begun, and now it would have to go on. "My life or yours, Aunt Pauline!" said Ciss to herself, thinking aloud as Pauline did. – "Then better your life should go under. You have had your turn, and more. If you can't live and let live, better you should die."

There followed a week of pure horror. Pauline did not recover. It was as if the thread that held her nerves in control had snapped, and now she was one shrieking discord of nervous misery. The doctor came and gave her sedatives, for she never slept. And he said her heart was irregular in its beat. It was a sudden collapse.

She was a dreadful sight to look at, like a creature which has suddenly lost its soul, and become a jangling arrangement of shrieking nerves. She could not be still; she never slept. All the time she paced about, nervously twisting. Her face was wrinkled and evil, hideous with malevolence. It was awful for her and for everybody. It was evident she suffered tortures of nervous jarring; no physical pain, but a shrieking insanity of the nerves. She no longer left her room, except to make terrifying pointless excursions round the rooms and corridors, like a mad-woman. She could not bear to see either Ciss or Robert. Ciss stayed nearly all the time in her own house. She felt terribly upset about Aunt Pauline. It seemed so horrible. Yet she could never feel really sorry. Aunt Pauline reeked with malevolence, and one cannot feel compassionate towards gibbering malevolence.

Once, when Ciss and Robert sat at dinner – for Ciss was hardly ever in the big house save at dinner-time – Pauline suddenly stood in the doorway, gibbering with malice, her eyes swinging sideways from Ciss to Robert with a jeering evil leer.

"Married yet? Celebrated the nuptials yet, on the q.t.?"◇ she rapped out.

Ciss and the servant froze with horror. Robert rose to his feet, but before he could get to the door, she had gone, throwing at him the most ghastly leer of hatred, a simulacrum of an inviting, luring glance. It was too ghastly. All that she had been of egoistic loveliness, she was now of sheer horror.

And from day to day she shrivelled, living on drugs, for the servants said she ate nothing.

Ciss knew that it was she who had flung the stone which had shattered the mirror of Aunt Pauline's loveliness. Sometimes, when she was very weary, she would have done anything to recall those words down the rainpipe. She wept in pure misery and terror of what had resulted. And then again she hardened her heart. Let it be so!

Robert would now sit in Ciss' rooms in the evening after dinner. They were both of them frightened and depressed, as if they had a tomb-stone on their souls.

"Do you think life is always a thing of repulsive horror, if one goes below the surface?" he asked.

"Don't say it!" she pleaded. "People are fearfully cruel. You don't know how cruel my father's self-made deacons were to him, in his chapel. They were base, and they so enjoyed torturing him, because he was a better man than themselves. They killed him, really. But he always said: I can trust my God, when my fellow-men are too much for me."

"What God did he trust?" said Robert.

"I don't know. But he did trust. He died in trust. And it seemed to me so much finer than other people, just trusting their own selfish will, and then collapsing."

"And do you trust?" said he.

"Somewhere I do, Robert." She laid her hand on his. "If I didn't I should feel so awful and guilty. But now, thank goodness, I can cry and get it off my heart."

He mused for a time. Then he said:

"So you trust in God?"

"Oh, I'm not religious," she said. "You know that. But some kind of a God, somewhere, somehow – without a name. Don't you think? Nothing churchy. I am a clergyman's daughter. I know too much about that."

"Probably it is so," he said.

Towards the end of the week, Pauline sent for her niece. Ciss found her aunt in bed. Pauline was trying to smile, but she only showed her teeth in a grin.

"Sit down!" she said.

Ciss sat and waited.

"I'm quite serious about wanting Robert to marry you," snapped Pauline. "Do you think he's going to?"

"I think so," said Ciss quietly.

Pauline looked at her with an awful grin of a smile.

"Well – " she said. "I hope you'll be prepared to earn your own living."

"I don't think I shall mind that," said Ciss quietly.

"Well – " Pauline fixed a jeering look on her niece. "That remains to be seen. I want to give you a present. I'm not leaving you anything."

Ciss did not answer this. Aunt Pauline took an envelope from under her pillow, and held it out. Ciss rose and took it, mumbling thanks.

"Better open it," said Pauline.

Ciss obeyed. It was a hundred pounds in notes. She flushed, saying:

"I really didn't want you to give me money, Aunt."

"Oh, precisely," said Aunt Pauline.

Ciss rose quietly, looking at her aunt.

"Thank you very much for the present, Aunt Pauline," she said. "Is there anything I can do for you?"

The two women looked into each other's eyes, Pauline grinning cunningly and horribly. But Ciss was saying with her eyes: "I don't mind the ugly things you do. You only make yourself uglier, and bring your own death nearer. You don't touch me." And filled with a heavy kind of grief, she left the room.

The next day Pauline was found dead in her bed. The doctor said, heart-failure.

When Robert came home he went up to see her. She was pretty again, but shrunken, like a little old child. Something very childish about the poor dead face, that smote his heart suddenly. And at the same time, that look of wilfulness and imperviousness had now fixed and gone cold, and chilled the heart. Fixed in her own will, and impervious, even in death. And at the same time, the pathos of a maid who has died virgin and unlived. It is the contradiction of a woman hardened to her own will: she never lives, she only knows what it is to force life. Because living, for a woman, means the gentle interpenetration of her life into other lives, other lives into hers. And this poor Pauline had missed. She had only used her will on other people.

This was how Robert saw her. Ciss wept bitterly, for the woman lost. Yet even so, she hated the look of immune self-will on the dead face.

"Oh Robert," she said, "I don't want to be like that!"

"No," he said. "I don't want you to be. – It is as you say, there must be some sort of a God somewhere, and some sort of divine justice. Otherwise it's not worth having – life. One can go so awfully wrong, without knowing. Nobody tried to keep mother right, when she was a little girl. And she didn't know how to keep me right, when I was a boy. If there's no God of any sort to appeal to, Ciss, you've not got much of a catch in me."

Pauline was spiteful even in death. She left Robert two thousand pounds only, and Old Brinsley; the house, but not the valuable *objets d'art*. These latter, with all the rest of her money, were to go to the founding of the Pauline Attenborough Museum.

RESOURCE NOTES

Who has written the short stories and why?

D. H. Lawrence's life

Lawrence's first short story to be published, a Christmas love story called 'A Prelude', won him a prize of £3 in a local newspaper competition in 1907 when he was 22. Lawrence was so keen to win that he got two of his friends to submit other stories of his under their own names. This was the start of an interest as a writer in the short story form, which continued until his death in 1930. From the beginning, Lawrence wrote stories to explore relationships, situations and ideas which interested him, but also to secure recognition and earn money as a professional writer with no other income.

As a young man, Lawrence was also an avid reader of short fiction. From the letters he wrote to friends, we know that he was interested in the stories of late nineteenth-century European writers like Anton Chekhov, Leo Tolstoy, Ivan Turgenev and Guy de Maupassant, and the earlier Honoré de Balzac, as well as contemporary writers in English such as Thomas Hardy, Henry James and his friend Katherine Mansfield. However, Lawrence was often critical of aspects of other writers' work and consciously tried to do new things with the traditional short story form as his career developed.

Throughout his writing career, Lawrence drew heavily on real people, places and experiences to create his fiction. Sometimes this got him into trouble when friends and acquaintances recognised themselves in his books. Lawrence always insisted, though, that real life only provided him with suggestions and hints which he then developed in quite different ways through his art. His early stories, such as the first three in this book, are all developed from events, settings and characters he came across in the first 25 years or so of his life which he spent in the small mining town of Eastwood, near Nottingham, in the Midlands of England.

Lawrence was the fourth of five children. His father, Arthur, worked in the local, privately owned coal mine as a 'butty' – a subcontractor in charge of a small gang of men. He was a convivial man, an excellent dancer in his youth and fond of animals and plants. He could hardly read or write and spoke the local dialect with a broad accent. Lydia, Lawrence's mother, came from a different background. Her family had once been well off and she had received much more education. As a result, she always spoke standard English, enjoyed reading books, sometimes wrote poetry and often went to lectures and debates organised by her local chapel.

The differences in the upbringing and personality of Lawrence's parents led to conflict between them even before he was born. Arthur Lawrence began to drink more, became physically aggressive to his wife and increasingly isolated from his children. Lydia brought up her children to fear and despise their father and established a particularly close bond with her youngest son, David Herbert, known as Bert when he was living at home. Lawrence later recalled that he'd grown up thinking his mother was absolutely right in everything she told him, and it was only later, after her death at the end of 1910, that he gradually began to see things more from his father's side and to appreciate some of his father's positive qualities.

The first two stories, 'The White Stocking' and 'Odour of Chrysanthemums', which were both rewritten several times before final publication in 1914, show Lawrence writing about the wife–husband relationship in ways which are influenced by his parents' experiences and his later reflections on them. 'Odour of Chrysanthemums' is based on actual experience, on Lawrence's Aunt Polly who lived in the house described in the story and whose husband was killed in a mining accident. However, the emotions explored are those that Lawrence imagines in retrospect in his own mother as she waits for the drunken miner to come home.

Like James Joyce's Dublin, Lawrence's Eastwood provided him with a wealth of characters, situations and incidents outside of his immediate family which he could use and transform through his fiction. The next story, 'Daughters of the Vicar', which was also redrafted finally in 1914, is based, as far as external settings go, on local families and their circumstances, which Lawrence knew. Memories of the community he was brought up in stayed with Lawrence throughout his career, however much he later disliked the place.

After training as a teacher and working at a school in Croydon, south London, for three years, Lawrence reached a critical point in his life during 1910–1912. In this period, Lawrence broke off his longstanding relationship with Jessie Chambers, saw his mother die slowly of cancer, fell seriously ill with pneumonia, ended a short engagement with another girlfriend and finally eloped to the Continent with Frieda Weekley, the German wife of his former university tutor. Frieda was to become Lawrence's partner and later his wife, in a relationship every bit as stormy as that of Lawrence's own parents. She also became an important influence on Lawrence's writing, as Jessie had been previously.

'The Prussian Officer' was written initially in Germany in 1913, and draws on the military locations and background of Frieda's family, the aristocratic von Richthofens. The setting and atmosphere contrast strongly with the earlier stories, suggesting how quickly Lawrence was able to assimilate what he called 'the spirit of place' of a foreign location and its new and very different social structures. 'The Prussian Officer' became the title story of Lawrence's first collection of short stories when it was revised and also published in 1914.

During the First World War, Lawrence and Frieda were stranded in England against their will. He later described the period as a long nightmare, which included being suspected of spying, partly because of Frieda's German connections. The war had a profound effect on Lawrence: he later said it destroyed all his hopes, both personal and for the future of industrial society. In the stories 'Tickets Please' (revised in 1921) and 'The Blind Man' (1918), Lawrence uses situations brought about by war: the employment of women on public transport and the effects of a war injury on a returned soldier. 'Hadrian' (1919) also features a man returning to his adopted home after the war. Characteristically, Lawrence uses the situations to investigate the personal and physical relationships both between women and men and between men.

After the war, Lawrence travelled around the world and lived for short periods in Italy, New Mexico in the USA, and France. In the final three stories he draws on his experience of more cosmopolitan middle- and upper-class social groups to explore different responses to the postwar situation.

Lawrence ran into a familiar problem with 'The Man Who Loved Islands' (1926). Compton Mackenzie, a writer Lawrence knew who bought and lived on a number of islands, objected that he was the model for the character. Lawrence replied that some of the circumstances were Mackenzie's, but 'the man is no more he than I am'. However, the story was not published in Britain until after Lawrence's death.

The next two stories in this selection, 'The Lovely Lady' (1927) and 'The Rocking-Horse Winner' (1926), were written as a murder/mystery and a ghost story respectively for a friend, Cynthia Asquith, who was compiling anthologies. Lawrence tackled the commissions in his own idiosyncratic way and had to admit that 'The Lovely Lady' was 'not very murderous' in the end. Both stories concentrate more on the psychological rather than the supernatural aspects of the events described.

Activity
Choose a story in which you feel Lawrence has made use of
real people, places or events. Use the index of a biography of
Lawrence (see Further Reading on page 332) to research more
biographical details behind the story. Decide how Lawrence
has changed things for the purposes of his fiction. Why has he
made these alterations?

Historical and cultural background
Lawrence's 25-year writing career coincided with a period of
rapid change and uncertainty affecting all aspects of life in
Western industrial society. The early decades of the twentieth
century saw technological advances such as the motor car, radio
and cinema being developed to create mass communication and
transport for the first time. Alongside this second industrial
revolution, new ideas about how society should be organised
became popular. This ferment came to a head in the First World
War of 1914–1918, fought between the European capitalist
nation states and later the USA, which gave rise to the Russian
revolution and the world's first Communist state. In the 1920s,
Communist and Fascist ideologies spread to other countries such
as Germany, Italy and later Spain, a development which Lawrence
witnessed at first hand and warned about.

In the arts there were corresponding developments which
challenged traditional methods and values. Modernism is the
name now given to this new approach to painting, sculpture,
architecture and music, as well as literature. It was characterised
by a desire to experiment, to reject old certainties and replace
them with a new relativism in the face of the challenge posed by
the mass culture of film, newspaper and radio. There was an
upsurge of interest in theories about the human unconscious being
formulated by Sigmund Freud and parallel discoveries about
primitive societies by anthropologists such as James Frazer.
Lawrence was particularly interested in these findings about the

importance of irrational forces within human individuals and communities.

In fiction, James Joyce and Virginia Woolf, and in poetry Ezra Pound and T. S. Eliot, were in the forefront of modernist writing in English. Lawrence shares with them a concern to establish new techniques in narrative and verse in order to express the uncertainties of living in a brave new world. However, Lawrence was always too much of an individualist to actually identify himself for long with any other writer or movement in his lifetime. As a poet, for example, he published work in both the conservative Georgian poetry anthologies, which tended to celebrate the traditions of English rural life, and the radical imagist ones, which were more international and experimental in approach. His own personal agenda was always very strong in whatever he wrote. There is no doubt, though, that Lawrence's writings were inspired by his times, and given a different historical and cultural context, he would have been a different and possibly less interesting writer.

✦ *Activities*

1 Construct a time line featuring some of the important political, cultural and technological developments of the period 1900–1930 (for example, the women's suffrage movement, the General Strike, publication of T. S. Eliot's *The Waste Land*, the beginning of British cinema and radio, the first mass production car). Plot the publication of Lawrence's stories and some of his major novels against these.

2 Aim to do some more detailed research into Lawrence's life, then, in pairs, role-play an interview with Lawrence. Try to establish the background influences on his writing, particularly the short stories selected here.

✦

What type of texts are the short stories?

The history of storytelling

Storytelling is older than literature: it emerges from an oral tradition of folk narrative which survives today in myths, legends and fairy tales. Children listen to stories and learn to tell them from a very early age. People tell stories every day of their lives, to themselves and to others, which is why narrative has been called 'a primary act of mind', an essential part of being human. Think of occasions when you've told stories over the past week, for example, as jokes, anecdotes, excuses, gossip, and so on.

Written stories, in prose or poetry, have a more recent origin. Geoffrey Chaucer's *The Canterbury Tales* from the fourteenth century is one of the first examples in English. 'Tales' have continued to be written since then, often appearing in ephemeral form in broadsheets, newspapers and magazines, sometimes being highly moralistic parables or fables, sometimes deliberately 'pulp fiction'. Like the novel, the short story can be written in different genres, such as ghost, horror, murder, detective, romance and science fiction. Here the reader expects the story to conform to certain rules and conventions, though often the skill of the writers is judged by how well they can vary the elements within the standard formula. The short story is sometimes said to be the most popular literary form today because of its widespread publication and large, varied readership. You might consider occasions when you read short fiction, for example stories in magazines or newspapers.

The literary short story

The literary short story in English, which Lawrence is consciously writing, has an even more recent tradition. It wasn't until the nineteenth century that writers began to exploit the potential of the short prose narrative, which could usually be read at one sitting and which was crafted so that it had 'a certain unique or single effect', 'a unity of impression', as the American writer Edgar Allan Poe (1809–1849) described it. Poe was one of the first writers to develop the form in English, and is often called the originator of genres such as the horror and detective story. His stories are characterised by strong plots, usually with a twist at the end, and often deal with extraordinary events. They have a definite beginning, middle and conclusion. Writers such as the American Kate Chopin (1850–1904), the British writer Saki (1870–1916), and more recently Roald Dahl (1916–1990), have continued in this tradition in their different ways. You may have encountered stories like this in school anthologies you've used or perhaps in adaptations for radio or television.

A rather different kind of literary short story has its origins later in the nineteenth century and at the beginning of the twentieth. When the stories of the Russian Anton Chekhov (1860–1904) began to appear in English translation towards the end of his life they became highly influential. Here were stories which often dealt with more humdrum experience, often concentrating on a particular situation or incident and its effect on the relationships of a group of characters, rather than having a strong linear plot. Often the ending was inconclusive or left to be imagined by the reader. This kind of story was once described as 'all middle, like a tortoise' (by John Galsworthy), which echoes Chekhov's own advice to writers: 'I think when one has finished writing a short story one should delete the beginning and end.' Katherine Mansfield (1888–1923), James Joyce (1882–1941) and more recently William Trevor (1928–) have continued this kind of short story, again in their own individual ways. Has this type of story also appeared in anthologies you've read or in radio and television versions you've encountered?

Lawrence's stories

As a self-taught writer of short stories, Lawrence was influenced from the start by his wide reading of many of the different kinds of stories mentioned above. His earliest attempts at the form were in a realistic, heavily-plotted mode, often rather sentimental in tone and written in an overblown style, imitative of late-nineteenth-century writers. However, he later heavily revised many of his early stories, producing the present versions of 'The White Stocking' and 'Odour of Chrysanthemums'. As he began to find his own voice, by focusing attention on critical moments in relationships rather than on plot details, he introduced a Chekhovian blend of realism and symbolism (the stocking and the chrysanthemums, for instance, are real items but with symbolic value), and evolved a sparer, less indulgent narrative style. 'The Prussian Officer' is a clear example of a story, written in a comparatively bare, unsentimental style, which is mostly 'middle', being about a master–servant relationship which changes irrevocably in a crucial instant.

As he developed, Lawrence used his increasing mastery of the short story form to explore themes and ideas which preoccupied him, particularly his concern that modern, industrial civilisation was destroying the instinctual side of human consciousness. He began to construct his personal 'philosophy' with its own symbolic system (for example, associating light and coldness with the rational and darkness and warmth with the passional). This symbolism is present in 'The Prussian Officer', but comes through even more strongly in 'The Blind Man'. Despite his acquired craft in the story form, sometimes the 'philosophy' is in danger of distorting the fiction at this stage. Think of the ending to 'Hadrian', for example. Do you find it abrupt and rather hard to accept?

In the last phase of his career, Lawrence consciously moved away from the symbolic realism of the short story as he had evolved it, and more towards the structures of fable, myth and fairy story, as in 'The Man Who Loved Islands'. He also for the first time engaged with the popular genres of the ghost and murder story, which Edgar Allan Poe had established. In an essay on Poe, Lawrence comments that 'Murder is not just killing. Murder is a lust to get at the very quick of life itself, and kill it' (in *Studies in Classic American Literature*, 1924). In 'The Lovely Lady', the murder is psychological and the lovely lady herself is guilty of it too, just as in 'The Rocking-Horse Winner' the ghostly voices are echoes of the children's unconscious wish for more money. Lawrence reinterprets the conventions of these genre stories in his own way, helped perhaps by the example of Henry James's psychological ghost story *The Turn of the Screw* (1898).

What counts as a short story?

Short stories are *not* necessarily defined by length! In this selection, for instance, the length varies from 'Daughters of the Vicar', which is more than 20,000 words, to 'Tickets Please', which is about 5,000. The difference between stories and novels is more to do with structure. Whereas the novel usually deals with a large number of diverse characters and events over an extended time span and divides its narrative into chapters, the short story is more unified and concentrated in its construction, attempting to work within a small frame. Think of it as the difference between a movie and a still photograph or series of photographs.

✦ *Activities*

1 In which of the two traditions, Poe's or Chekhov's, would you place the Lawrence stories which you have read from this selection?

2 Compare *either* 'The Rocking-Horse Winner' *or* 'The Lovely Lady' with other ghost or murder stories you have read. Prepare an argument to present to a small group either for or against the stories being considered part of these genres.

3 You have been commissioned by the BBC to select a Lawrence story for broadcast on the radio. The reading will

last 25 minutes and be broadcast in the evening. Choose a suitable story, list the reasons for your choice and record a sample extract on tape. The reading should be dramatised using different voices and it will be necessary to edit or shorten the text.

4 The situation in 'Odour of Chrysanthemums' was also explored by Lawrence in a play, *The Widowing of Mrs Holroyd*.

a Plan how you might adapt the story as a three-act stage play.

b Write the opening to the first scene of your adaptation, using stage directions and dialogue.

c Look at Lawrence's version of it or watch a video of the BBC TV production (1995). What has been lost or gained in your opinion by the change to a different form? What difference is made by the fact that in *The Widowing of Mrs Holroyd* there is another man, Blackmore, who is a rival to the husband?

◆

How were the short stories produced?

Methods of work

The book which established Lawrence's reputation as a fiction writer was *Sons and Lovers* (1913). When the book was first reviewed, Lawrence was infuriated by criticism of its 'formlessness': he had written to his editor 'it has got form – *form*: haven't I made it patiently out of sweat as well as blood' (*Letters*, 14 November 1912). However, critics have often repeated the charge that Lawrence was unable or unwilling to craft his work, which is seen as the flawed outpourings of a wild, untutored genius.

A closer look at Lawrence's methods of work makes this charge seem less valid. Lawrence *did* revise his writing, constantly and comprehensively. Each major novel, for example, was rewritten three or four times. The same process was applied to the short stories. However, what was different about Lawrence's redrafting from that of most writers was that he physically wrote out the whole of his text again by hand. He wasn't content to cross out or insert bits here or there; he started again each time. This was because the *rhythm* of the prose and of the story as a whole was very important to him and only in this way, by total immersion in the story, could he reshape it. Repeated rewriting was central to Lawrence's creative processes: it enabled him to *discover* what he wanted to say and how he needed to say it.

'The White Stocking' is a good example of how Lawrence transformed a story. It began as one of his entries for a competition in the *Nottinghamshire Guardian* at Christmas 1907 (in the 'Most Amusing' story category, which it didn't win!). At this stage it was no more than an anecdote from his mother's youth about an embarrassing incident that happened at a dance. Lawrence crafted it over the next seven years through five or six drafts into a convincing psychological study of the tensions of young married life presented in a carefully structured narrative form.

Publication

Once Lawrence had produced a finished draft to send to a publisher, that wasn't the end of the revising process. Much to the annoyance of his printers, it was Lawrence's habit to make substantial changes to the pages he was sent for proofreading. Usually his short stories were first published in literary magazines or anthologies before being collected into a book; this ensured an immediate and reasonably regular income, since book royalties only accumulated slowly. However, when Lawrence did publish a collection of stories he would thoroughly revise the magazine versions yet again before including them. When Lawrence rewrote a story after a long period of time, his redrafting often changed the text dramatically to reflect either his changed views or developing literary style. Often editors made him cut stories or tone them down for their magazines or anthologies, and Lawrence was able to reverse these changes later.

Lawrence published three short story collections in his lifetime: *The Prussian Officer and Other Stories* (1914) included the first four in this selection; *England, My England and Other Stories* (1922) contained the next three; and *The Woman Who Rode Away and Other Stories* (1928) included 'The Man Who Loved Islands' in its American edition. The other two stories selected here appeared in a posthumous collection, *The Lovely Lady* (1933).

✦ *Activities*

1 'Odour of Chrysanthemums' is the story in this selection which went through the most drafts (at least six) between its original composition in 1909, magazine publication in 1911 and book publication in 1914. In particular, Lawrence

changed the ending drastically. Here is the ending as published in *The English Review* in June 1911:

> It was this adolescent "he," the young man looking round to see which way, that Elizabeth had loved. He had come from the discipleship of youth, through the Pentecost of adolescence, pledged to keep with honour his own individuality, to be steadily and unquenchably himself, electing his own masters and serving them till the wages were won. He betrayed himself in his search for amusement. Let Education teach us to amuse ourselves, necessity will train us to work. Once out of the pit, there was nothing to interest this man. He sought the public-house, where, by paying the price of his own integrity, he found amusement: destroying the clamours for activity, because he knew not what form the activities might take. The miner turned miscreant to himself, easing the ache of dissatisfaction by destroying the part of him which ached. Little by little the recreant maimed and destroyed himself.
>
> It was this recreant his wife had hated so bitterly, had fought against so strenuously. She had strove, all the years of his falling off, had strove with all her force to save the man she had known new-bucklered with beauty and strength. In a wild and bloody passion she had fought the recreant. Now this lay killed, the clean young knight was brought home to her.

Compare this with the final paragraphs of the later version of the story.

a How has Lawrence developed the style of the passage?

b What imagery has been left out, in particular?

c How has the third-person point of view of the narrative been modified?

2 When Lawrence first wrote 'Daughters of the Vicar' in 1911, he called it 'Two Marriages' (this manuscript version is published in the Cambridge Edition of *The Prussian Officer and Other Stories*). He ended the story then with a page telling the reader what happened to Louisa and Alfred in their later married life (for example, they lived locally but she was socially isolated; he occupied himself with house and

garden and was quiet; they were happy together and had several children). Lawrence deleted this conclusion when he revised the story three years later. Why do you think he did this and what is your feeling about the present ending?

3 'The Lovely Lady' was cut to nearly half its original length when first published in the anthology of murder stories *The Black Cap* in 1927. The Cambridge text printed here is the first to use Lawrence's original text. All previous selections have used the abridged version. Look in an older anthology (for example, Penguin) and compare the two texts. Which version do you think is more effective?

◆

How do the short stories present their subjects?

Themes

Central to D. H. Lawrence's philosophy is a conviction of the importance of unconscious, emotional impulses associated with the body, which he felt were usually over-controlled by the mind. A healthier balance was needed, Lawrence felt, between irrational and rational forces within people. In his fiction, the unconscious impulses felt by characters are often associated with sensory experience, especially physical touch, and darkness, whereas intellectual control is associated with the sense of sight only and with light.

Often pairs of characters are presented in the stories who exemplify excessive reliance on mind and will power or on physical instinct. Think of Massey and Alfred in 'Daughters of the Vicar'; the Prussian officer and his orderly; Bertie and Maurice in 'The Blind Man'. Each pair seems to represent the two halves of a whole, as the final scene of 'The Prussian Officer' suggests, when the two men lie side by side in the mortuary. In the other two stories it is the dilemma of the central female characters, Louisa and Isabel, to try to reconcile the warring elements in the two men they encounter.

Lawrence seems to be suggesting the need for a better integration of mind and body, of what psychologists call the *ego* (the conscious self) and the *id* (the unconscious, instinctive forces in us). In a number of the stories, characters wake up or are woken up, literally in the case of Hadrian, to a new awareness of themselves and others. Sometimes the realisation comes in time, as with Robert in 'The Lovely Lady'; sometimes too late, as for the wives and mothers in 'Odour of Chrysanthemums' and 'The Rocking-Horse Winner'; or it is only dimly perceived, as with the orderly in 'The Prussian Officer'.

✦ *Activity*

Choose two or three stories from the first seven included here. Trace the theme of physical experience in conflict with intellectual experience by drawing up a chart for each story on a large sheet of paper:

Title of story:

Main character(s):

Reasons for conflict:

Incidents involving physical contact:

Resolution of story:

When you've filled in the chart, think about these questions:

a Another title for 'Hadrian' is 'You Touched Me'. Could this be used as a title for any of the other stories?

b Were you more struck by the similarities or the differences between the stories? Did you notice any similarities as you read the stories, or only afterwards?

c Consider the endings of the stories and the way they resolve conflict between characters. Are there any instances where you feel Lawrence's philosophy has distorted his fiction?

Issues

Lawrence links the destructive imbalance in his characters' psyches with the effects of modern, industrial society. Society, he feels, has exalted the individual will and intellect at the expense of a feeling of community and of connection with the natural environment. Lawrence's language and imagery link rationalism with coldness, separateness, alienation and individualism. 'The Man Who Loved Islands' is a parable about what happens when someone tries to be 'an island unto himself', and cuts himself off from both humanity and nature. Pauline, the 'lovely lady', illustrates how a domineering individual can psychologically murder or maim her own sons. The money-obsessed mother in 'The Rocking-Horse Winner' also has a 'little hard place' at the heart of her which her son dies trying to placate.

On the other hand, the unconscious is linked with warmth, with physical and communal life, being literally 'in touch' with yourself and other people. In some of the stories the conflict between the two kinds of consciousness takes place on the level of social class, as with the Lindley and Durant families in 'Daughters of the Vicar'. Similarly, in 'Hadrian' the two sisters think the adopted boy is 'common' and 'doesn't know his place' and Hadrian complains there is 'too much difference between the men and the employers' in Britain, unlike Canada. But a feature of Lawrence's stories is the variety of social classes he writes about, ranging from the mining family in 'Odour of Chrysanthemums', to the middle-class setting of 'The Blind Man', to the upper-class world of 'The Rocking-Horse Winner'. Lawrence was convinced that his analysis of Western civilisation's problems was valid at every level of society. He confessed himself to be, socially, an 'in-between', belonging completely to no one social class, finding the working class 'deep but narrow' and the middle class 'broad but shallow'.

Lawrence lived during the time of the women's suffrage movement and often referred to women's struggle for civil and political rights. He once said that he wanted to 'do his work for women' through his fiction writing. Certainly his fiction contains many women characters. However, Lawrence's portrayal of women and men has been strongly attacked by some critics as dangerously reinforcing stereotypical roles. George Orwell said that the moral of 'The White Stocking', for example, seemed to be 'that women behave better if they get a sock on the jaw occasionally' (*Tribune*, 16 November 1945).

Activities

1 Think about the main characters in the stories you have read. Where would you place them in terms of social class on this scale?

lower class / lower middle / upper middle / upper class

In his treatment of these characters do you feel Lawrence shows any bias for or against any particular social class? You may need to discuss what *you* understand by these terms, and to compare your definitions to Lawrence's.

2 Note how many of the stories presented here are mainly about women, and look at the main female characters in at least three of them. How often are women presented in a dominant role? Are they able to make choices for themselves or are choices made for them by male characters at important moments?

3 Make lists of the words most frequently applied to the main male and female characters in one of the stories you've read. For example, in 'The White Stocking':

Elsie	Whiston	Adams
little	warm	gallant
childish	slow	roué
etc.	etc.	etc.

Compare the words listed. Do the words tend to confirm or challenge traditional conceptions of masculinity and femininity? Now choose another story (for example, 'Daughters of the Vicar' or 'The Lovely Lady') and compile similar lists. How do these match up with the previous ones?

4 Imagine you are the editor of a school edition of Lawrence's stories. The publishers are concerned about possible charges of 'political incorrectness' from their advisory board of teachers. At a meeting with them you are asked to defend this present selection of stories in terms of their portrayal of gender roles, of old people (for example, Pauline Attenborough) and of people with disability (for example, Mr Massey or Maurice, the blind man) and their representation of violence. Compile a case in

defence of Lawrence, drawing on specific stories to back up your argument.

Narrative structure and language

Lawrence's fiction is sometimes criticised for being monotonous and dominated by his own voice and personality. In fact, Lawrence chooses to tell his stories in a variety of different ways. For example, 'The White Stocking' uses a three-part structure, with a flashback episode in the middle; 'Odour of Chrysanthemums' takes place over a matter of hours like a play; and 'Daughters of the Vicar' spans many years and is divided into fifteen sections. Lawrence is certainly capable of using a strong narrator presence, as in the ironic voice used in 'The Man Who Loved Islands' or the comic voice in 'Tickets Please'. However, he is also able to use third-person narration flexibly so as to put the reader inside the consciousness of a character, as in 'Odour of Chrysanthemums' or 'The Prussian Officer'. This technique is known as free indirect speech or thought, and blurs the boundary line between the direct speech of characters and the voice of the narrator. Lawrence often uses this free indirect style in a story to alternate between characters: in 'Daughters of the Vicar', for instance, you sometimes see their relationship from Louisa's viewpoint and sometimes from Alfred's. Similarly, in 'The White Stocking' the standpoint is sometimes Elsie's and sometimes Whiston's.

When characters do speak directly in the stories, Lawrence presents their voices using a variety of types of language, from informal slang between the husband and wife at the start of 'The White Stocking', to strong local dialect and accents in 'Odour of Chrysanthemums', to childish speech and more formal, upper-class conversation in 'The Rocking-Horse Winner'. Lawrence sometimes uses language differences between characters to suggest deeper conflicts, as with the contrast between Alfred Durant's dialect and Mr Massey's standard English.

Lawrence once wrote defensively:

> In point of style, fault is often found with the continual, slightly modified repetition. The only answer is that it is natural to the author: and that every natural crisis in emotion or passion or understanding comes from this pulsing, frictional to-and-fro, which works up to culmination.
>
> (Foreword to *Women in Love*, 1920)

The use of this kind of repetition is less pronounced in the short stories, but some readers are still irritated by it, feeling that Lawrence should have edited it out. As Lawrence explains, he is attempting to follow the rhythms of our emotions and to get inside his character's consciousness through this stylistic feature. Lawrence's prose often works rhythmically, like poetry, as well as on an intellectual level, and his methods of writing and revising emphasised this. However, if you look closely at passages of Lawrence's writing, you will see that often there is not straightforward repetition but the weaving of a complex and shifting web of words and associations. Lawrence chooses his words carefully: often in passages which appear to be just 'description' you will find meanings and associations which accurately 'place' the person or setting being depicted within a set of values.

Activities

1 'The Rocking-Horse Winner' begins: 'There was a woman who was beautiful ...'. 'The Man Who Loved Islands' starts like this: 'There was a man who loved islands ...'. These openings set up expectations in the reader of a fairy tale or mythic narrative. One common feature of these kinds of narratives is the 'rule of three': the story often develops through incidents which occur three times in succession. Often the initial situation in such tales involves a lack of something or a need which is resolved at the end (think of 'Hansel and Gretel', where the initial poverty which causes

the parents to abandon the children repeatedly in the woods is remedied by the discovery of the witch's gold at the end).

Trace the plot development of these two late stories and see whether they fit this pattern:

- initial situation/need
- first incident
- second incident
- third incident
- resolution.

Are there any other similarities with fairy tale or myth in these stories or others (for example, 'Tickets Please')?

How do the endings of the stories compare to the endings of fairy tales? How does the structure of 'The Lovely Lady' compare to the other two late stories?

2 Read closely the first four paragraphs of 'Odour of Chrysanthemums'. On a photocopy, highlight words and phrases Lawrence has used which you think have more than a simple descriptive meaning (for example, 'insignificantly trapped', 'stagnant light', 'passed like shadows'). How do these words and phrases gain extra significance in the context of the whole story as it unfolds?

3 Lawrence rarely wrote a short story in first-person narration. Choose one of the stories you know well and rewrite a passage from near the beginning in the first person ('The Prussian Officer' would be an interesting example).

What gains and losses do you think there are for the writer and for the reader in changing the point of view?

If the first-person narration continued right through, do you think it would become a different story?

Could the ending of your chosen story stay the same?

4 Choose one or two of the stories from the first five included here. Look at the dialogue between the main characters and note down which characters Lawrence has represented as

speaking Nottinghamshire English and which ones speak standard English. Make a table of your findings under these headings:

Character	Male/Female	Local dialect	Standard English

Is the local dialect spoken more often by male or female characters?

What qualities do the characters who speak in dialect display? Sort these into positive and negative ones.

What difference would it make if the standard English speakers used dialect?

◆

Who reads the short stories and how do they interpret them?

Early reviews

The earliest reaction to his stories was extremely encouraging for D. H. Lawrence. On the strength of reading the opening of 'Odour of Chrysanthemums' in 1909, the editor of *The English Review*, Ford Madox Ford, said he was convinced that Lawrence would be a major writer. When the story was finally published in that literary magazine, it impressed the publisher Martin Secker so much that he offered to publish a complete book of Lawrence's short stories.

The first press reviews were more mixed. The *Prussian Officer* stories published in 1914 (including the first four printed here) were praised as 'powerful':

> vivid, memorable … sincere in truthful passion and taut with painful life
>
> (*Glasgow Herald*, 17 December)

But most reviewers commented on the 'morbid' and 'brutal' aspects of the stories:

> Mr Lawrence does not fear grossness, but there are times when we may fear it for him; it must be understood that this is not a gentlemanlike book.
>
> (*Manchester Guardian*, 10 December)

This criticism of the 'sex and violence' in his work was one which Lawrence had to live with throughout his career.

The reaction to the *England, My England* stories in 1922 (including 'Tickets Please', 'The Blind Man' and 'Hadrian') was more sympathetic. Lawrence was by now established as a writer. One reviewer, for example, talked about:

the growth of the new English short story in the hands
primarily of Miss Katherine Mansfield, Mr D. H. Lawrence
and Mr [A. E.] Coppard. The greatest of these three is
undoubtedly Mr Lawrence, who stands isolated, without
precedent and progeny.

(*Saturday Review*, 24 June).

Lawrence's stories were now published in the USA, and he found
American critics much more positive than British ones. An
American reviewer wrote: 'the stories are all written in a flexible
style of fine shadings and swift, delicate strokes', which made
demands on the reader but gave a lot of pleasure to those who
responded (*New York Times Book Review*, 19 November).

Lawrence's later stories were mostly favourably reviewed.
'The Man Who Loved Islands' was called a masterpiece:
'fantastic, but really imaginative in its wealth of possible
meaning' (*The Times Literary Supplement*, 19 January 1933).
One critic praised 'The Rocking-Horse Winner' memorably as:
'like a Hans Andersen sophisticated by Freud, or Poe let loose
in the nursery', a first-rate story, 'bizarre, but powerful'
(*Nation*, 1933).

Later criticism

Lawrence's short stories have always lived in the shadow of his
major novels, which have received much more critical attention
since his death in 1930. The standing of the stories has
fluctuated along with Lawrence's reputation as a novelist. This
reached a low in the 1940s when Lawrence was neglected, but
revived in the mid-fifties with the work of the influential critic
F. R. Leavis and achieved a peak in the 1960s in the era of
'sexual liberation', when *Lady Chatterley's Lover* was put on
trial for obscenity and acquitted. The 1970s and early 1980s
saw another dip in Lawrence's popularity, when Marxist and
Feminist critics exposed what they felt were shortcomings in
Lawrence's treatment of gender and social class issues.

Both Marxist and Feminist criticism pointed to similar contradictions in Lawrence's attitude to society and to the place of women within it. For example, the Marxist critic Terry Eagleton wrote that:

> Lawrence's fiction represents one of the century's most powerful literary critiques of industrial capitalism ... Yet ... Lawrence was a major precursor of fascism ... These contradictions come to a crisis in Lawrence with the First World War, the most traumatic event of his life.
> (*Criticism and Ideology*, 1976)

Eagleton felt that after the war Lawrence began to believe in an authoritarian social order, which rejected the 'female' principle of compassion and care for others in favour of the 'male' principle of power and dominance over others.

Hilary Simpson also saw the First World War as a turning point in Lawrence's treatment of women. She thought that Lawrence, like many men at the time, found it hard to come to terms with the new-found freedom women gained during the war, when they took over traditionally male jobs and roles (like the women conductors in 'Tickets Please'):

> In Lawrence's postwar exploration of power relationships and 'savage energies', male dominance plays a crucial part. Lawrence develops in the twenties an explicit anti-feminism which is of a different quality from the more open-ended probings of love and power to be found in his earlier work.
> (*D. H. Lawrence and Feminism*, 1982)

Today there is growing interest in Lawrence as a writer who has something to say and a way of saying it which is relevant and interesting to our media-sophisticated and 'postmodernist' times. His explorations into male–female relationships and into the relationship between people and their environment (Lawrence was a 'green' before the term existed) strike a chord with many readers. Recently, Lawrence's short fiction has been rediscovered and given more attention in its own right. This has been helped by the establishment of reliable texts, like the ones printed here, which present the stories as close as possible to the way Lawrence wanted them, before editors and publishers interfered, and show the craft with which he worked at them.

Your own reading

Your reading of these stories will be unique. It is important to hold on to your initial impression of these short stories in your interaction with the texts as you read them. Jotting down reactions in a reading journal or on tape, before, during and after reading sessions, can help to preserve these responses. It's equally important to share your responses with other readers in the group or community of students you work with. Through this kind of collaborative discussion or activity you negotiate and modify the meanings you find in literary works. Remember also that each time you read a text (and short stories are easily reread) you will emerge with a slightly different interpretation, like a musician playing from a score.

Lawrence's advice to readers was:

> Never trust the artist. Trust the tale. The proper function of a critic is to save the tale from the artist who created it.
> (*Studies in Classic American Literature*, 1924)

He is directing your attention primarily to the stories themselves rather than what the writer or critic claims they are about. It's always helpful to be aware of different critical opinions, but you will never find one 'correct' interpretation.

Activities

1 How do you think Lawrence's stories would be reviewed by book critics today? Write a review of one or more of the

stories for a specific newspaper or magazine, or prepare a script to read on a radio arts programme.

2 Choose any short story and 'read' it from a Feminist point of view. You might find 'The White Stocking', 'Tickets Please' and 'Hadrian' particularly interesting to look at from this perspective.

3 Any adaptation of a literary text to another medium is a critical interpretation of it. 'The Rocking-Horse Winner' is the only story of the ones included here to have been made into a full-length film (1949). However, some of the stories have been made into TV drama. Imagine you have been approached by a TV channel to produce a series of screenplays based on Lawrence's stories. Choose six stories which you think would adapt well for a modern audience. Give your reasons for the choices you've made and suggest a general title for the series. Put your proposal to a group of students who should role-play TV producers, viewers' representatives and other interested parties who can give you feedback on your ideas.

Extension activity

Take one of the stories selected for TV adaptation and produce a storyboard roughing out the overall structure. Write part of one of the scenes from your storyboard. You'll find it helpful to look at some examples of screenplays first.

4 Research attitudes to Lawrence and awareness of his short stories among adult readers. This might be done through a written questionnaire sent to a number of people, or through spoken interviews with a smaller group (a local library or bookshop might help). Collate your findings. Are there any significant differences between age groups, social groups, sexes, etc.?

◆

GLOSSARY

The White Stocking

9   **What the Hanover:** a mild oath referring to the unpopular eighteenth-century Hanoverian royal family (the British sovereigns George I and George II)

18   **carte blanche:** literally, a white or empty card, meaning that Adams has a free choice of where to initial Elsie's dance card, so as to reserve her as his partner

18   *amourette*: a cupid or *amoretto*

19   *roué*: a man who has a lifestyle characterised by drinking, sexual activity and other excessive sensual indulgence

30   **backfire:** throw them to the back of the fire place
       trollops, trolley: slang expressions for a sexually promiscuous and slovenly woman

Odour of Chrysanthemums

38   **winter-crack trees:** late-ripening plum trees (Nottinghamshire dialect word)

39   **mash:** make the tea (dialect)

40   **bout:** fit of drunkenness (dialect)
       settler: clincher, point that settles an argument (dialect)

42   **ripping:** taking down the roof of a mine tunnel to make it higher
       waflin: waving or flapping (dialect)

43   **crozzled up:** shrivelled (dialect)

48   **Loose-a':** loose-all, the end of the shift in the mine
       bantle: batch (dialect)

49   **butty:** contractor, leader of groups of miners, like Lawrence's father

Daughters of the Vicar

62   **throng:** busy (dialect)
       chapel: The nonconformist chapels, such as those of the Methodists, were mainly working class, as opposed to the

Anglican churches which tended to be more middle-class places of worship.

64 **wideawake:** a soft felt hat with a broad brim and a small crown

65 **tundish:** funnel (dialect)

66 **John Wesley:** (1703–1791) the preacher who founded Methodism

71 **chétif:** puny (French)

79 **sensient:** Lawrence seems to have made this word up, as he sometimes did, perhaps out of a combination of 'sentient' and 'sensual'.

92 **bran bag:** a flannel bag filled with bran and warmed in the oven to make a kind of poultice, for applying to sore or inflamed parts of the body

93 **swaled away:** consumed or wasted away (dialect)

97 **gang-lad:** person who took empty tubs to the colliers at the coal face and took away full ones, carrying messages between different groups of miners
loose-all: See note to page 48.
sumph: sump, or well where water collected before being pumped to the surface
A green Christmas, a fat churchyard: proverbial expression suggesting that when cold weather comes *after* Christmas, more people are likely to die and fill the graveyard

98 **chair:** the cage-lift used for winding miners up and down the pit

99 **snap-bag:** a calico bag for carrying the miner's mid-shift meal (dialect)

The Prussian Officer

127 **Herr Hauptmann:** captain (German)

128 **cast:** squint

131 **Schöner:** The name of the orderly means, literally, 'handsome' in German.

Tickets Please

151 **Thermopylae:** a narrow pass in Greece, famous as the site of an heroic defensive action during the Persian war in 480BC

John Thomas: slang word for penis

Coddy: from 'cods', slang word for testicles

156 **He'll get dropped on:** Someone will get their own back on him (dialect).

on the *qui vive*: on the alert; on the look out

160 **Strange, wild creatures:** rather like the maenads, or mad women, who in Greek myth were followers of Dionysus (or Bacchus), the god of wine, and were supposed to have torn to pieces the poet Orpheus for interfering with their worship. Euripides' play *The Bacchae* is about a similar situation.

The Blind Man

174 **on the *qui vive*:** See note to page 156.

180 **a *littérateur*:** a literary man (French)

Hadrian

190 **Mary to Emmie's Martha:** a reference to an incident mentioned in the Bible (Luke, 10, 38–42) where Martha does the domestic chores while her sister Mary sits and listens to Jesus' words

192 **the armistice:** This agreement to end hostilities in the First World War was signed at 11 a.m. on 11 November 1918.

194 *sotto voce*: in an undertone (Italian)

Mannie: 'little man', a term of endearment for a young boy, here used sarcastically

203 **sliving:** scheming, stealthy (dialect)

The Rocking-Horse Winner

213 **the Ascot:** A famous horse called Sansovino won the Prince of Wales's Stakes at Royal Ascot racecourse in 1924.

batman: officer's servant

213   **blade of the "turf":** someone very knowledgeable about
      horse racing (slang)

214   **Lincoln:** the Lincolnshire Handicap run in the spring, the first
      big race of the flat-racing season

215   **Nat Gould:** journalist and novelist (1857–1919) who wrote
      mainly about horse racing

218   **Leger:** the St Leger race run at Doncaster in September

220   **Grand National ... Derby:** The Grand National is a famous
      steeplechase run at Aintree, near Liverpool, in March, and
      the Derby Stakes is run on Epsom Downs in June.

223   **as right as a trivet:** perfectly all right (a trivet is a three-legged
      stand for a pan)

224   **Malabar:** the name of a real racehorse of the time. Also the
      name of a king who received godlike powers for a period at
      the cost of his life, according to a book Lawrence knew well,
      The Golden Bough by the anthropologist Sir James Frazer.

The Man Who Loved Islands

227   **Abraham ... sands of the sea-shore:** 'I will ... make thy seed
      as the sand of the sea, which cannot be numbered for
      multitude', was God's promise to Abraham and his grandson
      Jacob in the Bible (Genesis, 32, 12).

230   **Hesperides:** the Isles of the Blessed in Greek mythology,
      where the three daughters of Hesperus guarded golden apples

232   **Hermes:** the herald and messenger of the gods in Greek
      mythology

237   **the lean kine of Egypt:** In the Bible Joseph interprets
      Pharaoh's dream of seven thin cows as meaning seven years
      of famine to come (Genesis, 41, 1–31).

240   **Orion:** constellation named after the hunter of Greek
      mythology who was killed by the goddess Diana and
      transformed into a group of stars

247   **Golders Green:** district in north-west London, used as an
      example of suburbia

The Lovely Lady

257 **Etruscan:** aboriginal people who lived in Italy prior to Roman domination. Little is known about their history but Lawrence became interested in their culture and beliefs in the 1920s, visiting the surviving Etruscan tomb sites in 1926 and writing a travel book, *Etruscan Places.*

258 **a Leonardo woman:** The Mona Lisa is the most well-known woman painted by Leonardo da Vinci (1452–1519).
whom age could not wither: a reference to Shakespeare's play *Antony and Cleopatra*, Act 2, Scene 2, lines 240–241: 'Age cannot wither her, nor custom stale / Her infinite variety'
renew her youth like the eagle: possibly a reference to the Bible (Isaiah, 40, 31): 'But they that wait upon the Lord shall renew their strength; they shall mount up with wings as eagles …'; or to the mythical bird the phoenix, which was supposed to be reborn from its own ashes
aspless Cleopatra: In Shakespeare's play, Cleopatra kills herself by clutching an asp, a venomous snake, to her bosom.

259 **make music for her:** Cecilia is the patron saint of music.
Queen Ann house: in the style of the early eighteenth century in England, when Queen Anne reigned
the Inns: the Inns of Court in London, the centre of the legal profession, where barristers have their offices or chambers

261 *Mexicana:* documents and artefacts relating to Mexico
Vice-regal Mexico: After its conquest by the Spaniards (1519–1521), Mexico was ruled by viceroys or representatives of the Spanish kings. The city of Vera Cruz later became a centre of the Spanish Inquisition.

263 **on the *qui vive*:** See note to page 156.
Renoir and Gauguin and Cézanne: Auguste Renoir (1841–1919), Paul Gauguin (1848–1903) and Paul Cézanne (1839–1906) were all French Impressionist painters.

265 **Orion:** See note to page 240.

272 **Madame Sans Gêne:** literally, lady without restraint (French), the title of a popular comedy by Victorien Sardou (1852–1922), later made into a film and an opera
beau ideal: ideal of a perfect type (French)

278 **apple tree:** a reference to the Garden of Eden as described in the Bible (Genesis, 3, 1–7)

280 *gamin*: street urchin (French)

281 **Chi lo sa, caro, se vale la pena:** 'who knows, my dear, whether it is worth it' (Italian)
Bravo … intelligenza: 'Good, yes, very good, poor little man! But a man like you he will never, never be. He's not a hero, he, neither in love nor in intelligence' (Italian).
nemmeno male: 'not even wicked' (Italian)

286 **Tinia threw his third thunder:** Tinia was the Etruscan god of thunder.

289 **girning:** grimacing (dialect)

291 **scotch:** a block or wedge

292 **pale:** fence or boundary (of Pauline's family). Robert can now go 'beyond the pale'.

293 **on the q.t.:** on the quiet, in secret (slang)

FURTHER READING

Selected works by D. H. Lawrence

Short stories
The Prussian Officer and Other Stories (1914)

England, My England and Other Stories (1922)

The Woman Who Rode Away and Other Stories (1928)

Love Among the Haystacks and Other Stories (1987)

Novellas
The Fox, The Captain's Doll, The Ladybird (1923)

St Mawr (1925)

The Virgin and the Gipsy (1930)

Novels
Sons and Lovers (1913)

The Rainbow (1915)

Women in Love (1920)

Lady Chatterley's Lover (1928)

All of these volumes are published by Penguin using the authoritative Cambridge University Press D. H. Lawrence texts. A larger selection of short stories based on older texts, with a helpful introduction, is *Selected Short Stories*, edited by Brian Finney (Penguin, 1982).

Poetry
Selected Poems (Penguin, 1972)

Selected Poems (Everyman, 1992)

Plays
Three Plays (Penguin, 1960)

Biography and criticism

Brenda Maddox, *The Married Man: A Life of D. H. Lawrence* (Sinclair-Stevenson, 1994)

John Worthen, *D. H. Lawrence: A Literary Life* (Macmillan, 1989)

F. R. Leavis, *D. H. Lawrence, Novelist* (Chatto and Windus, 1955)

Keith Sagar, *The Art of D. H. Lawrence* (Cambridge University Press, 1966)

Kingsley Widmer, *The Art of Perversity, D. H. Lawrence's Shorter Fiction* (University of Washington Press, 1962)

Julian Moynahan, *The Deed of Life, The Novels and Tales of D. H. Lawrence* (Princeton University Press, 1963)

George Ford, *Double Measure, A Study of the Novels and Stories of D. H. Lawrence* (Holt, Rinehart and Winston, 1965)

Keith Cushman, *D. H. Lawrence at Work: The Emergence of the 'Prussian Officer' Stories* (University Press of Virginia, 1978)

Michael Black, *D. H. Lawrence: The Early Fiction* (Macmillan, 1986)

Short stories by other writers

Edgar Allan Poe, *Selected Tales* (Oxford University Press, 1980)

Anton Chekhov, *A Woman's Kingdom and Other Stories* (Oxford University Press, 1989)

Henry James, *The Turn of the Screw and Other Stories* (Oxford University Press, 1992)

Thomas Hardy, *Wessex Tales* (Oxford University Press, 1991)

James Joyce, *Dubliners* (Cambridge Literature, 1995)

Katherine Mansfield, *Selected Stories* (Oxford University Press, 1981)

Roald Dahl, *The Best of Roald Dahl* (Penguin, 1983)

William Trevor, *The Stories of William Trevor* (Penguin, 1983)

CAMBRIDGE LITERATURE

✦

Ben Jonson *The Alchemist*

William Wycherley *The Country Wife*

William Blake *Selected Works*

Jane Austen *Pride and Prejudice*

Mary Shelley *Frankenstein*

Charlotte Brontë *Jane Eyre*

Emily Brontë *Wuthering Heights*

Nathaniel Hawthorne *The Scarlet Letter*

Charles Dickens *Hard Times*

Charles Dickens *Great Expectations*

George Eliot *Silas Marner*

Thomas Hardy *Far from the Madding Crowd*

Henrik Ibsen *A Doll's House*

Robert Louis Stevenson *Treasure Island*

Mark Twain *Huckleberry Finn*

Thomas Hardy *Tess of the d'Urbervilles*

Kate Chopin *The Awakening and other stories*

Anton Chekhov *The Cherry Orchard*

James Joyce *Dubliners*

Six Poets of the Great War

D. H. Lawrence *Selected Short Stories*

Edith Wharton *The Age of Innocence*

F. Scott Fitzgerald *The Great Gatsby*

Virginia Woolf *A Room of One's Own*

Robert Cormier *After the First Death*

Caryl Churchill *The After-Dinner Joke*
and *Three More Sleepless Nights*

Graham Swift *Learning to Swim*

Fay Weldon *Letters to Alice*

Louise Lawrence *Children of the Dust*

Julian Barnes *A History of the World in 10½ Chapters*

Amy Tan *The Joy Luck Club*

Four Women Poets

Moments of Madness – 150 years of short stories

Helen Edmundson *The Mill on the Floss*